D1610749

MEN
WHO MADE
LABOUR

With a Foreword by
Tony Blair

The Original Parliamentary Labour Party, February 1906
The Terrace of the House of Commons

Seated, left to right:
W. Tyson Wilson, Alex Wilkie, J. Ramsay MacDonald, Arthur Henderson, J. Keir Hardie, David Shackleton, Will Crooks.

Standing, left to right:
John Jenkins, Charles Bowerman, John Hodge, James Parker, George Kelly, Walter Hudson, George Wardle, George Barnes, Fred Jowett, George Roberts, Charles Duncan, T. Freddie Richards, Stephen Walsh, Alfred Gill, Philip Snowden, Thomas Summerbell, J.T. Macpherson, Thomas Glover, James Seddon, J.R. Clynes, James O'Grady, Will Thorne.

100 years on. The 2006 PLP photographed in the Chamber of the House of Commons, February 2006.

MEN
WHO MADE
LABOUR

The PLP of 1906 –
the personalities and
the politics

Edited by

ALAN HAWORTH *and*
DIANNE HAYTER

Routledge
Taylor & Francis Group

LONDON AND NEW YORK

First published 2006
by Routledge
2 Park Square, Milton Park, Abingdon, Oxon OX14 4RN

Simultaneously published in the USA
by Routledge
270 Madison Ave, New York, NY 10016

Routledge is an imprint of the Taylor & Francis Group,
an informa business

© 2006 Alan Haworth and Dianne Hayter

Typeset in Perpetua and Bell Gothic by
Florence Production Ltd, Stoodleigh, Devon
Printed and bound in Great Britain

British Library Cataloguing in Publication Data
A catalogue record for this book is available from the British Library

Library of Congress Cataloging in Publication Data
A catalog record for this book has been requested

ISBN10: 1–84568–047–2

ISBN13: 978–1–84568–047–3

To the memory of

Sir Frank Barlow CBE,

a former Secretary of the Parliamentary Labour
Party, whose interest in the victor of the Clitheroe
by-election of 1902, Sir David Shackleton, eventually
led to this book, and to the memory of the
29 Labour MPs elected in 1906.

Contents

Notes on Contributors

The late **Tony Banks** was MP for West Ham from 1997 to 2005, having previously represented Newham North West from 1983 to 1997. Prior to that, he had been Head of Research at the AUEW, and the Political Adviser to the Minister of Overseas Development in 1975. He was a GLC Member from 1970 to 1977 and 1981 to 1986 and its Chairman from 1985 to 1986. He was the Minister for Sports from 1997 to 1999. Appointed to the Lords as Lord Stratford, he died just after completing his chapter.

Hilary Benn has been the MP for Leeds Central since June 1999, and the Secretary of State for International Development since 2003. With a degree in Russian and East European Studies, he has been Deputy Leader of Ealing Council. He was a trade union Research Officer with ASTMS and Head of Policy and Communications at MSF. Prior to his election, he was Special Adviser to David Blunkett MP, the Secretary of State for Education and Employment, and from 1999 to 2001 was a member of the Environment, Transport and the Regions Select Committee, before becoming a Home Office minister.

Charles Clarke has been the MP for Norwich South since 1997. He read Mathematics and Economics at Cambridge and was President of the National Union of Students from 1975 to 1977. He was a Hackney Councillor and Chair of Housing. He was Chief of Staff to the then Labour Leader, Neil Kinnock, until the 1992 election when he became Chief Executive of a public affairs consultancy until he became an MP. He was a Junior Minister in the Department of Education, a Minister of State at the Home Office and then Minister without Portfolio and Labour Party Chair before becoming the Secretary of State for Education and Skills and subsequently, in 2004, Home Secretary.

Ann Clwyd has been the MP for Cynon Valley since 1984, prior to which she was the MEP for Mid and West Wales. She is the Chair of the Parliamentary Labour Party and, in 2003/04, was the BBC/*House Magazine* and the *Spectator* 'Backbencher of the Year' and also won the Channel 4 Political Award for 'Campaigning Politician of the Year'. Since May 2003 she has been the Prime Minister's Special Envoy to Iraq on Human Rights. She is Chair of the All Party Parliamentary Human Rights Group and Chair of the British Group of the Inter-Parliamentary Union. Before entering politics, she was a journalist with the BBC, and Wales correspondent for the *Guardian* and the *Observer*.

Ann Coffey has been the MP for Stockport since 1992. Born in Scotland, she studied Sociology at South Bank University and Psychiatric Social Work at the University of Manchester before becoming a Social Worker Team Leader with responsibility for fostering and adoption. She is now PPS to Alistair Darling MP, Secretary of State for Transport, having been the PPS to the Prime Minister (1997–98) and Shadow Health Minister (1996–97).

Jim Cousins has been the MP for Newcastle upon Tyne Central since 1987, having lived on Tyneside since 1968. He served on the Trade and Industry Select Committee Inquiry into the Iraq Supergun in 1990–92 and has been a member of the Treasury Select Committee since 1997.

Derek Foster was the MP for Bishop Auckland from 1979 to 2005, when he was appointed to the House of Lords. Before his election, he held senior positions in the voluntary and public sectors and served on Sunderland Council and the Tyne and Wear Metropolitan County Council, as well as being Chairman of the North of England Development Council. In Parliament, he has been PPS to Neil Kinnock, the elected Chief Whip (and thus on the Shadow Cabinet) from 1985 to 1995, joint Chair of the Education and Employment Select Committee (1997–2001), and was appointed to the Privy Council in 1993.

Alan Haworth was born in Blackburn, Lancashire in 1948. He was appointed to the staff of the Labour Party in 1975, working for the PLP. He has held a variety of posts in the Labour Party – including three years as a Constituency Secretary (Newham North East CLP) – and for several years was a member of the Executive Committee of the Labour Co-ordinating Committee. For 12 years from 1992 he was the Secretary of the Parliamentary Labour Party. He was elevated to the Peerage in 2004 as Lord Haworth of Fisherfield. He is author of 113 obituaries of former Labour MPs, some of which were published in *The Politico's Book of the Dead* (Politico's, 2003).

Dianne Hayter is a member of the Labour Party NEC. She was formerly General Secretary of the Fabian Society, Chief Executive of the European Parliamentary Labour Party and Chief Executive of two health charities. She is on the Board of the National Consumer Council and the Determinations Panel of the Pensions Regulator and is the former Deputy Chair of the Financial Services Consumer Panel. She is the author of *Fightback! Labour's Traditional Right in the 1970s and 1980s* (MUP, 2005) and various other publications.

Mark Hendrick became the MP for Preston in a November 2000 by-election and has been PPS to Margaret Beckett as Secretary of State for Environment, Food and Rural Affairs since July 2003. He was elected to Salford City Council in 1987 and served on the City Council for eight years. He was the member of the European Parliament for Lancashire Central from 1994 to 1999, where he served as Labour's spokesperson on economic, monetary and industrial policy, and Leader of the Socialists on the European Parliament's Economic and Monetary Affairs Committee.

Patricia Hewitt has been the MP for Leicester West since 1997. She worked for Neil Kinnock MP, Leader of the Opposition, from 1983 to 1989 when she moved to the Institute for Public Policy Reform (IPPR) as Deputy Director. She was Deputy Chair of the IPPR Commission of Social Justice. In 1998 she was appointed Economic Secretary at the Treasury, and in 1999 she was promoted to become Minister at the Department for Trade and Industry. Patricia Hewitt was appointed to the Cabinet in 2001, as Secretary of State for Trade and Industry, and Secretary of State for Health in May 2005.

John Hutton has been the MP for Barrow-in-Furness since 1992 and is now the Secretary of State for Work and Pensions. He was previously a minister at the Department of Health before joining the Cabinet as Chancellor of the Duchy of Lancaster in May 2005. Prior to entering Parliament, he was a senior lecturer at Newcastle Polytechnic having graduated from Oxford University.

Brian Iddon is the MP for Bolton South East. He has a PhD in Chemistry from Hull University and taught at both Durham and Salford universities. He was a Bolton Councillor for 21 years prior to his election to Parliament in 1997. He is a member of the Science and Technology Select Committee and also has a particular interest in education, health, the Middle East and Kashmir.

Sir Gerald Kaufman is the MP for Gorton, having been elected to Parliament in 1970. Educated at Leeds and Oxford, he was formerly Assistant General Secretary of the Fabian Society, on the political staff of the *Daily Mirror*, and political correspondent of the *New Statesman* before becoming Parliamentary Press Liaison Officer in Downing Street with Prime Minister Harold Wilson. He was a Minister from 1974 to 1979 (at Environment and the Department of Industry), made a Privy Councillor in 1978, was on the Shadow Cabinet (1980–92) and Labour's NEC (1991–92), and was Chairman of the House of Commons Select Committee on Culture, Media and Sport from 1997 to 2005, having been Chairman of the National Heritage Select Committee from 1992 to 1997.

Ruth Kelly is the MP for Bolton West, which includes a large part of the old Westhoughton Division. She became Education Secretary in 2004 (at the age of 36 – the youngest ever so appointed) after a short spell in the Cabinet Office and three years at the Treasury where she was, successively, Economic Secretary and Financial Secretary. Educated at Oxford and the LSE, she worked on the *Guardian* as an economics writer before joining the Bank of England. After her election in 1997, she became PPS to Nick Brown at the Ministry for Agriculture, Fisheries and Food.

Tony Lloyd has been an MP since 1983. Between 1983 and 1997 he represented Stretford and since 1997 Manchester Central. He studied at Nottingham University and Manchester Business School, lectured in Business Studies at Salford University, and was a Councillor on Trafford Metropolitan Borough Council (1979–84). He was Minister of State at the Foreign and Commonwealth Office (1997–99) and is now the Leader of the British Delegation to the Parliamentary Assembly of the Council of Europe and one of its Vice-Presidents.

Ian McCartney has been the MP for Makerfield since 1987, and Labour Party Chair and Minister without Portfolio since 2003. Prior to his election he was a Councillor on Wigan Borough and a Transport and General Workers Union lay official. In Opposition, he was a spokesperson on health and employment. In government, he has been a Minister at the Department for Trade and Industry where he was responsible for legislation establishing the National Minimum Wage, the Fairness at Work Act and the Competition Act. He was also Minister for Pensions at the Department for Work and Pensions and while Minister of State at the Cabinet Office he oversaw the 2002 Commonwealth Games, drugs policy and the Better Government for Older People initiative.

Alice Mahon was the MP for Halifax from 1987 to 2005. A graduate of Bradford University, she lectured at Bradford and Ilkley Community College and was a Councillor on Calderdale Borough Council. She has been PPS to the Secretary of State for Culture, Media and Sport, on the Select Committee on Health, and a member of the NATO Parliamentary Association. She is a member of Unison.

David Marshall is the MP for Glasgow East (from 2005) having represented Glasgow Shettleston from 1979 to 2005. He is a member of the TGWU, and a former transport worker, shop steward and Labour Party Organiser for Glasgow. He was Secretary of the Scottish Group of Labour MPs 1981–2001, Chair of the Transport Select Committee 1987–92, Chair of the Scottish Affairs Select Committee 1997–2001, and Chair of the British Group Inter-Parliamentary Union 1997–2000. He is Chair of the Executive Committee Commonwealth Parliamentary Association UK Branch and a member of UK Delegation to the Council of Europe and WEU, and is on the House of Commons Chairman's Panel.

David E. Martin teaches in the History Department at the University of Sheffield. A member for several years of the Executive Committee of the Society for the Study of Labour History, he edited the society's journal, the *Labour History Review*, from 1987 to 1998. Co-author of *Labour in British Society 1830–1914* (2000) and co-editor of *Ideology and the Labour Movement* (1979), he also contributed to the first ten volumes of the *Dictionary of Labour Biography* (1972–2000). He wrote sketches of Tony Benn, Roy Hattersley and other Labour Party figures for *The Oxford Companion to Twentieth-Century British Politics* (2002).

Chris Mullin has been the MP for Sunderland South since 1987. He has been Chairman of the Home Affairs Committee in the House of Commons and a Junior Minister in three government departments. He was previously the Editor of *Tribune*.

Giles Radice was the MP for Chester-le-Street from 1973 to 1983, and for North Durham from 1983 to 2001. He is now a Labour Peer in the House of Lords. He has written extensively on labour policy and history, most recently *Friends and Rivals* (Little, Brown, 2002), about Tony Crosland, Roy Jenkins and Denis Healey. He has been a committed European for many years.

Nick Raynsford has been the MP for Greenwich and Woolwich since 1997, having represented Greenwich from 1992 to 1997. He served as a Minister for Local and Regional Government, for Housing and Planning, and for London and Construction between 1997 and 2005, becoming a Privy Councillor in 2001. He was previously the MP for Fulham from 1986 to 1987 and a Councillor on Hammersmith and Fulham from 1971 to 1975. He was Director of SHAC, the London Housing Aid Centre, for a decade before his election. He is now Deputy Chairman of the Construction Industry Council and Vice-President of the Town and Country Planning Association.

Ernie Ross was the MP for Dundee West from 1979 to 2005. His earlier career was in engineering. He was a member of the House of Commons Select Committee on Foreign Affairs, Chair of the PLP Staff Liaison Committee, 1987–2005, and Chairman of the Board of Governors of the Westminster Foundation for Democracy.

Joan Ruddock has been MP for Lewisham Deptford since 1987. She rose to national prominence in the early 1980s as Chair of CND. Within Parliament, she was the first full-time Minister for Women under the new Labour government, and she now sits on the International Development Select Committee.

Jonathan Shaw has been the MP for Chatham and Aylesford since his unexpected election in 1997 to the newly created seat of Chatham and Aylesford, the bulk of which was previously a safe Tory seat. His 1997 majority of 2,790 was bettered in 2001 and in 2005 Jonathan gained a third successive term. Prior to becoming an MP, Jonathan worked as a social worker with Kent County Council and served as a Councillor for Rochester City Council. He has been a member of both the Environmental Audit Select Committee and the Education and Skills Select Committee before becoming the PPS to the Secretary of State for Education in 2005.

Marsha Singh has been the MP for Bradford West since 1997. Born in India, he has a degree from Loughborough University and was Senior Development Manager with Bradford Community Health Authority before his election. He is on the Select Committee on International Development and was on the Home Affairs Select Committee. He is Treasurer of the All-Party Kashmir Group and Vice-Chair of the All-Party Race and Community Group.

Jack Straw has been the MP for Blackburn since 1979. Now Foreign Secretary, he was Home Secretary from 1997 to 2001. A graduate of Leeds university, he was President of the NUS from 1969 to 1971 and a Special Adviser in the 1974–79 Labour government. He has also been an Islington Councillor as well as Deputy Leader of the ILEA (Inner London Education Authority).

Dennis Turner was the Labour and Co-op MP for Wolverhampton South East from 1987 to 2005 when he was elevated to the Peerage as Lord Bilston. He was previously a member of Wolverhampton Council for 20 years, serving as Deputy Leader from 1979 to 1986, and on West Midlands County Council from 1973 to 1986. Within the House of Commons, he was a Labour Whip in Opposition, PPS to Clare Short from 1997 to 2003 and Chairman of the Catering Committee from 1997 to 2005.

Dave Watts has been MP for St Helens North since 1997 and was PPS to the Minister (John Spellar) at the Ministry of Defence and then at the Department for Transport. He went on to be PPS to John Prescott, Deputy Prime Minister, and is now a Lord Commissioner and Government Whip.

He was previously Leader of St Helens Council from 1993 to 1997. He has been Labour Party Organiser, Research Assistant to Angela Eagle MP and John Evans MP, a shop steward at United Biscuits AEU and a St Helens Councillor from 1979 to 1997.

Shaun Woodward has been the Labour MP for St Helens South since 2001. Prior to his election, he worked for the National Consumer Council, and was the Editor of BBC TV's *That's Life*, a Producer of *Newsnight* and Director of Communications for the Conservative Party. He was elected as the Conservative MP for Whitney in 1997 but crossed the floor and joined the Labour Party in 1997. He is now a Minister in the Northern Ireland Office.

Foreword

Tony Blair

WHEN THE LABOUR Representation Committee was formed in 1900, its purpose was to secure a viable and credible Labour Party in Parliament. Keir Hardie and his allies knew that there could be little progress towards the party's progressive goals without power and that only through Parliament could the great reforms Britain needed be delivered.

That is why this centenary anniversary is so important to the Labour movement. Britain in 1906 was not yet a proper democracy. There was no universal suffrage. Women did not have the vote. But 29 Labour election victories meant that the voice of the people could never again be ignored as the famous picture at Westminster of the new MPs underlined. The 1906 election marked a crucial staging post towards building a fairer and better country.

Today, 100 years later, we can see the results of their pioneering endeavours. Labour, for the first time in its history, has won three successive election victories. The Parliamentary Party numbers not 29 but 353 MPs, who were photographed for the centenary in the Chamber of the House of Commons in February 2006. But all of us are aware of the debt we owe our predecessors and are proud to be following in their footsteps.

The Parliamentary Party of 1906 was a very broad church. MPs represented constituencies from right across Britain. Not all called themselves socialists. Many, like Arthur Henderson, were nonconformist radicals whose socialism owed more to Methodism than to Marx. But they overcame their differences to work together, based on a common commitment to using the power of government to enable people, regardless of their background, to realise their own potential. It is a belief that continues to drive this Labour government in very different times today.

The prospect of any Labour government in 1906, of course, was still a distant dream. The immediate challenge was to persuade the new Liberal administration to begin tackling the still Dickensian horrors of Britain at the time. The fledgling Parliamentary Labour Party succeeded in starting to build a fairer, kinder country because its MPs were ready to work with all those who shared their aims. Our party has always been at its most successful when it has looked outwards and has the courage to respond to changing circumstances. That remains as true today as ever.

Tony Blair

May 2006
10 Downing Street

Acknowledgements

The authors would like to pay particular tribute to the following, all of whom helped with researching or writing various parts of the book: Terry Ashton, Stephen Bird, Leyland Booth, David Boothroyd, Andy Bowden, John Chesshire, Christine Coates, Mark Davies, the Dundee City Council Local History Department, Jan Ferry, Claire Forrest, Rose Gibson of the Leeds Central Library, Andrew Howard Gill, John Grigg, John Gyford, the Staff of the House of Commons Library, the Labour History Museum, John Lloyd, Gillian Lonergan (Co-operative College), John Maxton, Frank Meeres (whose work is the basis of Charles Clarke's chapter), Gareth Myton, the Newcastle Local Studies and Family History Centre, Marcus Papadopoulos, Mary Presland, Paul Richards, Janet Setchfield (Secretary of Leicester West CLP who made available some of her private collection of historic papers to Patricia Hewitt), Tony Robinson, Greg Rosen, Ali Ross, Matthew Seward, Heidi Topman and the Thursday Group (St Helens' Historic Society).

Photo credits: Malcolm Brown (Henderson Medal), David Caplin (Bowerman plaque), Flying Colours (Jim Cousins MP), Eamonn McCabe (Ann Clwyd MP), Terry Moore (2006 PLP), National Portrait Gallery, London (George Henry Roberts), Jago Parker (Alice Mahon).

Introduction:
The Turning Point in the History of Labour

THERE CAN BE no one today who doubts the place of Labour in the country's politics and governance. A third majority government, a Commons majority of 66, and even – just achieved for the first time ever – Labour comprising the largest single group in the Lords, albeit far short of a majority. One hundred years ago, Parliament looked very different – and not simply because it was all male and white. It was only in 1900 that the trade unions, Fabians and the Independent Labour Party took their first tentative steps to getting working people into Parliament by establishing the Labour Representation Committee (LRC). Then in 1906, the sudden arrival of 29 Labour men led to the establishment on 12 February 1906 of the Parliamentary Labour Party – the PLP – whose centenary is celebrated in 2006, and to the metamorphosis of the LRC into the Labour Party.

This volume is not a history of the party since then. By contrast, it seeks to look at 1906 through the eyes of those whose arrival in Westminster we commemorate. Thus the obituaries of those 29 men, with one exception[1] written by their twenty-first-century successors, dwell on their origins, expectations, world vision and achievements in the context of early twentieth-century conditions. The achievements of this small band of pioneers are

---

1   The single exception is that of David Shackleton – first elected for Clitheroe in a by-election in 1902. The appreciation of Shackleton's life is written by Alan Haworth, former Secretary of the PLP. It is a remarkable story. Shackleton was elected to Parliament unopposed in 1902, unopposed even in his selection as a candidate. He is the first and only man ever to serve simultaneously on the Executive Committees of the LRC and the TUC and the only person in the history of the TUC to be elected to serve for a second term as Chairman – and this whilst he was de facto Chairman of the PLP. Later, in a most impressive second career, he became the first working-class Permanent Secretary of any government Department – the first ever Permanent Secretary at the Ministry of Labour – and the first Labour knight. Yet few people know anything about Shackleton. It was to remedy this astonishing state of affairs, and the simultaneous realisation that very little is known or at least remembered in the Labour movement about the majority of these founding fathers, that gave rise to the genesis of this book. To mark the centenary of the election of the Men who Made Labour in 1906, there is now a little more on the record, in 2006. Their successors have done them proud, and rightly so, for were it not for the achievements of these 29 men, there may not have been today's successors.

remarkable, not least because of the backgrounds from which they emerged. Along with the Lib-Lab MPs (working men elected under the Liberal banner) they mostly left school at 11, 12 or 13. Overwhelmingly they earned their living in hard manual work, with their intellectual curiosity and public involvement nurtured by the chapel, books, trade unions, the temperance movement and their experience of life. No maintenance grants, no sub-sidised fees nor university places for them; instead night school, Ruskin Hall,[2] libraries, newspapers and debates on how to improve the conditions they saw around them helped formulate their politics and fostered their desire to change things. David Martin's splendid chapter, reviewing the background of the 29 (together with J.W. Taylor who joined the PLP just days after its creation, but too late to be included in the iconic group photo-graph taken on the Terrace of the House of Commons and reproduced on the front cover) tells a tale of ordinary men who overcame poverty, illegitimacy, alcoholic parents, large families, unemployment and barren hopes to become extraordinary pioneers.

However, in the earliest days, there were other major challenges con-fronting them: the absence of universal suffrage, no salaries for MPs, the entrenched position of the Liberals – and the reaction to war. It was their differing responses to the 1914–18 war that caused their first major divide, more than a decade before the economic crisis of the 1930s that led MacDonald – Labour's first Prime Minister – to split off from Labour and plunge the party into opposition. So neither policy divides nor even party splits are new, although the effects of these – whether in 1914, the 1930s or the 1980s – are identical: extended periods of opposition. It thus took longer than anticipated for the party, first grouped in Parliament in 1906, to form sustained Labour governments.

Something of the surprise, and delight, at a majority government can be sensed from the two 1950s pamphlets reproduced (in slightly edited forms) at the end of this book: *Voice of the People* (commemorating 50 years of the PLP in 1956) and *Labour's Early Days* by Lord Shepherd.[3] These marvelled at Attlee's 1945 achievement, whilst the 1956 NEC celebrated the Jubilee with a service in Westminster Abbey; a reception, cabaret and dance[4] at the Seymour Hall, London, where speeches were given by Hugh Gaitskell, H. Scott Lindsay,[5] and leaders of the Labour Parties in the West Indies who happened to be in London for the Caribbean Conference; as well as ten commemorative events across the country.[6] By the mid-1950s, the party already had some major successes to honour. In Gaitskell's words:

> Poverty and insecurity have diminished, the welfare state has been built;
> many injustices . . . remedied, and, abroad, real progress has been
> made in the advance of our colonies to democratic self-government
> and independence. In all this, the Labour Party has been the driving
> force. It was the hard work and sacrifice of our pioneers which grad-
> ually won over public opinion towards accepting the ideals of socialism
> – ideals which . . . were regarded as impractical and even positively

2   Which Bowerman later helped establish as Ruskin College, serving on its Executive for several decades.
3   See pages 229 and 241.
4   No doubt reflecting the new Leader's enjoyment of the dance floor, Hugh Gaitskell having just taken over from Clem Attlee.
5   Who had been Secretary of the PLP until 1944.
6   NEC Report to the 1956 Labour Party Conference and *The Times*, 11 February 1956.

dangerous. Our older comrades had to strive against heavy odds and face much unpopularity.[7]

However, even as the party members celebrated in 1956, they recognised that the extraordinary victory of 1906:

> . . . so bravely won . . . [behind which] was a long, proud and often tragic history that reached back through the centuries; . . . a story of the human suffering of men and women . . . for the right to share fairly in the wealth they produced . . .[a] story in which the weapons of want, poverty, imprisonment and transportation had been wielded mercilessly to crush the spirit of freedom . . . a story of struggle, and more often than not a story of defeat, but now the first great victory had been won. Britain's Parliament, so long the prerogative of the rich and privileged, was at last to hear the voice of the people.[8]

Such sentiments had even been heard from the pulpit. Speaking in St Paul's Cathedral soon after the 1906 result, the Archbishop of York proclaimed:

> The great dumb mass of our working folk . . . has found its voice; it has exerted its strength, and comes forth challenging attention . . . Here are the men, at least, who have worked in pit and factory, whose friends are among the dwellers in our overcrowded cities . . . These men will bring first hand knowledge of the facts of life to the study of these problems. They will take care that amid all the business of politics 'the poor shall not always be forgotten'.[9]

Moving to the prosaic, the anniversary pamphlet goes on to recount the first 50 years of the PLP under headings such as 'The Test', 'Government', 'Tragedy' and 'Adversity'.

An early test for the party was in its response to the war, when MacDonald, Hardie and others turned away from supporting this conflict. By contrast, some of their number joined the government to support the successful prosecution of the war – at least two of whom maintained this viewpoint despite the deaths of their own sons in service. George Barnes' youngest son, Henry, was killed on the Western Front but this did not change his father's views. If anything, it reinforced his belief that, if such suffering and sacrifice were to be justified, the country had to unite. In 1918, Steve Walsh stood for election as a supporter of the coalition and its achievements in the war, notwithstanding the death of his son on active service. Barnes, Walsh and Wilkie supported conscription, whilst Charles Duncan, Arthur Henderson, Will Thorne, James Parker and the fiercely patriotic George Wardle joined recruiting campaigns, with James O'Grady even travelling to Dublin to help the army recruit there. Duncan went on a delegation to the United States to bolster American support for the war. Clynes persuaded the unions to agree not to strike until the war was over, and George Roberts helped end the 1915 miners' strike to assist the war effort. Furthermore, Clynes took a group of workers to Ypres to press the cause.[10] O'Grady, a Vice President of the patriotic British Workers' League,

---

7 Hugh Gaitskell, then Leader of the Labour Party, in his Foreword to *Voice of the People*, February 1956.
8 *Voice of the People*. See p. 230.
9 Quoted in *Voice of the People*.
10 Clynes did, however, save the workers' beer – albeit slightly diluted (see p. 42).

visited the Western Front several times while Roberts inspected the camps of German prisoners of war. Some of these MPs, such as O'Grady, were attacked by their local parties for their support of the war, and this was the motive behind Labour's first ever de-selection (of Roberts in Norwich in 1917). Likewise, John Hodge was later nearly de-selected in Gorton and it caused Parker to fall out with his local party members. In contrast, it was their opposition to the war that cost Philip Snowden and Fred Jowett the support of the electorate, and therefore their seats, in Blackburn and Bradford respectively in 1918.[11]

The other shadow over Labour's early years was the adversity of unemployment – the all-too-human impact of the world's economic crisis. Patricia Hewitt's piece on the role of her predecessor, Ramsay MacDonald, comments:

> The enormity of the economic crisis rattled the entire political class, not just Labour's leadership . . . For parliamentarians, brought up with the certainties of Empire, Monarchy and Parliament, it was beyond their comprehension or control. We . . . should try to understand the unprecedented circumstances that led to [MacDonald's actions]. When asked by the King to form a government, the son of a servant and a ploughman did not refuse.[12]

The Labour movement, early on, believed that 'the presence of aliens in Britain is not a cause of unemployment amongst British workers'.[13] Furthermore, it identified solutions including 'that local authorities should execute public work when the labour market was depressed'. This was a movement with an agenda for change, not simply a catalogue of complaints. It took time for a programme of policy positions to be developed, although the 1906 Manifesto (reproduced in the Appendix) highlights the issues of concern. First, the party had to develop an identity and philosophy of its own. In later years, both the communists and militants had to be kept out of the Labour Party, but at the beginning of the twentieth century it was the party's complete independence from Liberalism that was the issue, and from 1906 candidates had to agree to abstain from identifying themselves with or promoting the interests of any party not eligible for affiliation to Labour.

Another early issue, retold in the histories, was of the PLP's relationship with the NEC. At the 1906 annual party conference, the Parliamentary Party submitted the first of the Parliamentary Reports, which have remained a feature of annual conferences ever since. As Shepherd noted: 'The historical importance of this lies in the constitutional status acquired by the parliamentary party to the party conference. The Parliamentary Party, having direct access to conference, is not now, and has never been, subject to the direction of the National Executive Committee.'[14] The party's constitution was important in dealing with the selection of parliamentary candidates.[15] In addition to the de-selection of MPs (as with Roberts), the

---

11 Keith Laybourn, 'Philip Snowden (1st Viscount Snowden)', in Greg Rosen (ed.), *Dictionary of Labour Biography*, Politico's, 2001, p. 540.
12 See p. 129.
13 *Labour's Early Days*. See p. 248.
14 See p. 249.
15 An issue that returned in force in the 1970s and 1980s; Dianne Hayter, *Fightback! Labour's Traditional Right in the 1970s and 1980s*, Manchester University Press, 2005.

party had frequent changes of Leader – although normally by the Leader's own choice to stand down. However, in 1922 Clynes became the only Leader of the Labour Party to be voted out of office in the Parliamentary Party's 100-year history.

A more successful Leader – who held the post three times (although never as Prime Minister) – was Arthur Henderson. One of the party's major thinkers, he supported full enfranchisement, including of women – an issue on which he had little success within the party, which prioritised votes for *all* men over the granting of votes to women.[16] He also campaigned for elections to be held on the same day (rather than the 18 separate dates in 1906), payment of MPs and the 'prevention of the election of members by a minority of votes'.[17] Perhaps luckily for the Labour Party, this latter objective has never come to pass. Strangely unrecognised in Labour history is Henderson's position as a Nobel Peace Laureate – the only Labour Leader to have received this award.

One other part of the movement's history has now largely been forgotten – the desire to unite the unions and the party. Shepherd's pamphlet reminds us of such attempts, which only achieved 'an exchange of fraternal greetings at annual conferences' – a practice that continues today. Given the background of the MPs covered in this book, an ever closer working relationship was a very natural aspiration, despite the non-affiliation of certain unions. The LRC was set up so that the unions could have their voice within Parliament, not simply by lobbying it but in occupying it. Many of the 29 MPs continued their trade union work whilst in Parliament, all had a background of union activity and few would have made any distinction between their industrial and political work.

Bowerman, perhaps the prime example of this, had been Chairman of the TUC in 1901, and whilst an MP was its Secretary from 1911 to 1923. John Hodge, later to become the first ever Minister of Labour, had previously presided over the TUC. Shackleton – alone amongst all trade unionists – held the TUC Chairmanship for two years (1907 and 1908), again whilst an MP, as was Gill in 1907. Seddon presided during the war (1915). Others had held this most prestigious of union roles prior to their election: Jenkins in 1895 and O'Grady in 1898.

Many of the 29 had also held senior positions in their own unions, Hodge being President of the Iron and Steel Trades Confederation, Barnes the General Secretary of the Amalgamated Society of Engineers, Thornes and Clynes General Secretary and the President of the General and Municipal Workers' Union, Gill the Secretary of the Bolton Spinners Association, Shackleton the Secretary of the Darwen Weavers Association, Duncan first the General Secretary of the Workers Union and then Secretary of a section of the TGWU, Hudson President of the Amalgamated Society of Railway Servants (a very nineteenth-century name!) and Assistant Secretary when it merged into the NUR, O'Grady Secretary of the National Federation of General Workers, Seddon President of the National Amalgamated Union of Shop Assistants, Warehousemen and Clerks, Wilkie General Secretary of the Associated Shipwrights' Society, and Wilson Chairman of the Amalgamated Society of Carpenters and Joiners. Others were union officials (Glover and Hardie in the miners' union, Henderson with the Iron Founders and Macpherson the Steel Smelters' Association). For their part, Roberts and Summerbell were office holders in the Norwich and

16 See pp. 26, 256 and 258.
17 See p. 257.

Sunderland Trades Councils respectively. Union activity was not without its difficulties, and some experienced unemployment directly as a result of their union activity.

For all of them, though, their lifelong industrial and union experience led them to concentrate on safety and rights at work, hours of work, a minimum wage, pensions, unemployment and national insurance to cover sick pay. Given their backgrounds, two other issues dominated their early years in Parliament: education and school meals. It is perhaps fitting that, as Secretary of State for Education, Ruth Kelly writes about her predecessor's efforts in establishing the first school meals service via the Education (Provision of Meals) Bill, which received Royal Assent in December 1906.

Labour was not the only representative of working people in this election. There were also 'Lib-Lab' MPs: working men fighting under the Liberal banner, of whom a further 25 were elected, with the Labour and Lib-Lab candidates polling over half a million votes – 9 per cent of the national poll. The year 1906 thus saw a real change in composition of the House as the extended franchise began making its mark.

Given the origins of these new MPs, it is hard to imagine what they made of their arrival in what was then very much the capital of the Empire. At the beginning of the twentieth century, Britain was a staunchly three-class society – and it was clear from which of these three they had arisen. They arrived to experience the remains of Dickens' London, but also that of Virginia Woolf, with its assault on their senses, intellectually, noisily, internationally and 'in the bellow and the uproar, the carriages, motor cars, omnibuses, vans, sandwich men . . . brass bands, barrel organs . . . life'.[18] It must have been intimidating, bewildering and daunting to any stranger. How much more so to these men with their background in the pits, engineering or the great textile mills?

One silence in this book is the story of the women. Little was recorded – and thus goes unreported here – of their wives, some who remained in their home towns, sometimes with large families, often with little money. Others lived in London – and thus had to face the same social ascent as their husbands. Little wonder Beatrice Webb offered them encouragement and 'tutoring', but there is still too little known about how they rose to the challenge of the changes they saw in their husbands.

Some of the MPs extended their new worlds into government, and the very highest offices of State. Others ventured into the international community. Bowerman, for example, helped establish the International Federation of Trade Unions. Barnes, a prominent member of the League to Abolish War, was a negotiator at the Paris Peace Conference and one of the signatories of the Treaty of Versailles, a delegate to the first assembly meeting of the League of Nations in Geneva in 1920 and also helped establish the International Labour Organisation – which still exists today. Hardie was a delegate to the Second Workers' International, and Henderson, who had been President of the Labour and Socialist International, went on to became Foreign Secretary. Glover was a representative at an International Conference of Miners and also made visits to India and South Africa, whilst Hodge visited France, Australia and the USA. Gill, Wilkie and Shackleton were members of TUC delegations to the American Federation of Labor Congresses, and O'Grady took in Russia and India before becoming Labour's first Colonial Governor (in Tasmania, which brought him a knighthood, and then the Falklands). As boys, few would have been able to place

18 Virginia Woolf, *Mrs Dalloway*, The Hogarth Press, 1925.

these countries on a globe. As adults, they took their political beliefs onto the global stage.

Twenty-nine remarkable men, who rose to become Prime Minister, Home Secretary, Foreign Secretary, Chair of the PLP,[19] Party Chair, first Minister of Labour, Chancellor of the Exchequer and other ministers. Today, their successors as Home Secretary (Charles Clarke), Foreign Secretary (Jack Straw), PLP Chair (Ann Clwyd), Party Chair (Ian McCartney) plus Cabinet members Patricia Hewitt, Ruth Kelly, John Hutton and Hilary Benn[20] and the other ex-ministers, MPs and former MPs writing here, represent Labour in those same seats 100 years on – although only one seat, that of Ince (Makerfield), has remained without interruption in Labour hands throughout the whole century. The pages that follow tell of individual successes and set-backs, achievements and disappointments. In relating these personal stories, they recount a vital part of Labour's history without which we will understand little of its present, let alone its future.

Dianne Hayter and Alan Haworth

Dianne Hayter

Alan Haworth

19   A full list of all the PLP Chairmen and Secretaries, from 1906 to 2006, appears in the Appendix.
20   For whom 1906 marks a different personal centenary – the election of his grand-father (albeit as a Liberal MP) to Parliament.

Labour's Parliamentary Pioneers of 1906

W HEN THE CONSERVATIVE government of Arthur Balfour resigned from office in December 1905, four MPs sat as members of the Labour Representation Committee (LRC). They were Keir Hardie, who was returned as member for Merthyr Tydfil at the general election of 1900, Will Crooks, Arthur Henderson and David Shackleton, who had entered Parliament at by-elections. These four were successful at the general election of January 1906, along with 25 other men endorsed by the LRC.[1] At an early stage it was decided their strength warranted a change of title, to the Labour Party. Much discussion related to how the Liberals' landslide victory would affect the nation, and the likely policies of the new Prime Minister, Henry Campbell-Bannerman, but Labour's arrival at Westminster was also a subject of widespread comment.

A frisson of anxiety passed through the highest in the land. 'I see,' wrote the Prince of Wales to Edward VII on 20 January 1906, 'that a great number of Labour Members have been returned which is rather a dangerous sign, but I hope they are not all Socialists.'[2] Balfour, the defeated Conservative leader, also looked with disquiet on the new Labour Party. Campbell-Bannerman, he informed Lady Salisbury, 'is a mere cork, dancing on a torrent which he cannot control and what is going on here is the faint echo of the same movement which has produced massacres in St Petersburg, riots in Vienna, and Socialist processions in Berlin'. Another prominent Conservative, Joseph Chamberlain, wrote of 'the labour earthquake'.[3] But *The Economist* combined complacency with condescension. It allowed that the Labour MPs would bring to the House of Commons a large amount of direct knowledge of social and industrial questions, and, if treated with

---

1   The parliamentary party soon added a thirtieth member, J.W. Taylor, elected for Chester-le-Street with the support of a trade union not affiliated to the LRC. This essay draws on the author's '"The Instruments of the People"?: the Parliamentary Labour Party in 1906', in David Martin and David Rubinstein (eds), *Ideology and the Labour Movement*, Croom Helm, 1979.

2   Quoted in Harold Nicolson, *King George the Fifth: His Life and Times*, Constable, 1952, p. 94.

3   Blanche E.C. Dugdale, *Arthur James Balfour, First Earl of Balfour*, Vol. 1, Hutchinson, 1936, p. 329. Chamberlain's letter of 23 January 1906 appears in *The Autobiography of Margot Asquith*, Vol. 2, Thornton Butterworth, 1922, p. 82.

'firmness and sympathy, they may well prove a useful element in our parliamentary system'.[4]

While established opinion was caught in an uncertain mind, the Labour movement, for a short time at least, was jubilant. Demands for a strong working-class presence in government had been made even before the Chartists began their campaigns in the 1830s. The agitation continued, if irregularly, throughout the century. Apart from a few adherents of William Morris's socialist utopia, which marked down the Palace of Westminster as a storehouse for manure, debate centred on the means by which workers could achieve representation in the House of Commons. After the extension of the franchise to many, though by no means all, working men in 1867 and 1885, an influential section of trade unionists believed the interests of labour could be secured through the Liberal Party. Since the 1870s the party had accommodated a handful of 'Lib-Lab' MPs. Most of the men elected were trade union officials, who would also be assisted financially by their members' subscriptions. The Liberal Party benefited from a broadening of its electoral base, although the 'Lib-Labs' were expected to be loyal members of a party that sometimes accorded a low priority to the claims of labour.

Opposition to this arrangement had helped to secure the passing of the motion at the Trades Union Congress of 1899, which led to the establishment of the LRC in 1900. This body welcomed the affiliation of trade unions and socialist societies. Three of the latter joined: the Independent Labour Party (ILP), the Fabian Society and the Social Democratic Federation (but this Marxist group decided the LRC was too moderate and disaffiliated in 1901). However, the historical connection between organised labour and Liberalism did not end with the formation of the LRC, and in some respects it was reinforced. Secret negotiations between the LRC's Secretary, Ramsay MacDonald, and the Liberal Chief Whip, Herbert Gladstone, led to an arrangement that would operate at the next general election. Accordingly, in a number of constituencies LRC candidates did not face Liberal opposition, while in return Liberals were allowed straight fights with the Conservatives. Most of the LRC candidates elected in 1906 owed their seats to this agreement.

MEN OF THE PEOPLE?

The 30-strong (with J.W. Taylor added) Parliamentary Labour Party (PLP) contained men of differing opinions. As the Prince of Wales had hoped, not all were socialists. Then and subsequently the term 'socialist' could be problematic, but 18 MPs probably regarded themselves as such.[5] In the process of electing a leader, Hardie, the socialist veteran, obtained only one vote more than David Shackleton, whose interests were seen as mainly those of the trade unions. In spite of divisions between those closer to Shackleton's views and the ILP members (although some of these were also trade unionists), the personnel of the party shared much common ground, perhaps most strikingly in their social origins. In a political system that, apart from some of the Irish MPs and the handful of 'Lib-Labs', had long been dominated by the two main upper-class parties, the arrival of a group of working-class members drew much comment. Some of this overplayed their closeness to the realities of wage earning, as when the *Observer* of 21 January described them as 'toilers with horny hands'; for most, their days in factory and mine were some years in the past. Trade union officialdom in particular had provided higher paid, more secure and less physically arduous work. Of the 30 MPs, 23 were active trade unionists and eight of them were or had until recently been General Secretaries of their trade union.[6]

Yet collectively they could claim many years of direct and often physically exacting involvement in working-class life. Though most experienced some social mobility, their origins were distinctly working class. Possibly the only exception, and then at the lowest level of the lower middle class, was the father of T.F. Richards, a book canvasser (albeit an unsuccessful one). The classification of occupations is not without difficulty – there are no checks on the occupations stated on birth certificates and census forms – but it does seem that a disproportionate number of their fathers were skilled workmen compared with the working class as a whole. In consequence, these families would have been better-off than average, though having a trade did not always prevent unemployment and other hardships. Moreover, those who in childhood escaped first-hand experience of privation would have seen its effects on neighbours. Charles Duncan, for example, the son of a Middlesbrough 'labour aristocrat' (his father was a ship's pilot), explained that his conversion to teetotalism arose from the bacchanalian excesses he had seen in his youth. The experience of others was more direct. Will Thorne's father died in a drunken brawl; his mother married another heavy drinker whose violent temper decided Thorne to get away from home by going 'on the tramp' in search of work.

In the Victorian era families who fell into destitution so deep that nothing was left to take to the pawnshop, no credit remained at local shops and help from family and friends was exhausted had as a last resort the workhouse. This was a hated and feared institution, the shadow of which had fallen across several Labour MPs. Pauperism that required public provision was designed to carry a stigma, as Will Crooks and Walter Hudson, who both had childhood spells in the workhouse, knew at first hand. What was considered a stigma of a different sort was shared by Ramsay MacDonald and Keir Hardie – that of illegitimacy. Stephen Walsh's parentage was also obscure: at the age of four he was found wandering and eventually raised by an uncle. After the death of his mother, James Parker was also taken in by relatives. These support systems were widely necessary in working-class families.

Again in common with the working population, the formal education of most Labour MPs was meagre and often ended at an early age. Though some benefited from the Education Act of 1870, education was not made compulsory until 1880, and then only to the age of 10. Working-class children were expected to go early to work in an economy that offered many poorly-paid jobs to children not yet in their teens. Families often depended on these earnings. On the small wages of older children could rest the welfare of younger siblings. Large families had to squeeze into what they could afford to rent – frequently small and dilapidated houses. Both Crooks and Clynes were one of seven children and had direct experience of such

---

6   H.A. Clegg *et al.*, *A History of British Trade Unions since 1889*, Vol. 1, Oxford University Press, 1964, p. 387; William D. Muller, *The 'Kept Men'? The First Century of Trade Union Representation in the British House of Commons, 1874–1975*, Harvester, 1977, p. 5.

circumstances. Boys frequently went into the same occupations as their fathers, and this was the case with some of those who became MPs. Thomas Glover, for example, followed his father down the mine. Others had by their early teens worked in several jobs, and this too was an occupational pattern shared by many working-class boys who drifted from one 'blind alley' to another. Thorne's boyhood jobs were so numerous and disagreeable that at the age of 15 he vowed to do all he could to prevent other children from suffering the same hardships.

J.R. Clynes, the son of an evicted Irish peasant who became a labourer in Oldham, often recalled that as a 10-year-old he got up at 4.30 a.m. to go to work as a little piecer in a cotton mill; his wages, as a half-timer, were 2s 6d a week.[7] At 11 T.F. Richards began work as a half-timer in the file-cutting trade and, like Clynes, became a full-timer at 12. He too retained memories of early hardships, such as going to work without food and then pretending to his fellows that he had already enjoyed a 'splendid breakfast'.[8] David Shackleton and George Wardle both began as half-timers in textile mills at 9; A.H. Gill did the same on his tenth birthday; George Barnes entered a jute mill at 11. When the majority of these future MPs were growing up, in the third quarter of the nineteenth century, it was normal for working-class children to begin work at an early age, but on entering political life their early experiences were often turned to good account.

The working lives of the Labour MPs gave them, collectively, direct experience of many forms of industrial labour. Geographically, too, they covered a wide part of Britain, with some concentration in the North and Scotland. In the case of two of Labour's better-known MPs, Ramsay MacDonald and Philip Snowden, youthful effort led to membership of a higher social class, and some of the others had similar ambitions. G.H. Roberts had hopes of a career as a teacher only to be told he had not the strength. After two years as a pupil teacher G.D. Kelley contemplated becoming a clergyman, but to no avail, and, like Roberts, he was apprenticed to a printer. Thomas Summerbell entered the same occupation but on losing his job due to the introduction of linotype machinery he set up his own small business. The General Secretary of the Durham Colliery Mechanics' Association, J.W. Taylor, also had a printing firm that he operated with his brother. Although many were ambitious, almost all the early MPs had worked for several years among the industrial labour force.

A characteristic pattern in the more settled phase after early manhood was for advancement in the trade union that represented the workers in their industry. At the same time, many developed an interest in political questions, often those associated with the Liberal Party. Some achieved election to local councils, school boards, boards of guardians and, as it became policy to create more working-class JPs, appointment to the magistrates' bench. The public speaking and committee work that this involved was useful experience. As T.F. Richards observed, in nine years on the Leicester Town Council he was 'unconsciously qualifying . . . for Parliament'.[9] Local politics could also build a reputation among the electorate. For example, Thorne had been a campaigning West Ham Councillor since 1890. Thomas Summerbell also had a lengthy career in local government, having been

7   *Christian Commonwealth*, 9 February 1910; J.R. Clynes, *Memoirs*, Hutchinson: 1937, p. 29; and *When I Remember*, Macmillan, 1940, p. 5.
8   'How I Got On', *Pearson's Weekly*, 26 April 1906.
9   Ibid.

elected to the Sunderland Borough Council in 1892. In the same year Fred
Jowett defeated Conservative and Liberal candidates to become a Bradford
Councillor. Such duties often required day-time attendance, something that
was made possible in at least two cases – Jowett and Crooks – by a 'wages
fund' raised from supporters' contributions. But the most common path by
which these unpaid duties became possible was a full-time post as a trade
union official.

Here perhaps was a break with the mass of the working class. As a salaried
brain-worker the trade union bureaucrat belonged, in the Webbs' phrase,
'neither to the middle nor to the working class'. A recurring aspect of all
social democratic movements is the gap that can develop between the grass-
roots and full-time activists. The Webbs provided an account by an artisan
outlining how the full-time official could become estranged from his
members. Living in a 'little villa in a lower middle class suburb' he might
grow to look down on the workmen he passed as he walked to his office
in 'tall hat and good overcoat, with a smart umbrella' and to scorn the
unemployed 'as men who have made a failure of their lives'.[10] Certainly,
in dress and manner the representatives of labour did not lack respectability;
most had the demeanour of sober artisans in chapel.

If, during many years as trade union and minor civic functionaries, the
Labour MPs had not grown grey, most of them had at least entered into
middle age. The oldest was born in 1848, the youngest in 1872. Ten were
older than Hardie, the father figure of the movement. At the time of their
election to Parliament in January 1906 the average age of the group was
46, compared with an average of 49 for all members of the House of
Commons. It is likely that some of the differences between the parliamentary party and Victor Grayson, the independent socialist returned in the
Colne Valley by-election of July 1907, arose from his youth – he was only
26, and claimed to represent the coming generation – as well as his impa-
tience with what he regarded as the constitutionalism of the Labour Party.
However, although the trade union wing of the party feared his success
would encourage 'wilder' elements, his fellow ILP members tried to work
with him. Snowden and Clynes, for instance, sponsored him when he took
his seat.[11]

Before gaining, in the phrase they sometimes favoured, 'parliamentary
honours', their lives had often exemplified Smilesian virtues of persistence and self-denial, and even if early struggles might be over-coloured
when recalling the way they had 'got on', it cannot be denied that their
achievements were considerable. Of course, these very achievements distinguished them from the mass of the people that they were seeking to
represent. Though they had important first-hand knowledge and experience
of working-class life, some of their attitudes and ideas were untypical. Referring to their collective character, the author G.K. Chesterton observed:

> These men are not the representatives of the democracy, but the
> weapons of the democracy . . . They are the instruments of the people.
> They are not the images of the people . . . many of the Labour
> Members [are] men of a definite and even pedantic class; men whose

10 Sidney and Beatrice Webb, *The History of Trade Unionism*, Longmans, 1894,
    p. 457.
11 Grayson's insobriety was also a matter of disapproval. David Clark, *Victor
    Grayson: Labour's Lost Leader,* Quartet, 1985, ch. 5, analyses relations at West-
    minster between Grayson and Labour.

austere and lucid tone, whose elaborate economic explanations smack of something very different from the actual streets of London.[12]

As would be expected of a group of men who had reached the House of Commons, their intellectual horizons were wider than those of more typical workers. Among a section of the working class could be found a desire for knowledge and self-improvement, and the early MPs often shared similar aspirations. Most were familiar with the writings of John Ruskin and Thomas Carlyle, those two Victorian moralists whose strictures against bourgeois values were also to be found among the books in many middle-class households. The popularity of these authors was detailed in a survey conducted by W.T. Stead, a well-known journalist who was to die in the sinking of the *Titanic*. In 1906 Stead persuaded most of the Labour members to write briefly about the books that had influenced them. As well as Ruskin and Carlyle, among the favoured authors were John Bunyan, Milton, Shakespeare and Dickens. The Bible was also a popular choice.[13] On the other hand, although specifically asked about books, a number of MPs denied their influence had been strong. Shackleton stated his 'chief guide' had been the practical experience gained from work as a trade union official, although he had also found the *Manchester Guardian* useful. John Hodge too thought he had learned more from newspapers than books. To Henderson the best book was 'life'; and even an intellectual like Snowden declared that men had taught him more things than books. Thomas Glover made a similar point more bluntly, in the authentic tones of someone educated in 'the university of life':

> I am sorry to say that I have not gained my experiences out of books, but from the everyday experiences of how the workers have been treated by the employers and the class which do not work, and whose main object has always been to keep the working man as much in the dark as they can. I had to work in the mines from a very early age – nine years old when I started and very long hours – and the little I learned was at the night schools, and then by seeking to get into company always above myself and learning from them, which was most valuable to me.

Though more widely read and consequently possessing knowledge of subjects unfamiliar to the average worker, the Labour MPs were not separated from him by any mental gulf. At about the same time, an industrialist's wife, Lady Bell, inquired into the reading habits of Middlesbrough ironworkers and found that, of 200 households, 50 read novels only; 58 read newspapers only; 37 houses had inhabitants who were fond of reading; and in 25 were read books 'absolutely worth reading' – and these included Shakespeare, Dickens and Ruskin.[14]

12 G.K. Chesterton, 'Introduction' to George Haw, *From Workhouse to Westminster: The Life Story of Will Crooks, MP*, Cassell, 1907, pp. xv–xvi.

13 Stead wrote to 'Lib-Lab' as well as Labour MPs and got 45 replies, which he printed as 'The Labour Party and the Books that Helped to Make It', in *The Review of Reviews*, Vol. 33, 1906, pp. 568–82.

14 Lady Florence Bell, *At the Works: A Study of an Industrial Town*, Edward Arnold, 1907, ch. 7. How sections of the working population were lettered and self-improving in this period has been explored by Jonathan Rose, *The Intellectual History of the British Working Classes*, Yale University Press, 2001.

As a whole, the Labour MPs paid more attention to religious practices than their constituents. In the words of the French historian Halévy, they were 'devout Christians and moderate patriots'.[15] The only practising Roman Catholic was James O'Grady (who nevertheless informed Stead he had been influenced by the views of Karl Marx). Only two were Anglicans (perhaps offering some support to the assertion that the Church of England was the Tory Party at prayer). But several had nonconformist associations and some were lay-preachers (supporting another popular adage that the Labour Party owed more to Methodism than Marxism). Eighteen MPs claimed membership of nonconformist churches, although the denominational press, which along with other newspapers and magazines took an interest in the new party, identified only eight. The press mentioned Crooks, Gill, Hardie, Henderson, Hodge, Hudson, Jenkins and Taylor, but not Barnes, Clynes, Glover, Parker, MacDonald, Macpherson, Richards, Seddon, Shackleton and Wardle. Some of the latter group nevertheless do seem to have had close associations with nonconformity and their omission from the various yearbooks and directories is surprising. In any case, it is significant that almost two-thirds of the Labour Party should claim, however tenuously, nonconformist beliefs.

By contrast, it is generally agreed that the working-class made religious observation a lower priority than their social superiors would have wished. Many did practise what has been termed four-wheeled Christianity – travelling to church in a pram for baptism, a coach for marriage and a hearse for burial – and they often sent their children to Sunday schools (if only, verbal tradition insists, to allow parents a connubial hour together). There were pockets of infidelism, reflected in some of the writing of the great radical journalist Robert Blatchford. In some areas the chapel, if declining in its influence, was still strong. There was also much indifference towards organised religion. A sermon by a contemporary sympathetic to Labour was probably near the truth when he claimed:

> The poor are always 'religious' even to superstition . . . There is little agnosticism, still less deliberate atheism among them . . . Mr Blatchford's recent attempt at a resuscitation of 'determinism' has utterly failed to provoke any genuine response amongst the poor . . . It is against the 'Churches', not against Jesus Christ, that the minds of the labouring poor are set.[16]

Often the language of Labour politicians echoed that of the chapel, as in Philip Snowden's oration 'The Christ that is to be' – an address so popular that it was issued in pamphlet form. Snowden recalled those days of public speaking in an anecdote about a socialist in the Bradford area, a man who declared himself willing to go to the stake for his socialism as the martyrs of old did for their religion, who advised visiting speakers to 'keep it simple, and then when tha'rt coming to t'finishing up tha' mun put a bit of "Come to Jesus" in like Philip does'.[17]

15 Quoted in David Rubinstein, *The Labour Party and British Society 1880–2005*, Sussex Academic Press, 2006, p. 32.

16 F.L. Donaldson, 'The Church and the "Labour Church"', in William Henry Hunt (ed.), *Churchmanship and Labour: Sermons on Social Subjects*, Skeffington, 1906, pp. 93–94. There is an examination of Blatchford's atheism in Laurence Thompson, *Robert Blatchford: Portrait of an Englishman*, Gollancz, 1951, ch. 13.

17 Philip Viscount Snowden, *An Autobiography*, Vol. 1, Ivor Nicholson & Watson, 1934, p. 82; cf. also Colin Cross, *Philip Snowden*, Barrie & Rockcliff, 1966, pp. 35–37.

Closely associated with nonconformity was the conviction that drink was a social evil. Gambling was also frowned upon, if not quite as darkly as intemperance. All four of the MPs who had sat in the Commons before 1906 – Hardie, Shackleton, Crooks and Henderson – had temperance associations, though Hardie's went back to his Liberal days and his formal links had lapsed. But Crooks, a Congregationalist, and Shackleton and Henderson, both Wesleyan Methodists, were active in the cause. On being re-elected to the Commons in 1906 they supported the Trades Union and Labour Officials' Temperance Fellowship in its campaign against liquor. Henderson held the post of President and Shackleton was the Treasurer. MacDonald and T.F. Richards sat on the Executive Committee. Among its Vice-Presidents were Barnes, Crooks, Duncan, Gill, Hodge, Snowden, J.W. Taylor and Walsh. Some socialists argued drunkenness was a symptom of poverty, while others regarded alcohol as an important cause of destitution. The appearance of Labour MPs on temperance platforms, often in the company of Liberals, was Ben Tillett's central complaint in an outspoken pamphlet of 1908. He declared that instead of fighting capitalism and unemployment 'Messrs. Henderson, Shackleton, Snowden and others . . . have gone out of their way to play sneak on the working class'.[18] The support for temperance within the Labour Party was not commonly shared by working men, many of whom were regular and often heavy drinkers. The production of beer reached a record level in 1900, although after the turn of the century output declined and took up a correspondingly smaller proportion of working-class expenditure.

A century later, these nonconformist and temperance components of the Labour Party are scarcely visible. In 1906 both of these closely interwoven values were much more vigorous, especially in the North where the party was better supported. Being identified with nonconformity and temperance was unlikely to lose Labour many votes – the drink interest was solidly Tory – although it probably created an impression of aloofness among some potential supporters. On the other hand, where Liberal goodwill was involved, Labour's image of sobriety and earnest self-improvement was likely to be reassuring.

Though their language sometimes echoed that of the pulpit and was conciliatory, when fighting elections Labour candidates were shrewd enough to emphasise their special appeal to working-class voters. Thus, J.H. Jenkins claimed in his election address in 1906 that, 'as a working man . . . I have gained a thorough knowledge of working-class requirements, and I am in a position to voice their opinions'.[19] At Newcastle Walter Hudson declared he was a candidate 'because the industrial workers of the country required representation at Westminster'.[20] But Labour candidates also aimed at targets familiar to the hustings. There were few votes in praising foreigners; the South African War had aroused hostility to the Chinese and the Jews at a time when Jewish immigration was already being attacked. Nor were men raised in the heart of the Empire free of jingoism. Jenkins pledged himself not only to work for the restoration of HM Dockyards to their former position, but also for them to be extended. He was contesting Chatham and

18 *Is the Parliamentary Labour Party a Failure?*, Twentieth Century Press, 1908, p. 13. Tillett, who was later elected as a Labour MP, had come to prominence as a leader of the great dock strike of 1889. Jonathan Schneer, *Ben Tillett: Portrait of a Labour Leader*, Croom Helm, 1982, pp. 128–38, charts this phase of his career.
19 *Chatham, Rochester and Gillingham Observer*, 6 January 1906.
20 *Newcastle Daily Chronicle*, 9 January 1906.

probably also mindful of creating employment, but patriotic notes were sounded in constituencies with fewer martial associations. Seddon, for example, left no doubt about his loyalties in an election address at Newton; the Conservative government, he said, 'introduced un-English methods, reversed the most cherished traditions of the British race, left an indelible stain on the honour of old England, and shook the British Constitution to its foundations'.[21]

On the other hand, internationalist attitudes were stronger among ILP members. (A few years later, most held to their principles when war was declared against Germany.) Those on the socialist wing of the party were more sceptical about the benefits of the British Empire. Charles Masterman, a progressive Liberal, recorded the humorous patter of the moderate socialist Will Crooks, who spoke in a way that reached London working-class audiences, as when:

> He is recounting the difficulties of the Imperialist Missionary down in Poplar: to the first woman: 'Don't you know you belong to an Empire on which the sun never sets?' And the reply: 'Wot's the good of talkin' like that? Why, the sun never rises on our court'. To the second: 'You've got to learn to make sacrifices for the Empire'. – 'Wot's the good of talkin' about sacrifices when we can't make both ends meet as it is? Both ends meet! We think we're lucky if we get one end meat and the other end bread'. To a third: 'If you don't agree, you're Little Englanders'. – 'If I'm to pay another twopence a pound for meat, my children will soon be Little Englanders!'

Then, in a moment, Masterman continued, he would tell of a day in the life of the unemployed, of the monotony and wretchedness of the search for work:

> They all know it, they have mostly been through it; it is a shadow which hangs over them all. And a strange, impressive, hush falls over the vast assembly, and men cough, or rub their eyes, or turn away from each other's faces. 'Give 'em a chance', he will suddenly cry, with uplifted arm, and the tension thus released finds relief in thunderous volleys of applause.[22]

THE LABOUR MPS AND THE LIBERAL PARTY

For several years in the House of Commons there had been trade union leaders similar in character to those who took the Labour Party whip in 1906, but they had been classed as Liberals. Indeed, the careers of many of those designated Labour in 1906 had gone through Liberal and 'Lib-Lab' phases. Why had these new men not, like George Howell, Henry Broadhurst and Thomas Burt a generation earlier, remained with the Liberal Party instead of becoming associated with a relatively impecunious and insignificant committee for labour representation? Part of the answer must lie in the burgeoning of socialist propaganda since the 1880s, while the impact of wider economic changes also had an effect. But part of the answer lies in the nature of early twentieth-century Liberalism. At the local level Liberal

21 *Newton and Earlstown Guardian*, 19 January 1906,
22 C.F.G. Masterman, *The Condition of England*, Methuen, 1909, pp. 147–48.

associations were often unwilling to adopt working-men candidates, despite the advice of leading Liberals who since the 1867 Reform Act had sought to incorporate the labour movement into their party. This undoubtedly estranged some politically ambitious trade union leaders from Liberalism. But at the national level too many Liberals viewed the rise of Labour with some distaste. Although the radical wing of the party – reinvented as the 'New Liberalism' – claimed to represent the interests of the working man, its preoccupations were not those of the English working class. Conditions in north Wales had shaped the reforming zeal of David Lloyd George, the leading New Liberal. His targets – landlords, peers and brewers – were of less concern to the urban working class in England.

Further, some sections of Liberalism remained unprogressive. On the formation of Campbell-Bannerman's government Hardie criticised its 'seventeen land-owning peers and sixteen place-hunting lawyers'.[23] Also in the Liberal government were traditionally-minded libertarians such as John Morley, an opponent of a cause dear to most trade union leaders, the legal eight-hour day. Another Cabinet Minister, Henry Fowler, had not, in the words of his Private Secretary, 'the patience to suffer Radical and Labour members gladly'.[24] The 'Lib-Lab' John Burns, brought in as the first working-class Cabinet Minister and responsible for overseeing the poor law, was soon criticised for his reactionary attitudes.

Doubts about the capacity of Liberalism to pursue policies that would benefit the working class fitted in with an argument employed by all types of socialist. It held that the Liberal Party was the embodiment of the mid-Victorian bourgeoisie, but that the power of this class was being challenged by Labour, that Liberal commitment to individualism could not resist the tendency towards collectivism and that the Gladstonian shibboleths of peace, retrenchment and reform had become obsolete. In the words of *Justice*: 'Liberalism as a creed and as a force is played out.'[25] Socialism was destined to replace it. Such a view was not confined to socialists. Writing in *The Times*, one contemporary Liberal expected the ideas of the working class to be dominant in the twentieth century: 'I will,' he continued, 'hazard the prediction that the Labour party has introduced into the organism of middle class Liberalism, now, perhaps for the last time triumphant, the seeds of inevitable disintegration.'[26]

MacDonald, the Labour Party's chief theoretician, adopted a similar view of Liberalism. In writings that tried to establish a theoretical case for a party of labour, he presented socialism as an evolutionary force that would eventually replace existing society. Liberalism had its virtues, but its epoch was past: 'Socialism,' he wrote, 'marks the growth of Society, not the uprising of a class. The consciousness which it seeks to quicken is not one of economic class solidarity, but one of social unity and growth towards organic wholeness.'[27]

MacDonald, however, underestimated the importance of what he termed 'economic class solidarity' and the importance of the trade unions – organisations he had relatively little contact with – in the steady growth of the Labour Party. The genesis of the LRC was at the 1899 Trades Union

23 William Stewart, *J. Keir Hardie: A Biography*, Cassell, 1921, pp. 222–23.
24 Edith Henrietta Fowler, *The Life of Henry Hartley Fowler, First Viscount Wolverhampton*, Hutchinson, 1912, p. 500.
25 *Justice*, 6 January 1906.
26 'A Liberal Voter on the Liberal Victory', *The Times*, 31 January 1906.
27 J. Ramsay MacDonald, *Socialism and Society*, Independent Labour Party, 1905, p. 127.

Congress, and much of its early funding came from the affiliation fees of trade unions. Opinion among some trade union leaders and their more politically aware members was influenced by the pressure arising from increased foreign competition. This led some employers to seek higher productivity by introducing new techniques and tightening control of the labour force. Newer industrial processes made redundant some older skills and eroded differentials of status and pay. The unit of production became larger with amalgamations and economies of scale, and workers were increasingly likely to have to deal with salaried managers rather than a paternalistic factory or workshop owner. There was widespread disquiet about the changes taking place. In his Chairman's address to the LRC's 1902 conference, for example, W.J. Davis spoke of the 'displacement of labour by machinery', of workmen over 45 being told they were too old and of manufacturers compelling their workers 'to take out the finish, smoothness, and beauty, in order that they can get into the market cheap'.[28]

Trade unions were the main form of defence against these changes, yet they reinforced some of them; once a 'trade union rate' for a job had been negotiated with management all workers received it, despite variations in individual skill. The individual's bargaining function was replaced by a collective one, with all that such collectivism implied in terms of uniformity, solidarity and group consciousness. Some employers became more hostile towards trade unions, often invoking the law (the lengthy Taff Vale case in the early 1900s was one of several disputes that involved the courts). Criticisms of the unions were taken up in the press. A series of articles in *The Times*, appearing under the title 'The crisis in British industry', caused particular resentment. In this process of polarisation the LRC gained in strength; 127 unions, representing 50 per cent of the TUC's membership, affiliated to it within 12 months of the final judgement, and defeat for the railway workers, in the Taff Vale case.

In the general election of 1906 the Liberal Party benefited from the Conservative Party's adoption of tariff reform, a policy favoured by many manufacturers as a way of offsetting foreign competition. Liberal candidates were able to gain support by emphasising free trade – the 'big loaf or the little loaf' was a shrewd slogan with bread the main item of working-class diet. But in the longer term they were to lose their working-class base, as Liberalism was also to lose the support of most of the propertied class, which had been moving over to the Conservatives for some decades. In the short term, however, as agreed in the pact between Ramsay MacDonald and Herbert Gladstone, most Labour MPs were elected in tandem with Liberals.

In 1906, then, the Labour Party was a party supported largely by the trade unions, as was inevitable given the system under which elections were organised and financed. Although the majority of working-class men were not in trade unions, the actions of those who were struck some responsive chords. Socialists too were in a minority, but their agitations also could influence opinion. Economic changes were helping to ensure that both groups were moving in the same direction as the working class, which despite all its gradations and subtleties became more cohesive. Continuing urbanisation increased the size of working-class neighbourhoods in which families might identify common interests and values. Politically, it was a party of labour that came closest to representing these trends within society.

28 *Report of the Second Annual Conference of the Labour Representation Committee*, LRC, 1902, pp. 17, 19.

In this early phase, and subsequently, critics could point out failings in the Labour Party. The MPs of 1906 lacked parliamentary experience, frequently differed in their views, tended to opportunism and were weak in theoretical precepts. But in these characteristics they were not far removed from their supporters, and they were certainly closer than their political rivals to the everyday realities of working-class life. The words of a trade union organiser and socialist captured an element of the Labour Party at its advent:

> We now have men to represent us who know what it is to feel the pinch of poverty and the uncertainty of employment, whose homes for years have had the grim spectre of a rent lord hovering over them if work should fail, and who realise the depth of the shadow that falls in the evening of life, when grey hairs become a curse and men and women are no longer useful in the production of wealth for profit.[29]

The birth and early years of the Labour Party owed much to such sentiments, which gave rise to an unusually indelible reforming agenda. It provided, for good or ill, a point of reference for succeeding generations of activists.

David Martin

David Martin

29 Charles Coleman, 'The Coming of Labour', *Amalgamated Engineers Monthly Journal*, Vol. 2, 1906, p. 20.

G. N. BARNES. M. P.

George Barnes:
Labour MP for
Glasgow Blackfriars
and Hutchesontown,
1906–18, and for
Glasgow Gorbals,
1918–22

Chapter 1
George Barnes
1859–1940

GEORGE BARNES is sadly a much neglected and underestimated giant of the trade union and Labour movement. He was a pioneer of old age pensions and national insurance, of minimum employment conditions for women and young people, and of industrial safety and the right of combination.

He was an MP for 16 years, Chairman of the PLP, served as Minister for Pensions, and was a Member of the War Cabinet and a negotiator at the Peace Conference of Versailles. He helped establish the International Labour Organisation (ILO) as an agency of the League of Nations.

Born George Nicoll Barnes on 2 January 1859 at Lochee in Forfarshire, he was the second of five sons of James, a mechanic at a local textile mill and a Yorkshireman by birth, and Catherine Adam Langlands Barnes.

The Barnes family moved to Liverpool in 1866 when George was 7 years old and then to London in 1867. George attended Enfield Church School for two years and at the age of 11 he began working at a jute mill in Ponders End, Middlesex, which his father managed. The family returned to Dundee in 1872. Barnes worked at Parkers Foundry of Dundee where he completed his engineering apprenticeship before moving to Barrow-in-Furness where he got a job at the Vickers Shipyard.

However, the widespread unemployment in 'the black year of 1879' drove Barnes to London where after weeks of unemployment he had a number of short-term jobs including work at the Millwall Docks and in the construction of the new Albert Dock.

A maintenance engineer, Barnes gradually improved his skills by attending classes in engineering drawing and machine construction at Woolwich Arsenal. In 1882 he was able to obtain better work at Messrs Lucas and Airds in Fulham where he worked for eight years, joined the Amalgamated Society of Engineers and met Tom Mann and John Burns. In 1882 Barnes married Jessie, daughter of Thomas Langlands of Dundee, with whom he had two sons and a daughter.

On 13 February 1887 Barnes attended a demonstration in Trafalgar Square that turned into the riot known as 'Bloody Sunday'. It was at this demonstration that Barnes was badly injured when he was trampled on by a police horse. Barnes also attended meetings of the Social Democratic Federation and the Socialist League but rejected the idea of socialist revolution and refused to join either.

In the 1880s working-class political representatives stood in parliamentary elections as Liberal/Labour candidates. After the 1885 General Election, some socialists such as Keir Hardie began to argue that the working class needed their own independent political party. Barnes worked closely with other socialist trade unionists and in 1893 joined with Keir Hardie, Robert Smillie, Tom Mann, John Glasier, H.H. Champion and Ben Tillett to form the Independent Labour Party (ILP). The main objective of this party was 'to secure the collective ownership of the means of production, distribution and exchange'. In 1895, just two years after its establishment, the ILP had 35,000 members and George Barnes had become a leading figure. However, all ILP candidates, including Barnes, who stood in Rochdale, were beaten in the general election that year.

In 1889 Barnes was elected to the Executive of the Amalgamated Society of Engineers and was secretary of the powerful London Committee established on an ad hoc basis to promote the candidature of Tom Mann for the General Secretary of the union. Barnes acknowledged his debt to Mann on a number of occasions and once wrote: 'But for my connection with Mr Mann I dare say I should never have come into prominence in Labour circles, and very possibly I should have been content to go on working in the "shops".'[1] Just two years later this support was rewarded and Barnes was appointed Assistant General Secretary.

After three years, in 1895, Barnes resigned from the post to contest the position of General Secretary and was supported by a number of officials including Mann. He conducted a vigorous campaign and stood on a 'policy of direct parliamentary representation for the Society, increased militancy in trade policy, federation of all kindred societies, the transformation of the *Monthly Report* into a Journal for discussion of Society problems and for fettering the powers of the executive council which he claimed "enjoys a position of practical irresponsibility"'.[2] The contest was close with John Anderson, the then sitting General Secretary, polling 12,910 votes against Barnes 11,603. However, Anderson was dismissed the following year for wilful neglect of duty and in the union election that followed Barnes gained 8,000 more votes than Anderson who came second of the eight candidates.

Barnes was now a full-time union official. As General Secretary of the Amalgamated Society of Engineers (by now Britain's third largest union), Barnes was one of the country's most powerful Labour leaders. However, he had taken office at a time of great uncertainty for the engineering industry with the 'machine question' being the fundamental policy issue, this being whether the new machines would be operated by skilled workers. He led a national strike in 1897 in an attempt to win an eight-hour day but the strike ended in January 1898 without this having been achieved. Nevertheless, the strike was successful in establishing the principle of collective bargaining over conditions of employment. This changed the face of British industry, with much world industry being quick to follow. It is this that ensures his place in the history of the working classes.

In 1898 Barnes embarked on a fact-finding mission to Europe that convinced him that British engineers were the best in Europe but also that Britain was falling behind other industrial nations in wage levels and working conditions. He had long believed that real progress could only be achieved through working-class representation in Parliament.

1   *Pearson's Weekly*, 8 March 1906.
2   J.B. Jeffreys, *The Story of the Engineers*, Lawrence & Wishart 1945, p. 141.

On 27 February 1900, representatives of all socialist groups (the ILP, the Social Democratic Federation (SDF) and the Fabian Society) met with trade union leaders and, following a debate, the 129 delegates passed Keir Hardie's motion, which Barnes in his autobiography recalled 'I think I seconded', to establish 'a distinct Labour Group in Parliament, who shall have their own whips, and agree upon their policy'.[3] To make this possible, the Labour Representation Committee (LRC) was established and was made up of two members of the ILP of which Barnes was one, two members of the SDF, one member of the Fabian Society and seven trade unionists.

It was at this same meeting that Barnes made a speech arguing that not only working-class men should be selected as LRC candidates in general elections but that people such as Frederick Harrison and Sidney Webb had valuable qualities to contribute to the Labour movement. This motion was passed by 102 to 3.

A month after the establishment of the LRC, a ballot of all the members of the Amalgamated Society of Engineers produced only 2,897 votes in favour of affiliation and 702 against. This allowed the Society's Executive Council to postpone the issue; at the same time a resolution was passed whereby officers of the Society could not be eligible to stand as parliamentary candidates with financial support from the union. It was not until the following year that the decision to affiliate was accepted by a delegate meeting. Thus the Amalgamated Society of Engineers did not affiliate to the LRC until March 1902.

By this time the Taff Vale judgement had been upheld by the House of Lords and Barnes himself was much more realistic in appraising its consequences than many of his trade union colleagues. He fully supported the efforts of the TUC and the LRC to convince the Labour movement of the need for new parliamentary legislation.

In 1906 the Labour Representation Committee changed its name to the Labour Party. Barnes was a member of the LRC Executive Committee in 1904 and of the Parliamentary Committee of the TUC in 1906, the year he was first elected to Parliament.

In 1903 Keir Hardie introduced Barnes to the Blackfriars and Hutchesontown (later Gorbals) constituency, which covered the central areas of the City of Glasgow, North and South of the River Clyde. This seat had many engineers in its electorate, although this nearly resulted in him coming a cropper at the first hurdle when he instructed the engineers to return to work against their wishes during an unauthorised strike. Thus his campaign was a lively one embracing not only the rough and tumble of politics but also a heated industrial situation.

He fought the 1906 General Election on an ILP platform. The constituency had a large Irish Catholic vote, which in the previous general election of 1900 had gone to Andrew Bonar Law, the Unionist candidate, who defeated the Liberal candidate who was unsteady on the question of Irish Home Rule. However, Barnes received the official support of the Irish Nationalist Party and this, coupled with having travelled the country for four years as Chairman of the National Committee of Organised Labour for Old Age Pensions pushing this popular social welfare reform, saw him win the seat by a majority of some 300 votes over Bonar Law (who went on to become Conservative Prime Minister in 1922).

---

3   George Barnes, *From Workshop to War Cabinet*, Herbert Jenkins, 1923.

The Labour Party won 29 seats in the 1906 Election and on 12 February the PLP met for first time. Barnes derived more pleasure than anything else in his public career from his extremely active campaign for old age pensions and in February 1906 he made old age pensions the subject of his maiden speech. In 1907 he moved an amendment to the King's speech expressing his disappointment at the absence yet again of any reference to old age pensions.

In 1908 Lloyd George introduced the Old Age Pensions Act, which provided between 1 and 5 shillings a week to those over 70 and on incomes of not more than 12 shillings.[4] At the second reading of this Bill, Barnes spoke in favour of such reforms and of the general principles of the Bill but argued that the levels of benefits were not sufficient and opposed the pauper disqualification clauses and what later became known as the Means Test aspect of the reforms. He also believed that pensions should be universal and paid as a civic right to all fully qualified citizens.

By 1909 many Labour MPs, including Barnes, objected to the strong support that the leadership was giving to the Women's Social and Political Union (WSPU) and the National Union of Women's Suffragette Societies (NUWSS) in their fight for votes for women. Barnes argued that the party was being sidetracked from more important issues; it was this view that contributed to him replacing Arthur Henderson as Chairman of the Parliamentary Labour Party in 1910 after Henderson had been in the post for only ten months. During his period as Chairman, he had two outstanding questions to deal with. The first was the House of Lords with which Ireland was bound up and he believed that if the Irish Question had been settled the First World War might have been averted. The other was the King's Civil List, which he proposed should be turned over to the Public Exchequer. He believed that ample provision should be made for the maintenance of the dignity of the Crown but that the Duchies ought to be nationalised. In 1911 Barnes, who had been ill for most of his time as Chairman, was succeeded by Ramsay MacDonald.

In 1914 Barnes strongly supported Britain's involvement in the First World War. He believed that Britain had to defend its international obligations and uphold the authority of international law and the rights of neutral countries. During the first months of the war Barnes toured the country making recruitment speeches before going to Canada where he helped persuade trained mechanics to migrate to the UK to work in British industry replacing the skilled workers who had joined the army. He also took a special interest in the pensions and allowances being paid to families of recruits and demanded soldiers be paid a minimum of £1 per week.[5]

His youngest son, Henry, was killed fighting in the Battle of the Loos on the Western Front in September 1915 but this did not change Barnes views on the war. If anything, the death of his son reinforced his belief that, if such suffering and sacrifice were to be justified, the country had to unite. In 1916 he was one of only a small number of MPs to support military conscription.

Barnes was disillusioned with the way Herbert Asquith was running the country and in 1916 he helped David Lloyd George gain power. He was rewarded the same year by being made Minister for Pensions, making him one of only a few Labour MPs to attain a Cabinet post prior to a Labour government taking office. A condition of Barnes' acceptance of the post was

4   5 shillings would be about £20 in today's money; 12 shillings about £48.
5   About £78 today.

that the Royal Warrant for the Army should be revised; it was under Barnes' leadership that improvements in the payments to disabled servicemen were made and a new system introduced whereby some men could qualify for a pension linked to their pre-war level of earnings.

At the end of the war the Labour Party's National Executive Committee decided to withdraw from Lloyd George's Coalition government and this was confirmed at a Special Party Conference on 14 November 1918. In the 1918 General Election Barnes was opposed by John Maclean, the famous red Clydesider who stood as the official Labour candidate. Maclean was in prison having been sentenced for making seditious speeches. Barnes submitted a memo to the Cabinet suggesting Maclean's release which was forthcoming. Barnes defeated Maclean in a two-horse race by 6,811 votes.

Barnes subsequently resigned from the party in order to remain in charge of the Ministry for Pensions and formed the National Democratic Party with himself as its Leader. When Arthur Henderson went to Russia in 1917 to try to persuade the Kerensky government to continue in the war, Barnes replaced him as Minister without Portfolio in the War Cabinet where he remained until January 1920. Barnes believed that it was a mistake for the party to withdraw from the Coalition because it would mean relinquishing the opportunity to have some bearing on the Peace Conferences, the expectation of which had driven Barnes to fight for the continuation of the Coalition. Barnes was asked to attend the Paris Peace Conference as the government's Labour Representative and was subsequently one of the signatories of the Treaty of Versailles.

Since 1916 Barnes had been a prominent member of the League to Abolish War and during the final years of the war became very keen to establish an international machine fully supported by international law that would ordain and uphold the rights of working men. Towards the end of 1918 Barnes, along with other members of the Ministry of Labour, drafted a list of proposals that were to become the basis of the scheme that developed into the ILO. The Commission for World Labour set up by the Peace Conference took this British draft, the only detailed plan for a Labour Charter to be presented, as the basis for discussion. Delegates at the International Labour and Social Conference in Berne had been discussing certain 'minimum requirements' relating to education and employment of young people, women's working conditions, hours of work, dangerous work, the right of combination, conditions of immigrant workers, the legal minimum wage, unemployment and social insurance and the administration of the labour laws, many of which were included in Barnes' draft, which they wanted the League of Nations to incorporate into a 'Code of International Law'. Barnes steered the plan through 36 sittings of the Commission for World Labour and eventually saw it approved unanimously. The Labour Charter and the provisions for the ILO were later incorporated in Part 13 (often known as the Labour Chapter) of the Peace Treaty. This was Barnes' great contribution following the First World War and was regarded by him as his most significant achievement.

After heading the first ILO Conference in Washington in 1919, which, amongst other things, established a permanent Labour Office at Geneva, Barnes felt it was the time to leave the government; he resigned from the Cabinet for reasons of poor health in January 1920. His final years in the Cabinet had been difficult ones. His policies and personal position were criticised and his continued support and involvement in the Coalition government after Labour's withdrawal had made him unpopular within the Labour movement. It was later that same year that Barnes was made a Companion of Honour.

Barnes was also one of three British delegates to the first assembly meeting of the League of Nations at Geneva in 1920. However, unable to gain the support of the Labour Party two years later in the 1922 General Election, he resigned from the House of Commons.

He travelled extensively for the next few years and gave much of his time to the work of the ILO and to the Co-operative movement. He was Chairman of the Co-operative Printing Society for some time and continued his interest in the problems of industry. He published a book, *Industrial Conflict: The Way Out*, in 1924.

In August 1939 Barnes suffered a stroke. On Friday 19 April 1940 he fell into a coma from which he never awoke and passed away at his home, 76 Herne Hill, London, on 21 April 1940 aged 81, leaving behind his wife Jessie, son Robert and daughter Jessie. His burial took place at Fulham Cemetery.

Much of his legacy went up in flames when all of his papers were lost when his Herne Hill home was bombed in a German air raid. The life that most of us enjoy today and often take for granted exists only because of the labours of George Barnes and his colleagues of that era.

David Marshall
MP for Glasgow East

David Marshall

C. W. BOWERMAN. M. P.

*Charles Bowerman:
Labour MP for
Lewisham Deptford,
1906–31*

Chapter 2
Charles Bowerman
1851–1947

CHARLES WILLIAM BOWERMAN was a life-long trade unionist, whose passions were workers' rights and education. Little is known of his family background, though 'his father was a tinplate worker, who having gone to London for the Great Exhibition of 1851 decided to settle there'.[1] Charles Bowerman was born that year on 22 January probably in Honiton, Devon, but it was London that shaped his fortunes.

His education was typical of those who became grass roots leaders at the time: five years at a national school, followed by an apprenticeship and a subscription to Cassell's monthly educational and scientific publications. By the age of 21 he was a journeyman compositor on the *Daily Telegraph*, where he remained for 19 years. During this time he steadily advanced his position in the London Society of Compositors (LSC) winning his first election to become Secretary of the News Department. Within a few years he was involved in the LSC's Reform League, set up to challenge the conservatism of the union and its Secretary Drummond. In 1892 the League won three seats on the executive, the old guard resigned and the following year Bowerman was elected General Secretary. His victory was attributed to his 'engaging personality and enormous appetite for hard work'.[2] Bowerman's life as a working-class radical had set its course.

Entries on Charles Bowerman frequently appear in reference works of these early days of the Labour movement. They record his many trade union offices but nothing personal. In one photograph, he appears distinguished and formally dressed, sporting a moustache and a hairstyle of the kind later favoured by Lord Lucan. At the age of 25, and newly established in his career as a compositor, he married Louisa Peace. Of his wife nothing appears to have been recorded except that she gave birth to no fewer than five sons and seven daughters and died before her husband. In 1894 the family moved to 4 Battledean Road, London N5 (Islington), which was to remain Bowerman's home for over 50 years and which today bears a commemorative plaque.

---

1   *Dictionary of Labour Biography*. This chapter draws heavily on John Saville's entry for Charles William Bowerman in Joyce M. Bellamy and John Saville (eds), *Dictionary of Labour Biography*, Macmillam, 1979.
2   *AEU Monthly Journal*, June 1927.

Bowerman's commemorative plaque

Bowerman's election as General Secretary of the LSC led to three decades of activity at the top of the union movement. He attended his first TUC conference in 1893, becoming Treasurer in 1899 and Chairman in 1901. But it was his support for Labour representation that was to shape the next phase of his life. Elected to the TUC's parliamentary committee in 1897, he found himself taking the chair at the Swansea TUC following the Taff Vale judgement in which the railway company successfully claimed damages against the railmen's union. He advised Congress to 'make haste slowly' as the parliamentary committee had no specific proposals to make. However, with 'a judicious amendment of the rules . . . it will be possible to avert many of the difficulties created by the decision of the House of Lords, especially in the direction of protecting the funds of unions'. Summing up, he advocated 'the imperative and absolute necessity of securing increased representation in the House of Commons'.

Like many of his peers, Bowerman knew the value of education to the working class and devoted much of his time and effort to it. He played a significant part in establishing Ruskin College, Oxford, and later represented the parliamentary committee of the TUC on various committees of the college.

He was actively involved in the opposition to Balfour's 1902 Education Act. He opposed the destruction of the School Boards and the continuation of religious control of education policies. Such issues were at the heart of his ambition to become a Member of Parliament. Three years after attending the founding conference of the Labour Party in 1900 and a year after joining the NEC of the Labour Representation Committee (LRC), he won a ballot to be a parliamentary candidate. He was already an LCC Alderman and a well-known political figure in London – it only remained for him to find a seat. He did not have to look far; across the river, the Deptford and Greenwich Trades Union Council was initiating a search for a Labour representative.

Bowerman received recognition from the LRC and was adopted by the local Trades Union Council as the candidate for Deptford. At the time, a secret pact between the Liberal Chief Whip, Herbert Gladstone, and

Labour's Ramsay McDonald was designed to provide a straight run against the Conservatives for Labour and Liberal candidates in about 30 seats each. In Deptford, the LRC candidate was not to be so favoured – the Liberals insisted on their own 'Stop Bowerman' candidate. As a consequence, the sitting member, Conservative and Unionist A.H.A. Morton, reputedly approached the election with an unwarranted degree of complacency. On 5 January 1906, the local *Brockley News* published a letter from Charles Bowerman in which he set out a mini manifesto:

> As a Labour man with 33 years' continuous connection with my trade organization, and being privileged during that period to occupy various official positions, I can at least claim to possess some knowledge of the pressing needs and requirements of the workers of all grades, and my energies would be directed most strenuously towards promoting any and all social legislation having for its object the 'greatest good of the greatest number'.
>
> I am in favour of the Disestablishment and Disendowment of the Church of England. Religion should be free and no sect receive State support.
>
> In my opinion, education in our schools should be secular. Religion is not a matter for the State.
>
> I strongly advocate the Nationalisation of the Land, Railways and the Canals.
>
> I am in favour of the establishment of a Minister of Labour, controlling a department whose duty should be to deal with the serious question of the unemployed.
>
> I am in favour of raising the minimum wage of Government Workers to a standard of 30s weekly in the London district.
>
> With confidence I place myself in your hands . . . it is the first and bounden duty of a successful candidate to represent the electors who have honoured him with their confidence. I appeal to the brain and manual workers of Deptford for their support during the contest.

Contemporary accounts in the *Kentish Mercury* record campaign meetings at New Cross Hall – Bowerman's meeting presided over by a Christian minister – 'a meeting so large that it overflowed into the corridors until the outer gates had to be shut'. 'Organised radical rowdyism' was recorded at the Conservative candidate's meeting at the same hall.

Seventy-seven per cent of the electorate of 15,397 turned out, giving Labour over half the votes cast and relegating the Liberal candidate to third place. The *Kentish Mercury* recorded a crowd of 5,000 outside the Town Hall when the result was declared and wrote: 'Mr Bowerman proceeded to his central committee rooms at the Deptford and Greenwich Trades Club but was too tired to make a speech.'

Bowerman resigned as General Secretary of his union on taking his seat and became Parliamentary Secretary of the LSC. In January 1910, reflecting on his role as an MP, he said he was in Parliament as a trade unionist. He would 'extract all the practical part of the Socialist programme' and work in harmony with 'what are known as the more extreme men'.[3] He remained true to his word, supporting moderate Labour policies and actively pursuing a wide range of national and international Labour issues.

3   *Christian Commonwealth*, January 1910.

It is possible his first contribution in the Commons was not recorded. Hansard did not start producing a verbatim account of proceedings until 1909. There is no indication that Bowerman's first recorded intervention on 9 May 1907 on the London County Council (Electric Supply) Bill was his maiden speech. The speech bears an asterisk, indicating that it had been revised by the Member in question. It reads rather oddly as in most of the text Bowerman is speaking not as himself but for 'those for whom he spoke'. He is opposing the Bill, not because he does not want the County Council to take control of the electric supply but because the intention was to 'ask the House for certain powers, and after these powers had been obtained to lease them to private companies'. Referring to those he represented Bowerman said:

> they believed that if the question had been fairly presented the County Council would have had the consent of the ratepayers of London to the running of an electric supply. They had before them the evidence of their capacity to run one of the best tramway services in this country, and if they could do that successfully . . . surely they had a right to assume . . . they would make an equal success of the electric supply.

He went on to predict that, if the County Council allowed its powers to pass to private hands, it would only be a matter of time before 'they would have to make overtures to those private companies, with the result that Londoners would find themselves compelled to buy them out at some extravagant rate'.

Bowerman did not advance any constituency interest in this speech but Deptford had a very significant connection with electricity. Sebastian de Ferranti built the world's first modern high pressure station at Deptford in 1889, introducing a new age in the scale and capacity of electricity generation. Deptford is also distinguished as the terminus for the first urban railway in the world and the oldest surviving urban railway outside central London. Railways were one of Charles Bowerman's many industrial interests, and his first recorded parliamentary questions, in 1906, concerned rail fares: 'I beg to ask the President of the Board of Trade if his attention has been called to the increases in fares on the District Railway, which press heavily upon working-class families; and if he will cause inquiry to be made into the matter and appoint a committee to make recommendations thereon.'

Lloyd George replied:

> Yes, Sir, I have had this matter under careful consideration. The question whether the workmen's fares now charged by the railway company are unduly high is one that can be dealt with under the Cheap Trains Act, 1883. I am informed by the London County Council that their Housing Committee is in correspondence with the railway company, and that failing a satisfactory settlement, the Council will be recommended to make a representation to the Board of Trade under the Act. Full investigation would then be made into all the circumstances either by the Board of Trade or by the Railway and Canal Commissioners.

However it was Deptford's last remaining connection with Henry the Eighth's great naval shipyards that occupied much of Bowerman's time. On the banks of the Thames, close to the steps where Drake is thought to have alighted on his return from the new world, were the Royal Victoria Victualling Yards. In constant use by the Navy from 1742, the yards finally closed in 1961 and the modern Pepys estate was built soon afterwards.

Typical questions asked by Bowerman in his early years in Parliament related to the conditions of workers in the Victualling Yards and numerous aspects of naval contracts. Another major constituency concern was the Deptford Cattle Market – a subject not only of questions but also speeches. In May 1907 he was pressing the Board of Agriculture to remove the restriction on cattle imports from Holland and Denmark, arguing that both countries had been free of foot and mouth disease for four or five years and their exports should be allowed into Britain. He said he was appealing from 'a purely Labour point of view' and, referring to a recent visit to Deptford, said 'so far as disease was concerned, it was not possible for any disease to come out of the market . . . The system of inspection was so stringent . . . [and the market had] cost nearly half a million to build.'

Two years into his parliamentary career Charles Bowerman is recorded as speaking on the Elections and Registration (London) Bill proposed by backbench Liberal MP Willoughby Dickinson. The issue was the registration of electors, with Bowerman arguing passionately that 'workmen were being disenfranchised year after year by the absurd and unnecessary difficulties which were being placed in their way'. Describing the average London workman's day, he said 'he had to be at his work in ninety-nine cases out of 100 before eight o'clock in the morning. He had probably to travel from seven to ten miles to get to business.' As a result 'workmen rushed from their work to the polling booth on election days, and, though reaching the place in time to record their votes, they were not able to vote because of the large crowd assembled there'. Such was the deficiency of the law that reference had been made to the case in which the decision of the revising barrister depended upon the answer to the question 'whether the wife of the claimant shook the front door mat'. In common with the fate of most private members' bills today, it never reached the statute book.

Bowerman stood again for Labour in 1910 adding to his previous aims the abolition of the House of Lords; resistance to Tariff Reform; adult suffrage; Home Rule for Scotland, Ireland and Wales; and removal of poor law disqualification. By this time he was a national figure and, in 1911, he was elected Secretary of the TUC. When the outbreak of war seemed inevitable, Bowerman and Arthur Henderson convened a special TUC conference, which established the War Emergency Workers National Committee. The aim was to put the maximum trade union support behind the war effort in the hope of a swift end. He became one of the secretaries of the Joint Labour Recruiting Committee in 1915 and supported conscription in 1916. That year he was made a Junior Whip – and a Privy Councillor about which 'universal was the pleasure and approval of everybody connected with him' on receiving this 'well deserved honour'.[4]

Throughout the war years, Bowerman remained active in both the TUC and Parliament. At Westminster he kept up a barrage of questions on the war effort at home; at the TUC he concentrated on international affairs. Links were maintained with the European trade unions and in 1919 he participated in setting up the International Federation of Trade Unions. He was also closely involved in the consultation that led to the formation of the International Labour Organisation (ILO). He attended its

4   *AEU Monthly Journal*, June 1927.

first conference in Washington in October 1919 and played a significant part in formulating the House Convention, which proposed a 48-hour working week in all countries.

The Rt Hon Charles Bowerman went on to fight another six general elections, representing Deptford continuously from 1906 until 1931. His major concerns are reliably recorded in Hansard but I wonder what other contact he had with Deptford's people and places, even then a multi-ethnic and multicultural society. Was he at the 1907 opening of the Deptford Town Hall with its magnificent marble and wrought iron staircases or the Carnegie-endowed and elegant Deptford Library in 1914?

The Albany Institute might well have been of interest, having been established in 1899 by the Deptford Fund to raise and improve the poorer part of Deptford, 'religiously, intellectually, morally and socially'. Did he ever, I wonder, visit the great entertainment palaces of the Broadway Theatre and New Cross Empire with their combined seating capacity of three and a half thousand people?

While little appears to be recorded of the less public side of his life, tributes to him suggest a man of warmth: 'In every respect Bowerman has been and is a remarkable man; his courtesy, amiability, energy, disinterestedness and charm of manner have endeared him to all who have had the privilege of his friendship.'[5]

In 1919 he was made a JP for the Finsbury Division and it was this interest, together with London's municipal affairs and the print industry that sustained him in the later years of his life. At the age of 72, in 1923 he stepped down from the secretaryship of the TUC under its newly introduced age limitation. In 1931 he stood for Parliament for the last time, aged 80. He was defeated in a two-way contest with the Tory D.A. Hanley, swept away in an anti-Labour tide but still polling over 45 per cent of votes cast. As a tribute to his 25 years as Deptford's MP, a new street was named Bowerman Way.

Charles Bowerman maintained his interest in Ruskin College, serving on its Executive Committee to the end of his long life. Likewise, his commitment to the print industry saw him, still serving as the Chairman of the Co-operative Printing Society aged 95.

He died at home on the 11 June 1947, aged 96. George Rowles' obituary of him for the LSC referred to him as 'our Charlie' and 'a worker to the end'.

Joan Ruddock
MP for Deptford

Joan Ruddock

5   Ibid.

J. R. CLYNES. M. P.
COPYRIGHT PHOTO EDWARDS

J.R. Clynes: Labour MP for Manchester North East, 1906–31, and for Manchester Platting, 1935–45

Chapter 3
J.R. Clynes
1869–1949

JOHN ROBERT CLYNES joins Ramsay MacDonald, Philip Snowden and Arthur Henderson as one of the most noteworthy and illustrious MPs that formed the Parliamentary Labour Party (PLP) in 1906. In a parliamentary career that spanned over five decades, he became Leader of the Labour Party and a Member of the Cabinet in three separate governments.

Born in Oldham in 1869, he was the eldest of two boys in a family of seven. His father, Patrick Clynes, never earned more than 24 shillings in a week,[1] yet ensured that all of his children received the elementary education to which he had not been entitled. But the family was poor and Clynes and his siblings spent much of their childhood in hunger. He started working part-time at the age of 10 at the local mill as a 'piecer'; at 12 he gladly gave up his formal education to work full-time so as to bring in much needed extra income. It was his experiences of the harsh conditions in the mill that got him interested in the rights of workers and the burgeoning trade union movement.

Despite not enjoying his formal education, Clynes was an avid reader who was fascinated by language. He spent endless nights reading through and copying down words and their meanings from a dictionary on which he had invested two weeks' wages. At a young age he was reading Dickens, Ruskin, Mill and Shakespeare. He started his political education reading the local newspaper to three old blind men and listening to them debate the articles. Their opinions on workers' rights and just rewards impressed the young Clynes. His chaotic ideas began to take shape and he began to believe deeply that people deserved a fair return for their hard endeavours.

He became involved in political movements when listening to a group discussing the Irish National Question. His Irish father had been a tenant farmer but was evicted in 1851; this injustice led him to seek out the group. At the first meeting, enraptured by the debate going on around him, the young Clynes stood up and denounced the lot of mill workers. Encouraged by the main speaker, Clynes began to transcribe his thoughts onto paper in the form of a long series of letters to a local Oldham paper, under the pseudonym of 'piecer'. The inspiration for his letters came from the men

---

1   Less than £100 in today's money.

and women who had 'been through the mill' in the phrase's most literal context. He wrote vividly about the brutality of their living and working conditions and made suggestions as to potential reform. His letters were almost always published and the editorial often alluded to them and even endorsed the opinions of the anonymous writer.

Piecers were treated the worst of all the mill workers. At 15 Clynes went on a one-man strike, refusing to work overtime cleaning and oiling the machinery for which he would not be paid. He avoided being sacked because he powerfully and succinctly convinced a sympathetic foreman of the injustice of this practice; from then on he was allowed to arrive later than his colleagues. Not satisfied with improving his own lot, he subsequently established a Piecers' Union alongside the main Cotton Operative Workers' Union. The union was difficult to maintain, not least because the membership was made up of young and inexperienced workers who would normally become spinners as they got older.

In 1891 he was spotted by Will Thorne, founder of the National Union of Gas and General Workers, at the inauguration of the Lancashire branch of the union. So impressed was Thorne by Clynes' oratory skills and extensive knowledge of the conditions in the factories, he instantly enlisted him to work for the Lancashire branch.

Having left the gruelling labour of the mill, new opportunities presented themselves to Clynes. Union activity was considered on the borderline of criminality, with those partaking in it running the risk of imprisonment. Over the next few years Clynes spent much of his time travelling to congresses and conferences that were to become the foundation of the Labour Party. He was present at the founding Congress of the Independent Labour Party (ILP) at Bradford in 1892; the following year he attended the Belfast Trades Union Congress where nationalisation of land and industry was supported. He fervently believed that one day all workers would work together for the greater good.

He fiercely advocated the new party at union and Labour meetings, especially against those loyal to the Liberals or Tories. He believed that the Labour Party was the natural remedy to social problems and wrote in his memoirs: 'to champion oppressed humanity against them and to teach them that gold cannot be eaten or drunk or even turned into happiness, the Labour Party was evolved. It was of all the productions of the Victorian era most un-Victorian – a living proof that every evil produces its own remedy.'

He held variously the posts of Secretary and President on the Oldham Trades and Labour Council (the second largest in the country) and was selected as its representative on the Oldham Chamber of Commerce. He was considered a brilliant negotiator by both the union members and employers alike and often said that he enjoyed listening to both sides of the debate so as to understand any issue fully. The fact that Clynes was extremely well read helped him transcend those class barriers that were imposed on society, and employers tended to listen. He preferred arbitration to all-out strikes. Strike action did become a common feature of union work but Clynes witnessed workers during long strikes reduced to levels 'below that of paupers or prisoners'. He was later described as being the 'epitome of industrial moderation' in his work when he became the President of the National Union of Gas and General Workers (which later became the General and Municipal Workers' Union).

Clynes became a Magistrate in 1904 and stood as a candidate for Oldham Council but was never elected. However, his reputation across Lancashire led several councillors from Manchester City Council to approach him to stand as their candidate in the Manchester North East seat in the 1906

Election. They had been greatly impressed by his involvement with the Labour Representation Committee and the ILP and by his ability to speak well. He accepted and embarked upon what must have been one of the most enthralling election campaigns that Labour has ever fought. Clynes even got the chance to kick off for Manchester United in the first-half of a game at their former stadium in Bank Street, Newton Heath – something of which his present day successor is extremely envious! In the second half, the Liberal candidate for Manchester North West, a certain Winston Churchill, kicked off for their opponents. United, of course, won – a good omen for Clynes.

Yet Clynes suffered, as did many of those early candidates, from class snobbery. On one occasion when out canvassing, he visited the house of a retired military officer who responded negatively: 'I am a gentleman, Mr – er – Mr Clynes . . . I have always been a gentleman, and a gentleman I intend to remain until my dying day. I consider it my duty, sir, to do my best to see that a gentleman is returned to Parliament for North West Manchester', to which Clynes replied, 'Thank you for your promise. I am sure you will never regret the confidence you place in me.'[2]

Nevertheless, the Labour Party did hold the popular appeal in Manchester. Clynes' hard work and shining speeches paid off; he was returned as the Member of Parliament for Manchester North East, comfortably beating the sitting Tory Cabinet Minister, Sir James Fergusson.

Like many of his Labour colleagues in Parliament, Clynes fell into financial difficulty. The unsalaried position of MP suited those with inherited wealth or business interests. Labour members, a few aside, had to rely on the support from their respective unions. Clynes found it difficult paying for accommodation and travel but he was assisted by his union. This arrangement was seriously threatened following the Osborne Judgement in 1910. Inevitably, he had to live far from Westminster in order to be able to afford accommodation – well outside the 'division bell' area.

He spent most of his early years in Parliament listening to debates and learning about the alien customs and ceremonies within the Palace of Westminster, a far cry from his background as a piecer in the cotton mills of Oldham. He maintained his union activities in his spare time, and readily spoke in Parliament to help the non-unionised workforce. He resolutely believed that the state should provide support for the unskilled non-unionised workforce and worked towards this objective.

On the eve of the First World War, Clynes was one of many in the PLP who spoke out against the foolishness of military action. However, once war had been declared, he joined forces with Arthur Henderson and formed the leadership of the party, following the resignations of Keir Hardie and Ramsay MacDonald. He helped establish the Industrial Truce, getting the unions to agree not to strike until peace had been declared. He argued against Labour Members entering a coalition following the split in the Liberal government and returned to Manchester to avoid being asked, although Henderson became a Cabinet Minister. Nevertheless he continued to work with the government. Despite the Industrial Truce, there were stoppages in the factories due to appalling conditions and pay. Clynes took a group of workers from military equipment factories on a fact-finding mission to Ypres, believing that labourers needed to see the appalling conditions of their comrades on the front so as to cease their stoppages. He also

2   E. George, *From Mill-Boy to Minister: The Life of the Rt Hon J.R. Clynes MP*, T. Fisher Unwin Ltd, 1918, p. 59.

wanted to demonstrate the dangers of war profiteering and to convince factory workers not to cut corners when manufacturing military equipment, to the advantage of the owners, as this made the war even more perilous for those on the front.

Towards the end of the war, his position on entering government changed, when he was asked to be the Parliamentary Secretary to the Food Controller, Lord Rhondda. Clynes had been one of the first to suggest food rationing and at the beginning of the war had been accused of scare-mongering. But Lord Rhondda had been impressed by hearing Clynes speak about the real danger of food shortages. These shortages allowed a few to make massive profits by speculating at the expense of labour on the front and on the home front. Clynes proposed price capping and nationalisation of both food and its transportation supply links. He reluctantly accepted the post, convincing himself that he should put his criticism into construc-tive action on a subject close to his heart. In his time at the Department, the costs of production and transport were carefully monitored, and the prices of commodities were fixed, thus cutting out profiteering. People were fined for getting food on the black market. He established 2,000 Food Committees across the country to ensure a better distribution of food, insisting that every committee included a housewife and a Labour repre-sentative, and that they worked with Co-operative Societies. Full rationing was introduced for the first time, which even affected the King. Clynes also set up the Consumers' Council. One biographer suggested that it was prob-ably his own childhood hunger that drove Clynes tirelessly to ensure that every man, woman and child had enough to eat. The food crises that were averted due to the Ministry's work convinced Clynes that the state was fully capable and, moreover, a better producer and distributor than a private owner or corporation.

For his endeavours, he was made a Privy Councillor and, when Lord Rhondda suddenly passed away in July 1918, Clynes took his Cabinet post of Food Controller.

At one point the American Food Authorities asked the British govern-ment to ban the brewing of beer to save on the short supply of grain. Clynes argued fervently against this, knowing that it would cost the war: 'To the working man beer is food, drink and recreation; he takes it in moderation, and would fiercely resent any attempts to abolish it. The inn is his club; very often there is no other place where he can meet his friends, since his home is too frequently nothing better than a collection of overcrowded bedrooms.' He believed that riots would ensue and attributed the Bolshevik Revolution, in part, to the prohibition of vodka in Russia. The slogan 'More beer, and better beer, and sell it cheaper!' followed him around and he even earned a place in *Punch*. Despite this, the beer had to be watered down, although he claimed the actual quantity was no worse than before.

His position in the Cabinet became untenable shortly after the war. Lloyd George had betrayed the wartime coalition by calling a snap election, capi-talising on the war victory. Moreover, many within the Labour Party, Clynes included, were extremely uneasy about the harsh terms of Armistice. A Conference vote prohibited Members remaining in government; Clynes was left with the choice to leave either the government or the Labour Party. He immediately tendered his resignation to Lloyd George.

At the December 1918 Election, both Ramsay MacDonald and Arthur Henderson lost their seats. William Adamson became the Leader of the Parliamentary Party, with Clynes its Vice-Chairman. Following Adamson's resignation in 1921, Clynes became Leader/Chairman of the PLP, and entertained the thought of becoming the first Labour Prime Minister. Under his leadership Labour gained 67 seats in the 1922 General Election, taking the number of Labour MPs to 142, and making Labour the official opposition for the first time in its history.

However, his hopes of becoming Labour's first Prime Minister were quickly thwarted. In the PLP leadership contest, the newly re-elected Ramsay MacDonald won by five votes. Clynes had been tipped to win and later claimed that some of his supporters, predominantly from union backgrounds, failed to turn up at the vote believing that his leadership was assured. But MacDonald held the support of the Clydesdale group and the more left-wing Members who had been dissatisfied that Clynes had not regularly led the party on walkouts of Parliament. He thus became the only Leader of the Labour Party to be voted out of office in the Parliamentary Party's 100-year history. He did, however, accept the post of Deputy Chairman, which he held until 1931.

Following the December 1923 Election, Stanley Baldwin formed a minority Conservative government. Labour, with 193 seats, proved a powerful challenge, and it was Clynes who moved a vote of no confidence in the debate on the King's Speech in January 1924. The vote forced Baldwin to resign and enabled Ramsay MacDonald to form the first ever Labour government.

Clynes was made Lord Privy Seal and Deputy Leader of the House and moved to 11 Downing Street – very different to his childhood accommodation in Oldham. He was left predominantly in charge of both the government and formulating legislation as MacDonald, having appointed himself Foreign Secretary, spent most of his time at European Congresses.

There was tremendous hope that this first Labour government would bring about great social transformation. But the Tories and Liberals had sufficient numbers to obstruct any piece of legislation that would have heralded the changes that the government desired. Labour was not even the largest party in the Commons, and was blessed with neither the time nor the numbers to give it the legitimacy of the present government to enact radical social change and greater equality. Bills were introduced to improve working conditions and get some 200,000 people back to work. Furthermore, unemployment benefit was increased from 26 to 42 weeks. Nevertheless, it was only Wheatley's Housing Act that had any lasting social significance. After only eight months, MacDonald was forced to call a general election, which left the Labour Party somewhat fractured over the ensuing years. Clynes was again erroneously tipped to take over from MacDonald.

Clynes was to get his third chance at government in 1929 when Labour polled 8.5 million votes. MacDonald formed a second weak minority government and once again Labour 'faced a period of rule subject to Liberal permission'.

Clynes became Home Secretary; although the Home Office was not at the forefront of policy making, it gave him the chance to concentrate on issues close to his heart. He was head of the factory inspection system, allowing him to use his own experience of the mills in Oldham to draft legislation 'whereby workpeople could be protected not only from their employers' desire for greater profits, but also their own blind readiness to work themselves into early graves earning overtime money by merciless assiduity in unhealthy occupations'. He regularly got advice from colleagues in the union movement and he visited factories and other workplaces to gain a better insight into working conditions.

He saw his position as Home Secretary as being to uphold the law even where he did not agree with it or felt it was unjust. This was exemplified with capital punishment to which he was morally opposed. He was only able to suggest the quashing or revoking of the sentence if there was an error in the way a person was convicted or if new evidence cleared the person, and abided by this. Had Labour had more time in power, he argued in his memoirs, he would have attempted to change the law.

Clynes, like Henderson, advocated a step-by-step approach to socialism; he was interested in making the party 'not only socialist, but successful'.[3] His philosophy was one of negotiation and he was always ready to seek a compromise between different groups. He was no 'Trot'; indeed as Home Secretary he refused Trotsky permission to seek asylum in the UK, although this may have had more to do with the Labour government's policy of re-establishing diplomatic relations with Stalin's Soviet Union.

He attempted to reform the overcrowded prison system and introduce education to give offenders the opportunity to find alternative means of living once released. He also brought in the Electoral Reform Bill, which was based on the alternative vote, but this was heavily defeated in the Lords, and Clynes was lambasted for introducing it.

Labour's time in office was overshadowed by world events. It did not take long for the international depression to affect the British economy; at one point over two million people were unemployed. The government was heavily criticised for borrowing excessively to pay for unemployment bene-fits. Initially, the Cabinet and the TUC remained united, refusing to reduce unemployment pay or impose wage reductions. Nevertheless, as the economic crisis deepened, both MacDonald and his Chancellor, Snowden, began to advocate dramatic cuts to resolve it. MacDonald, without con-sulting his Cabinet, formed a National Government to implement these changes. Snowden followed, but Clynes and Henderson chose not to turn their backs on those who had voted for them, and so abandoned power rather than see unemployment benefits cut by a few shillings.

The split in the party was a personal blow to Clynes. He had been in Parliament for 25 years as a colleague and friend to those who had chosen to part company with the Labour Party. Clynes was once again asked to stand as Leader but refused, convincing Arthur Henderson to take the post. At the subsequent election, Clynes became one of the 213 Labour MPs who lost their seats. Only 52 Members were returned, the Tories speculating that the Labour Party would not survive the crisis.

Clynes was extremely critical of MacDonald's record in government, writing in his memoirs: 'Up to that time he had given much to the building of the movement. But he always owed it more than he gave. The highest place, the greatest praise and an authority which was almost absolute had been surrendered to him.' He accused him of being cowardly in govern-ment. As Prime Minister in the second Labour Cabinet 'he was less a leader than a medium for collecting opinions'. Clynes claimed not to be sour about the PLP leadership election, yet there is an evident tone of bitterness in his writings. He believed that MacDonald, on forming the National Govern-ment, had ratted not only on those who had voted for him, but also on the party in general.

In his years outside Parliament, Clynes dedicated himself to union activity but was elected MP for Manchester Platting Division in 1935. A total of 160 Labour MPs won their seats, proving wrong the Tory prophecy that the Labour Party was dead. He was again asked to be Leader of the

3   J.H.S. Reid, *The Origins of the British Labour Party*, University of Minnesota Press, 1955, p. 159.

Opposition but refused and took a backbench role, being 66 years old at his re-election. He served a further ten years in Parliament, and was called upon during the Second World War to dedicate his expertise as Food Controller in the First World War to the Food Supply Select Committee. He stood down at the 1945 Election having reached the age-limit on MPs set by his union.

He was only to briefly witness the enactment of real social change brought about by the newly elected Attlee government in 1945, change of which the fragile Labour governments in which he was so senior could only ever have dreamed.

In retirement he complained bitterly in a letter to *The Times* of the 'means-test', which meant that he was not entitled to anything from the House of Commons ex-Members' Fund despite having paid into it since its inception. He had been finding it difficult living on the money given by his union especially as he had to pay for help for his wife who had been seriously disabled since being injured during the blitz. A personal fund was started for him into which even Churchill, the politician whose career largely had overlapped with as Clynes, paid.

He died in October 1949 at the age of 80. His life mirrored the burgeoning 'new unionism' Labour movement at the end of the nineteenth century and the nascent Labour Party in the twentieth century. His wife of 56 years, Mary, died just five weeks later. He was the last surviving of the 29 who entered Parliament in 1906.

Tony Lloyd
MP for Manchester Central

Tony Lloyd

W. CROOKS, M. P.
COPYRIGHT PHOTO HAINES

Will Crooks: Labour MP for Woolwich, 1903–21

Chapter 4
Will Crooks
1852–1921

IN MANY WAYS the life and career of Will Crooks is, in microcosm, the story of the emergence of the Labour Party as a transformational force in British politics. He came from a background of severe poverty in London's East End, where part of his childhood was spent in the work-house. As a young man he experienced the insecurity and hardship of working-class life, which in turn propelled him into organisation and agita-tion on behalf of his fellow citizens. He played an important role in the development of trade union activity, including the London dock strike of 1889. Along with George Lansbury, he was a leading figure in the Labour and socialist movements in Poplar, pioneering the use of municipal power bases to improve conditions for working people. His skills as an orator and his moral fervour shaped in part by his non-conformist Christian background won him widespread popular support and in 1903 a spectacular by-election victory in Woolwich.

In Parliament he campaigned single-mindedly on behalf of the poor and unemployed. Although against the South African war, he did not join those Labour MPs whose pacifist and internationalist instincts led them to oppose the declaration of war in 1914. On the contrary, Crooks, whose constitu-ency contained the world's largest armaments factory, toured the country extensively during the Great War, promoting the war effort and recruitment campaigns. A practical, hard-headed reformer rather than a dreamer or rev-olutionary, he made a substantial contribution over many years up to his death in 1921 to improving the life chances and living standards of working people in east London. Despite this he has received surprisingly little atten-tion in histories of the Labour Party. It is therefore appropriate, on the cen-tenary of the Labour Party's emergence as a substantial parliamentary force, to pay tribute to one of the party's great pioneers. Preparing this chapter, I have drawn heavily on George Haw's biography of Crooks, *From Workhouse to Westminster*, first published in 1907, and more recent papers from Paul Tyler, currently mayor of the London Borough of Greenwich, and I would like to acknowledge their contributions with gratitude.[1]

---

1   George Haw, *From Workhouse to Westminster: The Life Story of Will Crooks MP*, Cassell, 1907 (from which the quotes are taken) and Paul Tyler, 'Will Crooks MP, Local Activist and Labour Pioneer', Greenwich Industrial History Society, Issue 30, 2003.

Will Crooks was born in April 1852 in a one-room home near the docks in Poplar. He was the third of seven children. The family suffered severe poverty after Will's father George lost an arm in a steamship accident when his son was just 3 years old. When Will was 9, he was forced, along with his father and four of his siblings, into the workhouse, while his mother tried to maintain the rest of the family outside. The bitter experience of Poor Law schooling and the separation of his parents remained with him for the rest of his life: 'Every day spent in that school is burnt into my soul.'

Crooks' mother, Charlotte, eventually managed to raise sufficient money to reunite the family and to pay the penny a week necessary for Will to attend the George Green School near the East India docks. He read widely, including the works of Dickens and other social commentators, as well as Scott and Bunyan. This in turn informed his own later activity promoting working-class consciousness through Sunday morning gatherings outside the East India dock gates – known as 'Crooks' College'. Here he developed his public speaking skills, in which he combined the moral fervour of the evangelist with a down to earth cockney sense of humour. His appeal and ability to sway audiences earned him a growing reputation in the emerging Labour and socialist movements in Poplar. He spoke on the basis of his own direct experience:

> My University has been the common people . . . the man trained as I have been amid the poor streets and homes of London, who knows where the shoe pinches and where there are no shoes at all, has more political knowledge of the needs and the sufferings of the people than the man who has been to the recognised Universities.

Will had to work from an early age initially in labouring jobs and the docks, though he became on his mother's insistence apprenticed to a cooper. He twice tramped to Liverpool in search of work as a result of being refused employment in Poplar because of his political agitation.

In 1892 Crooks became one of the first Labour members of the London County Council (LCC) and a year later he was elected to the Poplar Board of Guardians, the very same Board that had forced him and his father into the workhouse 32 years before. As a local representative Crooks focused on practical measures to improve living standards for working-class people in his area. His first election address pledged that he would: 'Seek especially to represent the interests of the working classes who form three-fourths of the taxpayers of Poplar'. It advocated municipal ownership or control of water, tramways, markets, docks, lighting, parks and the police. He pledged support for 'all measures which would help to raise the standard of life of the poor, especially in the way of better housing and a strict enforcement of the Public Health Acts'.

His first speech on the LCC was on the principle of a Fair Wages Clause where his wording insisted:

> That all contractors be compelled to sign a declaration that they pay the trade union rate of wages and observe the hours of labour and conditions recognised by the London Trades Unions, and that the hours of labour be inserted in and form part of the contract by way of schedule, and that penalties be enforced for any break of agreement.

More specifically he highlighted the low wages paid to some of the park attendants, citing the example of the Red Lion Square park-keeper who was paid only 13 shillings a week. To the taunt from another member:

'the man's not worth more; he's got a wooden leg', the Labour bench
responded: 'Yes but he hasn't got a wooden stomach.'

Similarly, on the Board of Guardians he set about raising standards and
attacking the inhumanity of the Poor Law. Giving evidence to the Poor Law
Commission in 1906, he described what he saw on his first visit as a Guardian:

> We found the conditions of things in the house almost revolting. The
> place was dirty. The stores were empty. The inmates had not sufficient
> clothes, and many were without boots to their feet. The food was so
> bad that the wash-tubs overflowed with what the poor people could
> not eat. It was almost heart-breaking to go round the place and hear
> the complaints and see the tears of the aged men and women.
>
> 'Poverty's no crime, but here it's treated like crime', they used to
> say. Many of them defied the regulations on purpose to be charged
> before a magistrate, declaring the prison was better than the work-
> house.

On attempting one visit to the workhouse, Crooks and George Lansbury
were refused entry by the workhouse master. The protest that they raised
forced a change in the regulations so that Guardians were guaranteed access
to the workhouse at any reasonable hour.

From 1897 to 1906 Crooks held the Chairmanship of the Poplar Board
of Guardians and used the position to drive radical reforms to the workhouse system. The old tell-tale pauper's garb was replaced with decent
homely clothing. 'Skilly' was replaced with more wholesome food. Crooks
developed arrangements for baking bread on the premises to ensure a better
and cheaper supply of bread than could be obtained outside. Despite this,
his critics argued that he was incurring additional expense to be met by the
ratepayers. 'Yes,' Crooks replied, 'but to economise on the stomachs of
the poor is false economy. If it's only cheapness you want, why don't you
set up the lethal chamber for the old people? That would be the cheapest
thing of all.'

In 1900 he was elected to Poplar Borough Council and became Mayor
of Poplar the following year, the first Labour Mayor in London. His work
with Lansbury in seeking to raise working-class living standards marked the
beginnings of 'Poplarism', which led the Labour controlled council into
conflict with local ratepayer alliances over their spending commitments.

Improving the quality of life in east London with new parks and open
spaces such as Island Gardens at the foot of the Isle of Dogs opposite
Greenwich was one of his priorities as was the construction of the Blackwall
Tunnel to facilitate cross-river transport. This advocacy of the project was
acknowledged in the *Municipal Journal*:

> As one of the representatives of the Poplar District he has turned his
> membership of the Budget Committee to good account by giving to
> the tunnel his special attention. No Councillor has been so frequent a
> visitor to the various works and it is doubtful whether any outsider
> went so many times into the compressed air.
>
> The workmen had just cause to bless the Poplar County Councillor.
> It was owing to Mr Crooks' efforts that a revised schedule of wages
> was adopted. The result of this was that the contractors paid an addi-
> tional £26,000 in wages.

His popularity as a champion of working people in Poplar and east
London explains his selection as Labour candidate to contest the Woolwich

parliamentary seat. When he accepted the nomination he had anticipated at
least two years before the next general election but, in just the same way
as occurred to me in Fulham in 1986, Crooks was thrown almost immediately into a by-election – in his case prompted by the resignation of Lord
Charles Beresford, the Tory MP for the area who left to take up command
of the Navy's Channel Squadron.

After the decline of Liberal influence in the area in the late nineteenth
century, Woolwich had become a safe Conservative seat. Sir Edwin Hughes,
who had represented Woolwich since 1885, had been returned unopposed
in 1900 and Lord Charles Beresford had inherited the seat also without a
contest. However, it was soon recognised that the 1903 by-election would
be a closely contested one. Crooks launched himself immediately into an
energetic campaign, seeking to attract the support of all progressive opinion
in the constituency. John Burns MP, who had served with Crooks on the
LCC, came to give his support, attracting a crowd of over 5,000 and
boosting hopes of a Labour victory.

The Conservative candidate, Geoffrey Drage was forced onto the defen-
sive, and made a serious tactical mistake seeking to justify low wages in
parts of the Royal Arsenal with the argument that half a loaf was better than
no loaf at all. The Labour campaign seized on this as a key theme: 'No half-
loaf policy for us; we want the whole loaf.' To ram home the point, Crooks'
supporters carried poles around the streets of Woolwich, some topped with
loaves and some with half-loaves to represent the different party policies.
The loaf became the symbol of the fight, a highly appropriate one given
Crooks' own record in improving the quality and supply of bread in the
Poplar workhouse.

On polling day itself, miniature loaves baked specially for the occasion
were everywhere in evidence. Men wore them in their buttonholes, boys
in their caps and women on their dresses. As a marketing ploy, New Labour
could not have surpassed the achievement. The outcome was a massive
Labour victory, far beyond expectations. A seat that had been held by the
Conservatives for 20 years with majorities (when elections were held) of
up to 2,800, returned Will Crooks with a majority of 3,229.

The by-election prompted entirely understandable press speculation
about the significance of the Labour victory. *The Times* said: '[T]he questions bound up with the existence of an organised Labour Party which have
been hitherto regarded as chimerical are coming to the front in practical
politics.' While the *Pall Mall Gazette* commented: 'Mr Crooks' return is
first and most obviously an indication of the growing strength of the idea
of an organised Labour Party, such as under the name of socialism is so
potent a force in continental politics.' Within three years the 'chimera' had
become a reality with the emergence of a substantial Labour block of MPs
returned in 1906.

In Parliament Crooks focused initially on the same issues as he had cham-
pioned on the LCC, Poplar Council and the Board of Guardians. His maiden
speech, delivered two weeks after his election, highlighted the fact that
capacity at the Royal Arsenal in Woolwich was lying unused, while work
was being allocated to external contractors: 'The government has no right
to use the money of the nation in building machinery and to allow it to
stand idle in the interests of outside firms, no matter who they are or what
influence they may have.'

This clear commitment to public sector employment as against out-
sourcing, which was to characterise Labour's stance for most of the ensuing
century, was accompanied by an attack on low wages:

I maintain that it is not cheap for the government to pay men 21 shillings a week, although other employers may be able to get them for that amount. If the men had more money, they would be able to get better house accommodation and the ratepayers would be saved the substantial sums now paid under the Poor Law for medical orders for people brought up in overcrowded houses.

Other causes that he promoted in his early months in Parliament were the payment of MPs to facilitate the election of more working men and the enfranchisement of women:

It is because in all my public work I aim at making the people self-reliant, able to think and act for themselves that I want women to have the power and the responsibility that the possession of the vote gives . . . we entrust to women as teachers and as mothers the all-important task of educating the future citizens. How absurd, then, to hesitate to give to women the rights of a citizen.

Linking the issues of poverty and the franchise, Crooks frequently mentioned an incident that occurred when he protested at low wages being paid to women in Deptford, claiming that 14 shillings a week pay for widows with families in government workshops was starvation wages. An official insisted that at least the pay was constant. 'So you see,' Crooks commented, 'that Government officials think starvation's all right so long as it's constant. Do you think this system of constant starvation would be tolerated for a day if women had the vote?'

Crooks rapidly earned the respect and goodwill of members on all side of the House as described in *Vanity Fair*:

His tact and common-sense served him as well in the House as they had done in settling labour disputes in Poplar. By never debating any subject but those on which he has special knowledge, and by his perfect good temper and modesty, he became one of the men whose politics arouse no personal animosity on the other side.

In the 1904 Session of Parliament, Crooks pressed the Conservative government to take action on behalf of the unemployed and successfully argued for the Local Government Board to co-ordinate relief across London. In the following year the government conceded the need for legislation on the relief of unemployment and established a Royal Commission on the Poor Law. Maintaining the pressure, Crooks and his wife organised a march by 6,000 women – wives and sisters of unemployed men – on the Local Government Board with the slogan 'work for our men – bread for our children'. Although the government refused more money, Queen Victoria launched a public appeal 'to all charitably disposed people in the Empire, both men and women, to assist me in alleviating the suffering of the poor starving unemployed during this time. For this purpose I head the list with £2,000'. The appeal raised a total of £150,000, enabling the London Distress Committees to maintain their programmes of work and relief throughout the winter.

The following year the general election swept the Conservatives out of power and saw the election of a Liberal government and a substantial Labour block of 29 MPs for the first time, paving the way for more effective government measures to tackle unemployment and poverty. Crooks himself was returned with a comfortable, albeit reduced, majority.

Crooks had secured his by-election victory by rallying the support of progressive opinion and he was supportive of measures that involved co-operation between Labour and the Liberals. This, at times, put him at odds with more ideologically minded colleagues. In 1911 he fell out with the TUC over his support for one measure – the Labour Disputes Bill – seeking to curtail strikes. In this Crooks was following the same line that he had advocated years before, speaking to the Labour Co-Partnership Association where presciently he said:

> I want men who groan under the injustice of so much in our industrial system to understand that they can do much for themselves. By combi-nation and co-operation they can run businesses of their own . . . trade unionists are now learning that instead of spending money on strikes it is better to spend it in starting workshops of their own. The time has come when Labour leaders and others might well cease talking to the workers about their power and begin talking to them about their responsibilities.

Crooks remained a Member of Parliament until 1921 when ill-health, which had dogged much of his later career, forced him to resign his seat. Within six months he was dead.

Eighty-five years later the area he represented in Parliament is under-going a remarkable transformation. The Royal Arsenal, the core of Woolwich's economy in his time, where 80,000 people worked at its peak during the First World War, closed its doors more than 20 years ago. It is now undergoing a dramatic regeneration programme with new houses and businesses being created to fill the void. New transport links across the Thames are once again being planned and constructed – the first since Crooks' time, opening up new employment and social opportunities for the people of Woolwich. By contrast with the electorate of his time, Woolwich is now a profoundly multi-cultural society. The poverty that was so endemic in Crooks' time is still not eradicated, but living standards are rising, bolstered by a minimum wage and substantial investment in improved public services – all of which would unquestionably have given him great satisfac-tion. For Will Crooks' great legacy – a passionate commitment to tackling poverty and unemployment and improving the condition of working people in East London – is still an inspiration to his successors and a driving force of the twenty-first-century Labour Party.

Nick Raynsford
MP for Greenwich and
Woolwich

Nick Raynsford

CHARLES DUNCAN. M. P.

COPYRIGHT Photo Russell

Charles Duncan: Labour MP for Barrow-in-Furness 1906–18, and for Clay Cross 1922–33

Chapter 5
Charles Duncan
1865–1933

THE VICTORY in Barrow-in-Furness by Labour's Charles Duncan
in the 1906 General Election was described in the local *North West
Daily Mail* as 'more than defeat – it was slaughter' for the Tories.
The result when announced to a 10,000 strong crowd that stood outside
the Barrow Town Hall on that historic night was flashed on a lantern screen
and read: 'Duncan (Lab) 5,167 : Cayzer (Con) 3,395'.

But this was neither the end nor the beginning of the story. The beginning could more accurately be described as being when J. Keir Hardie
addressed the members of the Barrow Fabian Society and the public at a
packed meeting on the evening of Sunday 16 October 1892. The Barrow
Fabian Society had been formed in 1884 but it was only after the magnificent 'Politics of the Mad House' speech that Keir Hardie gave that evening
that it was resolved by those present to form the Barrow branch of the
Independent Labour Party (ILP), which pioneered the setting up of the
Labour Representation Committee (LRC) in 1898, with the Barrow branch
being represented at the LRC Conference of 1900. A local newspaper report
of that Sunday evening meeting said: 'A great meeting was held in the Jubilee
Hall in the evening to hear a continuation of Mr Keir Hardie's morning
address. The building was markedly insufficient to accommodate those
desirous of hearing him, not even standing room being available.' Reporting
the full moving and inspiring speech it ended: 'Mr Hardie concluded his
address by remarking that if they (the people present) were faithful and
courageous, honest and true to Labour, they would succeed in making the
pathway easier for those who came after them (loud applause).'[1] No one
reading that full speech could have any doubt about why the Labour Party
and movement in Barrow then went on from success to success.

Charles Duncan was born on 8 June 1865 at 93 Stockton Street, Middlesbrough, the son of a river pilot on the Tees, Alexander Duncan, and Jane
Dobson. His father's regular wage meant that Duncan stayed in full-time
education until he was 16. Declining to follow in his father's footsteps, he
first worked in shipping with a view to becoming an engineer before taking
up an apprenticeship back in Middlesbrough at the Teesside Iron and
Engine Works. On completion of the apprenticeship he worked for a short

---

1 The *Barrow Herald*, 18 October 1892.

time at the Elswick ordnance factory on the Tyne, where he joined both the Amalgamated Society of Engineers (ASE) and the ILP. He had become a socialist from an early point, not least due to his wide reading and continued education. In 1890 he married Lydia Copeland.

Towards the end of the nineteenth century, he became one of the most prominent ILP members in Middlesbrough, organising a soup kitchen for the unemployed in 1891 and being elected to the local Board of Poor Law Guardians shortly thereafter. In 1895 he was elected to Middlesbrough Town Council and three years later became branch secretary of the newly-formed Workers' Union (WU), which was described by *The Times* as an 'organisation for the large mass of nondescript and miscellaneous labour which remained outside the scope of the craft and industrial unions covering the more or less homogenous and well-defined industries'. A full-time union official from 1898, he achieved a weekly minimum wage of 21 shillings[2] for council employees and in 1900 encouraged a strike by WU members employed by the council who were campaigning for a closed shop. The strike failed and the staff were sacked. Partly as a result of this episode, Duncan did not seek re-election to the council and turned his attention to his growing influence within the WU. He had already become National President and towards the end of 1900 was appointed General Secretary and moved to London. The following year the union's founder, Tom Mann, moved to New Zealand, leaving Duncan as the dominant figure in the union, a position he maintained for the best part of three decades.

After initial difficulties in maintaining the WU's financial position, he eventually built up the organisation partly by reversing union policy and introducing funeral and sickness benefit schemes; the union's membership steadily rose in the first few years of the twentieth century to around 5,000.

Through his sponsorship by the ASE, Duncan received the approval of the LRC to be its candidate in Barrow-in-Furness in 1906. It seems that Keir Hardie and Ramsay MacDonald were not especially enamoured with Duncan and had intended to give the Liberals a clear run in Barrow in return for standing aside for Labour elsewhere. However, Duncan was selected as the candidate and received Liberal support in the election.

Leading up to the 1906 campaign, Duncan and his agent Arthur Peters (later to be Labour's first National Agent) established the *Barrow Pioneer*, a monthly journal with a guaranteed circulation of 5,000 – a fantastic achievement in days of low wages, poor education and prejudice. The first edition recognised the responsibilities entrusted to the party, which included 'electing one of its own representatives to swell the ranks in the House of Commons in the new Parliament. We shall' said the *Pioneer*, 'use every legitimate means through these columns with that aim in view and without fear or favour, and the cause of humanity will find us among its ever-growing army of champions.' And champions they were. In the 1906 general election, Duncan easily defeated the Conservative Sir Charles Cayzer, achieving more than 60 per cent of the vote.

Duncan's first contribution in the Commons recorded by Hansard is on the 16 March 1906, on the Parliamentary Elections (Disqualification Removal) Bill, which sought to reverse the Medical Relief Act 1885's 'dis-enfranchisement of working men who were compelled by sickness to apply for medical relief'. Hansard records that Duncan 'said it was a cruel thing that such an enormous number of men should lose their votes in this way through circumstances over which they had no control. He hoped a

2   About £90 in current money.

division would be taken, so that they might have an opportunity of showing the people of this country that they mean business in this matter.'[3]

Appointed a Labour Whip, Duncan became renowned in the Commons for his dress sense – many years later, obituaries made particular reference to his reputation as one of the 'best-dressed Members of Parliament'. He was a strong supporter of the First World War, backing conscription and speaking on recruitment platforms. He was appointed to a number of war economy committees and in 1916 signed the manifesto of the pro-war British Workers' League. Lloyd George included Duncan on a delegation to the United States to press for continued US support:

> The members of the British Labour Mission, who arrived here [New York] on Sunday, are doing admirable work, both in interviews and in speech, in clearing away American misapprehensions. The Mission consists of four men – Messrs Charles Duncan, J. Butterworth, D.L. Mosses, and W.A. Appleton . . . Mr Duncan then took up the thread of the argument and told the newspaper representatives that the Pacifists numbered about 40,000 in Great Britain adding: 'If the dear Pacifists of America love peace they will not attempt to send delegates to London'. This statement was called forth by the report that a number of notorious Pacifists here of the Lochner, Scott, Nearing, and Hillquit type had met and appointed delegates to attend the conference in London. Mr Duncan said that the report must be a joke, but he warned American Pacifists that British Labour would give them a very inhospitable reception.[4]

Duncan held Barrow with decreasing majorities, falling to 520 votes in the second 1910 election before being defeated in 1918 by 299 votes by Robert Chadwick. Many of the MPs defeated in the 'coupon' election had been anti-war. However, in Duncan's case, his defeat is credited to the withholding of support by local militants, mainly from Duncan's own trade of engineering, encouraged by the Barrow Labour Party.

Duncan had remained General Secretary of the WU throughout his parliamentary service and by the outbreak of war its membership had risen to 140,000 following significant industrial unrest. Increasing membership meant increasing income, which was in turn used to further boost recruitment drives. Duncan maintained a strong grip on the union and ensured it continued with a relatively moderate line. The war further increased membership (including many women) and when the National Amalgamated Workers' Union was formed in 1919 it had nearly 500,000 members, became the largest trade union and planned further amalgamations. However, this was to be the union's peak. Following a financially misjudged benefit scheme and the onset of recession, membership and income dropped. The General Strike further damaged the union's finances and, when membership fell below 100,000 in 1929, the WU merged into the Transport and General Workers' Union. Duncan became Secretary of the WU branch of the larger union, a position he held until his death.

Duncan had meanwhile continued to try to return to the Commons. In February 1920 he stood in the Wrekin by-election caused by the death of the Coalition Liberal MP Sir Charles Henry. The Liberals came third in the contest, but Duncan was beaten into second place by 538 votes by

3   House of Commons Hansard, 16 March 1906.
4   *The Times*, 14 February 1918.

Independent candidate Charles Palmer, who had the backing of Horatio Bottomley and his Independent Parliamentary Group. Palmer died before the year was out, and in a two-handed contest in November 1920 Duncan was more decisively defeated by the Independent Conservative and military personality Major General Sir Charles Townshend.

Duncan finally returned to the Commons in 1922 for the Derbyshire seat of Clay Cross, and held the seat with comfortable majorities for 11 years.

His service as MP for Clay Cross does not seem to have been particularly assiduous, however. His obituary in the *Derbyshire Times* said:

> He held the Clay Cross constituency with the minimum of effort. He visited the division very seldom between elections and during a contest he never seemed to worry or put in a third of the time addressing meetings that his Labour contemporaries in other constituencies did . . . It was remarkable that he had such a hold on the division because he was unknown in it before 1922, and as General Secretary to the Workers' Union he had not the local claims for recognition which, say, a representative of the Derbyshire Miners' Union would have had.

Duncan lived his last years in Golders Green and he died on 6 July 1933, in Manor House Hospital Hampstead. *The Times* referred to his reputation for sartorial elegance and said that he 'retained to the end an alert and upright carriage which belied his age. In his youth he was something of an athlete and was a keen cyclist, winning many prizes in road racing and on the track.'[5] Two years after his death a plaque marking his service to the Labour movement was unveiled at Transport House by senior Labour figures including Arthur Henderson, who took over Duncan's Clay Cross seat following his death.

Charles Duncan's initial Barrow victory of 1906 was undoubtedly a significant contributor to Labour being the natural party to represent working people's interests both in Parliament and on local councils in Barrow and the Furness area. Labour, and more importantly the people of Barrow and Furness, have been well served by the representatives chosen to stand on the party's behalf. Formidable campaigns have often seen off the much better funded campaigns of opponents. A history of the first 50 years of the Labour Party in Barrow, written by the late Jack Mowatt and Albert Power, reflects that looking back at the campaigns of the past, we can recall that, at great turning points in history, when the floodtide of public opinion is running high, there exists among the people a sense of purpose, which communicates itself to young and old alike. At such times new visions, new tasks and new responsibilities challenge the people. They draw strength from the past in reaching to the future.

At the centre of all that is done are the people who, in the quietness of themselves, determine who shall govern and to what purpose. After all the speeches have been made, and the last election leaflet read, it is the people who are the arbiters of the future. It is they who shape the destiny of the yet unborn and they who build tomorrow on the foundation of today as we have built upon the example of our great pioneers.

When Duncan and his 28 Labour comrades were elected in 1906 there were the valiant few who gathered around the inspirational leaders and founders of our party. Today we are millions. We have grown – not beyond the dreams of our forebears because they did not dream such growth; they

5   *The Times*, 7 July 1933.

knew it was inevitable because they knew the truth of the message they had
and they had faith in the sense of the people they sought to serve.

Although Charles Duncan and many of his comrades are those whose
names history records as being the champions of the people, there are many
more whose invaluable contributions are, for one reason or another, neither
recorded nor ever recognised. There are as many unsung heroes and hero-
ines now as there were then and the debt owed to them is immeasurable.
It is now our turn to maintain the faith, the courage, the honesty and trust
in Labour that Keir Hardie urged us to have so many years ago.

John Hutton
MP for Barrow

John Hutton

ALFRED HENRY GILL. M. P.

Alfred Gill: Labour MP for Bolton, 1906–14

Chapter 6
Alfred Gill
1856–1914

ALFRED HENRY GILL was elected junior Member of Parliament for Bolton in 1906 along with the senior Member, Liberal George Harwood. He was re-elected twice in 1910, in January and December, and died in post as the senior MP for Bolton, aged 57, of heart failure brought about by an acute form of anaemia, at 61 Hampden Street, Bolton, on 27 August 1914. He had suffered a heart attack in June 1913. Gill was buried in his adopted town, in the non-conformist part of Heaton Cemetery, following a funeral service at Halliwell Road Wesleyan Chapel on 31 August.

Gill's majorities in his three general elections were 3,723 (1906), 4,385 (January 1910) and 1,411 (December 1910). At the time of his death he was Vice-Chairman of the Parliamentary Labour Party.

On the wet wintry night of his first election victory, on 22 January 1906, 10,000 people gathered in Bolton's cobbled and gas-lit Victoria Square and the surrounding streets to hear the Mayor make a historic announcement from the Town Hall steps, and to celebrate that victory. The horse trough had been emptied to prevent party activists 'ducking' their opponents, and the crowd was warmed up by speakers who had brought orange boxes from which to deliver their speeches. All present sang and chanted. This was a historic occasion: Bolton's first Labour Member of Parliament was about to be announced.

Gill's victory would not have been possible had Ramsay MacDonald, the secretary of the Labour Representation Committee (LRC), and Herbert Gladstone, Liberal Chief Whip, not agreed that, in a handful of two-Member constituencies such as Bolton, the Liberals would only put up one candidate and support the other Labour candidate.

Alfred Henry Gill was born at 36 Oldham Road, Rochdale, on 3 December 1856. From the age of 7 he helped his father, cotton spinner and newsagent John Gill (his mother was born Mary Stott), to deliver and sell newspapers on the streets before entering a cotton mill owned by Messrs Samuel Radcliffe and Sons (later to become the Eagle Spinning Co.) as a half-time 'little piecer' at the age of 10, becoming a full-timer at the age of 13. He was educated at St Mary's Elementary School, Balderstone.

In 1879, Gill moved to Oldham, where he worked for eight years at the Moss Lane Spinning Company, Heyside. During this period he became interested in the Co-operative movement, which led to his appointment to the

Education Committee of the Crompton Co-operative Society, of which he later became a Director and, in 1885, its Chairman. On Jubilee Day 1887, he left for a better position, though still as an operative cotton spinner, at Newtown Mill, Pendlebury (actually in the 'Bolton province'). During this period Gill improved his education by studying science at night at the Salford Technical School, and became a member of the Technical Instruction Committee of the Swinton and Pendlebury District Council. One of Gill's favourite hobbies was to invite a number of his fellow workers to his home at night and pass on what knowledge he had gained himself.

Then, in 1896 at the age of 41, he was appointed from a field of 15 candidates, following a rigorous examination and a vote, as Assistant Secretary to the Bolton Operative Spinners' Association, then the largest organisation of its kind in the country, if not the world, and the wealthiest single trade union in the country. In May 1897, he became its General Secretary, a position he held until his death. On 24 August 1912, Gill had the privilege of opening the Spinners' Hall on St George's Road, Bolton. That magnificent edifice still stands and has just received its first major refurbishment, although it is now in multiple use.

Gill's intimate knowledge of the cotton industry and his popularity with the workers allowed him to settle countless disputes without the need for strike action. He became skilled at navigating the complicated list of piecework rates in the local cotton industry, which employers used to underpay their employees. It was these skills that led to his appointment to various organisations in the Labour and trade union movement, and to the Bolton Magistrates Bench, in 1899, and the Education Committee of the Borough of Bolton.

He began attending the Trades Union Congress (TUC) in 1897 and served on the TUC's Parliamentary Committee (1903–07). In 1907, he presided over its Annual Congress in Bath. He was one of the TUC fraternal delegates chosen to attend the Annual Convention of the American Federation of Labor, in Toronto in November 1909, travelling on to give evidence on the operation of the Workmen's Compensation Act before the New York State Commission and to meet President Taft at the White House.

Gill was from the people and of the people – a very popular self-made man. It is not surprising therefore that he spent his entire parliamentary career fighting for improvements in the factories in which he had worked. In the 1906 election campaign, he pledged to devote his time to three main causes: trade union law; free trade; and opposition to 'Chinese labour ordinance', although he endorsed other causes during his parliamentary career, including pensions, reducing working hours, health and safety in factories, temperance (he was teetotal throughout his life), better educational opportunities, mining royalties, a land tax and reform of the House of Lords. He preferred pacifism to aggression.

Maiden speeches were not delivered in 1906 as they are today, but Gill did not waste much time in making his first speech, supporting the Second Reading Debate of the Notice of Accidents Bill, on 3 March 1906. At that time cotton operatives were regularly injured by the fast-moving machinery, and accidents were not always reported when they happened. Indeed, the law of the day required a period of 14 days to elapse before an accident was reported. Gill argued successfully that this should be reduced to no longer than 3 days. This victory became significant later when Gill fought for amendments to The Workmen's Compensation Act.

As with most new MPs, it took Gill a few years to gain momentum. His most productive years, measured by his contributions in the Official Record, were 1911–13. However, from the moment he arrived in Parliament in

1906 he brought to the attention of the government the unsatisfactory pay and working conditions of those working at Bolton Post Office, and he campaigned for a new Post Office to be built. Although the government made him promises, he died before the opening of the new Post Office in November 1916.

Health and safety dominated his time in Parliament. Injuries in the cotton industry were common with people – including women and children as young as 12 (half-time 'little piecers') – often losing fingers and whole limbs. Young boys fell into the boiling water of the unfenced 'kiers' in the bleaching and dyeing industry. Men in the carding sheds rarely worked beyond the age of 40. The dust from the cotton fibres caused asthma, chronic bronchitis and emphysema, which were further exacerbated by the high humidity. Gill constantly called for an increase in factory inspectors, but expansion of the industry outpaced their employment by the state.

At every opportunity Gill called for better ventilation in factories (especially for dust extraction in carding and stripping sheds), better lighting on staircases and in the darker rooms, anti-locking devices over the cylinders of carding engines, and fences or guards wherever there was moving machinery that could cause injury. He argued that lime-washing walls helped to make rooms brighter.

He was a keen advocate for the provision of a Museum of Safety Appliances and one was built in Horseferry Road, Westminster, during his time in Parliament, as well as for tripartite conferences on workplace health and safety involving employers, employees and factory inspectors.

Gill was a keen supporter of the Workmen's Compensation Act, a landmark piece of legislation that provided for compensation when workers were injured at work. In 1899, he had given evidence before the Royal Commission into the operation of the Act. He was against 'averaging', whereby compensation was based on the average annual wage because 'short time', when workers were laid off, was common in the cotton industry, and he argued that compensation should be payable from the date of the accident.

Throughout his parliamentary career, Gill was critical of the 'medical referees', who examined the workers, because they were in private practice and biased towards the insurance companies who paid the compensation. He believed that they should be employed by the state. Workers had to pay their own doctors for medical certificates (they cost 1s – over twice the daily wage of 4 to 5d[1]), which amounted to a small fortune as the factory managers required them on a regular basis, something that was not allowed in law. Workers also had to pay their own surgeon's bills. In contentious cases the trade unions ended up picking up the bills for compensation. Factory owners and their insurance companies did everything possible to wriggle out of compensation payments, even accusing workers of 'malingering'.

Gill constantly raised questions about the Workmen's Compensation Act and asked for committees of inquiry into its application. His last speech in Parliament was on 20 May 1914, when his parliamentary colleague Tyson Wilson (who had represented the Westhoughton Constituency since 1906) moved that a Committee of Inquiry be set up. On that occasion the Parliamentary Under-Secretary of State for the Home Department promised that one would be created.

---

1   One shilling would be nearly £4 today – but with a daily wage of less than half that.

It was through the efforts of parliamentarians like Alfred Gill that the Workmen's Compensation Act was significantly amended. 'The insured workman, be he spinner, miner or engineer, has Mr Gill to thank for the first sovereign he draws in compensation, for it is owing to his individual efforts that payment of compensation begins in the first full week succeeding the injury' noted one commentator.

Workers in the cotton industry worked a 55.5-hour week; Gill supported a reduction to 48 hours. Eventually, the Factory and Workshops Act (1901) Amendment Bill of 1907 implemented these shorter hours. In the debate he argued that productivity had increased as the machinery had speeded up.

One of Gill's constant campaigns was against the illegal practice of 'time cribbing'. Cotton factory managers were illegally running machinery, in contravention of the Factory and Workshops Act, until the finishing times of their operatives, which meant they were working unpaid overtime to clean their machines. The good employers were against this practice because it was anti-competitive; Gill saw that employment could be increased considerably throughout the cotton industry if the practice was stopped. He constantly asked questions about this. However, it was difficult to stop 'time cribbing' because the bad employers had scouts to watch for the approach of the factory inspectors.

Cotton operatives worked at piecework rates and the Particulars Clause of the Factory and Workshops Act demanded that employers provide 'particulars' of the way in which their wages had been calculated. Gill campaigned for this practice to be extended to other industries.

Because of the rapid expansion of the cotton industry, the usual sources of fibre, the USA, Egypt and India, could not keep the Lancashire mills in full production. In 1913, Gill supported production in the Sudan. He supported the Public Works Loans Bill in 1907 because it provided money to build a railway in Nigeria that 'would be of great benefit to the Lancashire cotton trade'. Gill was a member of the British Cotton Growing Association from its inception.

Gill's passion for his workers in the cotton industry led him to vote against his party's line just once, in 1912, on the School Attendance Bill. This raised the age at which young people began work from 12 to 13 and was aimed at 'half-timers' who worked in the mornings and attended elementary school in the afternoon. The trade unions were also against the Bill. Gill argued that these young people did not sleep in school in the afternoon, as alleged, and that the evils of the half-time system had been exaggerated in the debate.

The National Insurance Bill, introduced in 1911, was another landmark piece of legislation. On 24 May 1911, Gill described it in one of his most important speeches as 'the boldest attempt to deal with industrial problems which has ever been made'. The Bill allowed workers to pay contributions to Friendly Societies and benefit from pay-outs when they were off work sick. It also introduced maternity benefit, which Gill described as 'one of the finest benefits in connection with the Bill'.

In a speech on 31 January 1913 during the Third Reading of the Trade Unions (No. 2) Bill, which restored the rights of unions to establish political funds, removed from them by the 1909 Osborne Judgement, Gill said: 'Reference is made to socialism and our party is spoken of as a Socialist Party. This party is not a Socialist Party. There are socialists in it and there are those who are not socialists.'

On 8 July 1912, Gill spoke in favour of the Franchise and Registration Bill and one person one vote. Women had to wait for some time before they became enfranchised. He argued that general elections should be held on one day, that officials ought to be paid to run elections, that plural voting should be banned, all MPs should take their pay, 100 Irish representatives should be in Parliament until Home Rule for Ireland was achieved, that local authorities should actively encourage men to register, and that people with property or with a better education should not be given more electoral power. At that time the qualifying period for registration was two and a half years at the resident address. Gill argued that six months would be better. If a person moved in 1912, even across the road, they disenfranchised themselves for two and a half years.

Gill believed passionately in Home Rule for Ireland. During the Second Reading of the Government of Ireland Bill, on 1 April 1914, he argued that Protestants and Catholics had a lot of common interests – more than the interests that divided them.

He was also passionate about reform of the House of Lords, a debate that has lasted over 100 years. There were constant battles with the Upper House at that time over Finance Bills. Indeed the elections of 1910 were precipitated by this. The frustration of the Lower House led to the Parliament Act of 1911 and to exclusion of the House of Lords from discussions about Budgets. This was one of the topics in Gill's third address to his constituents in the Temperance Hall in Bolton, on 15 January 1909, when one wit in the audience cried: 'We want revolution, not reform.' Nothing changes. 'Should the Peers or the People rule?' was a common cry from Gill on the hustings. Candidates at this time held an incredible number of election meetings compared with today.

Gill was briefly concerned with animal welfare. Carters commonly looked after two carts and two horses, which Gill tried to prohibit in Bolton, a policy already adopted in places such as Heywood, Manchester and Salford. The problem was that, when the first horse and cart stopped, the second horse bumped into the back of the first cart, which was regarded as cruel by the Society for the Prevention of Cruelty to Animals.

Gill was not a great platform speaker. In Parliament he commanded attention not for his rhetoric but for his sound contributions based on experience and fact. In his own modest words: 'I prefer to work rather than talk . . . and I can look back with satisfaction on the little that I have done for my fellow workers in Bolton and Lancashire generally.' We can also look back in satisfaction, not only at his contribution but on those of all 29 Members of Parliament who founded the Parliamentary Labour Party in 1906, at the beginning of what became an important reforming period for working men and women.

Gill's wife (born Sarah Ellen Greenwood), son (Herbert) and four daughters (Mary, Emily, Ada and Lucy) survived him and he left effects to the value of £3,750. Descendants of Alfred Henry Gill still live in Bolton and I am grateful to his great grandson, Andrew Howard Gill, for helping me to construct this obituary.

Dr Brian Iddon
MP for Bolton, South East

Dr Brian Iddon

THOS. GLOVER. M. P.

COPYRIGHT

Thomas Glover:
Labour MP for
St Helens, 1906–10

Chapter 7
Thomas Glover
1852–1913

P RESCOT, WHERE WILLIAM GLOVER and his wife Isabella came to live not long before their youngest child, Thomas, was born in March 1852, was a small but flourishing Lancashire town, some eight miles east of Liverpool. At the centre of a large sprawling parish and also of a thriving watch-making industry, Prescot stood where the road to east Lancashire (our A58) forked off north-eastwards from the main Liverpool–Warrington highway (our A57).

Situated at the western edge of the South Lancashire coalfield, Prescot had its coal mines, and it was to work on one of these in Fall Lane that William Glover had come with his family. The colliery belonged to David Bromilow whose mining interests were scattered in and around the infant but expanding industrial town of St Helens, three miles north-east of Prescot.

William Glover had worked at the coalface in another Bromilow pit, at Blackbrook, two miles beyond St Helens' centre, for at least a decade before Thomas was born, and in 1854 the family returned to Blackbrook with their six surviving children. There William was now employed as an 'underlooker', an underground official, nowadays a 'deputy', a position he held there for at least the next 20 years.

Seven years later, the census shows William's parents to have been added to the household and suggests his two older sons had died. The surviving boys, William Jnr and Thomas, were described as scholars. In fact their schooldays were all but over. Having been started fairly near home at a church school, Thomas's final three years' education took place at the Cowley British School in the centre of St Helens – quite a walk for a small boy.

Thomas left school at 9. The Mines Regulation Act permitted boys of 10 to work underground and, as he recalled years later:

> I then went to work down the Blackbrook colliery. My first job was to tent [mind] the [ventilation] door for the ponies which took the empty tubs into the working places of the coalgetters and brought full tubs back. I sat and opened the doors commencing to work at 6 am and working until 5 pm and 6 pm, never seeing daylight in the winter, only on Sundays. My next job was to drive the ponies, after which I became a waggoner [responsible for coupling and shunting the coal tubs underground], then a drawer [directly assisting the collier, by loading the hewn coal into the tub] and at the age of 18 years I was a coal getter [a fully-fledged collier, working directly at the coal face].

That he progressed so rapidly from stage to stage – few achieved collier status before they were 21 – reveals Thomas Glover as possessing both physical strength and reliability.

The year 1868 had brought changes that directly and indirectly were influential in Thomas Glover's life. The whole area, as that new year dawned, formed part of the parliamentary constituency of South Lancashire. One of its three representatives was then William Ewart Gladstone, Leader of the Liberal Party. In the July 1868 General Election, with the constituency, now South-west Lancashire, halved in size and returning two members only, Gladstone lost his seat, and had to contest and win Greenwich to remain in Parliament and serve as Prime Minister. Doubled in number by the 1867 Reform Act, voters in the St Helens Polling District showed themselves Conservative by preference, with that party's candidates successful in each succeeding election, including those following St Helens becoming a single-member parliamentary borough in 1885 – until Thomas Glover's electoral victory in 1906.

Meanwhile, February 1868 had seen St Helens receive its Charter of Incorporation, and in May the town's first councillors (three for each of the borough's six wards) were elected and aldermen chosen. Too young to vote, 16-year-old Thomas Glover was already an active trade unionist who had swiftly become Secretary of the Blackbrook Lodge of Miners (part of the St Helens' Miners' Association formed in 1868) and was immersed in industrial action, prompted by a proposed 10 per cent reduction in miners' wages.

'In 1868,' he later wrote, 'we had a great strike in Lancashire and at that time we were connected with what was known as the National Unions and the members expected to receive strike pay which they did for one week only. Then we were told there was no more money and after ten weeks stoppage the men were beaten and went back to work.'

Did news of the meetings held at the Mechanics' Institute, David Street, Manchester early that June reach Thomas Glover, as back at the coalface he must have been pondering the implications of the strike, with its withering effect on Lancashire's various district miners' unions? With 34 delegates representing some 118,000 trade union members, the Trades Union Congress had met for the first time.

Young in becoming a coal-getter and in assuming union responsibilities, Glover was also young to marry. During 1872 their first son, William Edwin, was born to Thomas and his Birmingham-born wife Fanny Siddons (whom he had married at Perry Barr Church in 1871). By 1873 he was employed in another Bromilow pit, at Laffak-Garswood, as a check-weighman, a post he held until the colliery closed in 1881. Distinctive tallies were attached underground to the tubs of coal produced so that each miner's output could be identified for weighing at the surface – the task of the check-weighman. Fulfilling this role for eight years shows the complete confidence in which Thomas Glover was held by both his fellow miners and their employers.

Speaking in the House of Commons in 1909 in the debate on the Check-weighman's Bill, when a check-weighman's failure to provide a man with proof of weight was mentioned, Glover's familiarity with the work speedily put matters right: 'In this case the man was not working by contract or piece-work. He was working by day-wage, and therefore needed no weighing at all.'[1]

---

1   Hansard, 1909, col. 1355.

By the time the Laffak-Garswood pit closed in 1881, there were five young Glovers to be supported by Glover, who at once went back to work at the coalface in another local colliery. That same year his efforts on behalf of the fledgling St Helens and District Miners' Union, which at its formation had appointed him Secretary, were credited with achieving weekly rather than fortnightly or even monthly pay, and a 10 per cent wage increase, through strike action.

When John Cross, the miners' agent for the district, died in 1884 (the year before St Helens gained separate parliamentary representation), Glover was elected to take his place. He was admirably suited for the post for he had, as he told a reporter for the *St Helens Lantern* in 1888, 'gone through every stage of a miner's life, short of being manager'. In the same interview he also revealed his political thinking – calling himself a 'Liberal' and a 'Radical' and asking: 'Did you ever know a *thinking* working-man who was anything else? A real "Conservative working-man" ought to be put in a museum as a curiosity. Yes,' he concluded, 'I am strongly in favour of sending Labour MPs to Parliament.. He could not have foreseen that almost 30 years later an interviewer for the *St Helens Labour Record* would write of him: 'As Mr Glover, now that the Parliamentary recess is on, has to resume his duties as Miners' Agent, and is in a state of (almost) perpetual motion through the Lancashire District, he has not much time to spare for anything outside his routine work.'

Glover's own direct sortie into local politics came in the 1890 municipal elections. Highly dissatisfied with the apparent agreement between the opposing Liberals and Conservatives to leave seats uncontested he, John Smith, a chemical worker, and Robert Hunter, Secretary of the Glass Bottlemakers Trade Protection Association, contested three wards. In total the three Labour candidates had a majority of 22 votes over their capitalist opponents, and by roundly defeating William Windle Pilkington (a major partner in the glass-making firm, and Mayor 1901–02), Robert Hunter became St Helens' first Labour councillor.

Accepting defeat, Thomas Glover acknowledged that the contest, in which he had declared his support for an eight-hour working day for those trades desiring it, had been a fair fight. He had also urged the abolition of mining royalties and the desirability of having working men as magistrates. Barely two years later, he himself became the first such person appointed to the St Helens' bench, and he was also made a county magistrate in June 1909. Again he was the right man in the right job. His personal qualities – tact, fair-mindedness and good judgement – were much emphasised when the court met immediately after his death in 1913. He was described as 'fearless in his administration of justice' and (to quote the Magistrates' Clerk) 'an absolutely honest and conscientious man, a man of sound commonsense without any fads, and he did his work on this Bench as well as any magistrate could'.

Just before contesting the municipal elections, both Hunter and Glover had been much involved in the successful launch of the St Helens Trades Council. Delegates from 24 skilled and unskilled trades, with members totalling 3,855, inaugurated the Council in October 1890 with Hunter its Chairman and Glover its Secretary – a temporary position he had held in 1885 when an unsuccessful attempt to found a Trades Council had been made. Writing to the press at that time Thomas Glover assured readers that '[p]olitics has never been allowed to be introduced at any of our meetings'.

When, on a splendidly sunny day in September 1891, St Helens Trades Council organised a major demonstration and mass meeting, crowds formed to watch and applaud the procession that wound its way around the town centre. Perhaps some onlookers recognised, seated among other trade unionists in the carriage that led the way, none other than Tom Mann, President of the Dockers' Union, which had struck so successfully in 1889.

After the procession, with its banners and brass bands and headed by the miners' contingent, had reached the open-air destination, a mass meeting was briefly addressed by Robert Hunter. Glover then outlined the Trades Council's development, inviting more trades to affiliate. Resolutions were moved supporting increased working men's representation on local bodies, and the eight-hour working day – themes developed in the major speech by Tom Mann with which the meeting concluded.

Meanwhile, in 1889 Thomas Glover, who for five years had doubled as both its agent and Secretary, gave up the latter position in the St Helens and District Miners' Union. By then the union, though keeping its agent and funds separate, had affiliated to the Lancashire and Cheshire Miners' Federation (LCMF) created in 1881. With the formation of the Miners' Federation of Great Britain (MFGB) in 1890 and the return of Sam Woods (a prominent miners' agent who was both President of the LCMF and Vice-President of the MFGB) to Parliament as a Lib-Lab MP for the Lancashire constituency of Ince following the General Election of 1892, coal miners were gathering both industrial and political strength.

This they demonstrated in 1893, striking successfully for 16 weeks against a 25 per cent pay reduction – a period during which, as in other stoppages, Glover refused to draw his salary as miners' agent (then £156 per annum[2]). In 1897 internal restructuring, as part of which all its agents were brought under central control, further strengthened the LCMF whose delegates in 1904 elected Glover as their Treasurer. This unpaid office, to which he was annually re-elected, he fulfilled diligently until his death.

There were many other calls on his time, from canvassing energetically in Haydock, a mining district within the Newton constituency, for the (unsuccessful) Liberal candidate in 1892, to serving for six years on the Board of Guardians for Prescot Poor Law Union, whose large administrative area included St Helens. Characteristically, when in 1902 Thomas Glover found he could no longer devote to this the time he felt necessary, he resigned from the Board. By then he had spent four years as a member of the Assessment Committee, at a time when all St Helens' poor rate assessments were being revised.

For Glover and his contemporaries, belonging to a Friendly Society could provide a small cushion against hard times, and as a very young man he became an Oddfellow. His membership lasted more than 40 years, and of it he wrote: 'I passed through all the Chairs being a past Grand Master of the St Helens Branch, being the second youngest in the kingdom.' By then improvements to workmen's compensation and the provision of old age pensions, enacted by the Parliament in which Glover had sat, had begun to reduce hardship in the community.

Whilst repercussions from the formation of the Labour Representation Committee (LRC) in 1900 percolated through to St Helens Trades Council and the LCMF, Thomas Glover was representing not only the 62,000 strong LCMF but also the MFGB's 600,000 members in Paris, Brussels, Liege and Amsterdam at the gatherings of the International Conference of Miners.

In Lancashire, where Sam Woods had successfully entered Parliament as a Lib-Lab MP, relations between the miners and the Liberal Party were becoming uneasy, as suggested mining candidates were spurned. The only

2   About £13,500 a year today.

mining body to do so, the LCMF sent delegates to the 1900 inaugural meeting of the LRC but then had cold feet. Only in 1903 when they planned to adopt four mining candidates did they affiliate.

Following Hunter's success in 1891, only one of the infrequently contested seats in St Helens' municipal elections fell into Labour hands before 1904. That year two wards returned Labour members, one of whom was George Parr, Secretary of the recently re-invigorated Trades and Labour Council, which, in association with the town's Socialist Society, had approached the LRC regarding the possible adoption of a direct and Independent Labour candidate for the parliamentary borough of St Helens. On 29 August 1903, strongly supported by the miners, Thomas Glover was adopted to contest the seat.

In November 1905 five further Labour candidates won election to the Council, all of whom, plus the existing Labour councillors, distributed themselves around the polling stations, as did Glover's brother and nephew when, barely two months later, the General Election took place. Also that November, a packed and enthusiastic pro-free trade meeting, chaired by veteran St Helens industrialist David Gamble, had been rousingly addressed by the then Liberal MP Winston Churchill, who harshly criticised the Tory government's Protectionist Tariff policy. For Glover, moving the vote of thanks, Churchill's subsequent remarks were significant. Seeing it as a great new feature in the next election, Churchill wished the Labour Party well, believing it had a great and important duty and work to perform in the world.

Formally adopted as an Independent Labour candidate on 21 December, Thomas Glover had circulated his election address by 5 January, three days before Parliament was dissolved. He sought protection for trade union funds (following the Taff Vale Judgement) and amendment of the Workmen's Compensation Act, an end to Chinese 'slave' labour in Transvaal mines, protectionist tariffs and brewers' tied-houses, and advocated an eight-hour day for coalminers, old age pensions, Land Tax reform and considerable local self-government in Ireland.

Sir Henry Seton-Karr, the Conservative candidate and son-in-law to glass-maker William (Roby) Pilkington (1827–1903), had represented St Helens at Westminster ever since defeating David Gamble at St Helens' own first parliamentary election in 1885. A keen supporter of protectionism, he saw a Liberal-Radical regime as leading to domestic disturbance and imperial disunion. This prompted Glover to explain, at one supporters' meeting, that Independent Labour MPs would form a separate party, though prepared to support any government's measures benefiting the country's workforce.

Nothing but rain greeted voters on 16 January, election day. Unlike the Conservatives, Labour supporters had very few conveyances to carry them to the polling stations, and came on foot, particularly later when work was done. Remarkably, of the votes promised to the canvassers, almost 99 per cent were cast. To entertain the estimated 15,000 assembled to await the results, a series of pictures were thrown on a large screen attached to the Town Hall tower. Then figures flashed on it: 'Glover 6,058 – Seton-Karr 4,647', and for the winning party celebrations began.

Reflecting on his first year in the House of Commons, Thomas Glover commented favourably on the respect with which the Labour members were treated, the value of their contributions, particularly in Committee, and the Labour legislation initiated. Though critical of the lack of close scrutiny of major departments' expenditure, the hereditary House of Peers thwarting the will of the people, and time lost in excessive talking, often on local topics better served by devolution, St Helens' new MP had only praise for the tact, sagacity and sympathetic leadership of the Prime Minister (Campbell Bannerman).

Of himself he was to write:

> While a Member of Parliament I sat on grant and select committees and occasionally spoke in the House on mining matters [following the report on the Maypole Colliery explosion, whose devastating effects he had immediately witnessed, he spoke forcefully on the mines' inspectorate's inadequacies] and asked several questions [seeking particulars of coal production, mining and industrial injuries, and hounding the progress of the Coal Mines Eight Hours Bill], and whilst a Member of Parliament the Miners' Federation of Great Britain found me a salary of £350,[3] with a further sum for a second-class travelling contract from St Helens to London.

The General Election of January 1910, fought following the Lords' rejection of the 1909 Budget, felt very low-key in St Helens. 'More like a municipal election' was one comment. Nevertheless, over 93 per cent of those eligible cast their votes. They retained the Trades Council's unanimous choice for candidate, Glover, who had campaigned for the Budget and restraining the House of Lords, by a majority of 795 votes over the Tory Rigby Swift. Eleven months later, with a turn-out of 90 per cent, the situation was reversed. Glover, campaigning on whether the peers or the people should rule, in no way associated Rigby Swift with a local newspaper's 'scurrilous' campaign against him. But he did blame that, and the Tories' cessation at 5 p.m. of providing conveyances for voters' use, for Swift's slender 262 majority.

No longer their parliamentary champion, Glover continued to serve his community as a magistrate, and as miners' agent and treasurer, until his death from diabetes in January 1913. Tributes paid then, and by so many, make the St Helens motto he knew, *Ex Terra Lucem* (loosely interpreted as 'from the earth light', referring to the town's underlying coal measures) appropriate for the first Labour MP, the collier Thomas Glover.

Shaun Woodward
MP for St Helens South

Shaun Woodward

---

3   Roughly £28,000 in today's money.

*J. Keir Hardie:
MP for West Ham
South, 1892–95, and
Labour MP for
Merthyr Tydfil,
1900–15*

JAMES KEIR HARDIE. M. P.

COPYRIGHT Photo Russell

Chapter 8

J. Keir Hardie

1856–1915

JAMES KEIR HARDIE was born in Lanarkshire on 15 August 1856, the illegitimate son of a farm servant, Mary Keir. He overcame poverty to devote his life to struggling against many of most powerful social and political injustices of the day. Perhaps more than most politicians, an understanding of his early life is fundamental to understanding the man.

Despite the mythology, Hardie was neither illiterate nor uneducated, but self-taught. His obituary in the *Aberdare Leader* proudly declared that he was no 'illiterate ignoramus', having 'graduated with Honours in the school of tribulation'. His mother's influence steered him towards the Young Templars Movement, whose pledge he took at the age of 16. Its advocacy of self-help and self-discipline, and the equal treatment of women, influenced him greatly. As an older man, Hardie offered the following advice to a miner seeking to better himself: 'drink less, read . . . and think more'. He practised what he preached.

His was the last generation not to receive compulsory education, and he began work aged eight. His step-father was injured at work, and the family came to rely on Hardie's income, earned working twelve hours per day, seven days per week as a bakery message boy. He also helped care for his chronically ill elder brother, Duncan. For Hardie, politics and morality were intertwined. More than merely understanding hardship, Hardie experienced its daily, humiliating and debilitating grind. In later life, he described how, on arriving fifteen minutes late for work for the second day running, he was summarily dismissed by his employer, who fined him a week's wages in order to make him 'more careful in the future'. The cruel indifference of his boss (in light of the fact that the family relied on his income and his brother was to die of his illness very shortly afterwards) surely affected him profoundly.

Religion shaped his psyche and informed his later actions. Despite his parents' atheism, Hardie's own moral sense was hugely influenced by his particular interpretation of the Christian faith. He despised what he termed 'churchianity', claiming that 'the rich and comfortable classes have annexed Jesus', making him a 'symbol of respectability rather than a force to combat social evils'. In his 1906 election address to Merthyr Tydfil, he argued that 'religion should be voluntary', and that religious education should occur outside school in order to put education 'beyond the reach of sectarian disputes'. It is fascinating to read this devoutly religious man, who some would say identified himself with Jesus, and whose worldly actions were enacted with a religious zeal, caution against religious influence in schooling. Present-day advocates of the expansion of faith schools might reflect on his words.

Hardie's particular view of Christianity shaped his view of socialism, to which he 'converted' while active in unionism in the coal mines. Religion, morality and politics became synonymous for Hardie. He stated that 'socialism is the modern word for Christianity'. For Hardie, to be truly Christian was to be a socialist – not the socialism of theoretical Marxism or economic theorising, but of activism and agitation in seeking to better the lives of the poor and to empower them, through democratic politics. Hardie wrote, in typically rousing language, that 'socialism, [and we must infer – religion] I say again, is not a system of economics. It is life to the dying people.'

Hardie was to see these 'dying' people at first hand, while working in the Lanarkshire coalfields from the age of 11 as a trapper – younger boys were often employed to open and shut the doors to keep the mine's ventilation system working. Hardie's ability to empathise with suffering can be seen in his befriending of a pit pony, who responded only to his gentle cajoling, and whose teeth marks were visible on the wrist watch that he wore for decades. However, after witnessing appalling conditions and many fatal accidents, his sense of outrage at these injustices began to be channelled into action. As a self-educated man, a temperance movement activist and an eloquent public speaker, Hardie was chosen to became secretary of the Hamilton District Branch of the Lanarkshire Miners' Union in 1878, aged 21. This led to his prompt sacking and blacklisting, and from this moment on he was a full-time trade union and political activist.

Following his marriage to Lillie in 1879, there was no time for a honeymoon due to his involvement in a miners' dispute – an early indication that the pursuit of a career in politics was to damage his family, whom he left alone for long periods in Scotland, on a relatively meagre allowance.

Hardie's notoriety as a union agitator led to his first journalistic job – with the *Cumnock News*. Journalism was to be a central plank of Hardie's activism. He wrote damning columns for the *Cumnock News* under the pseudonyms 'Trapper' and 'Black Diamond'. He published a 'Good Pits Guide', encouraged readers to write in with grievances, and used his paper to campaign on many disparate issues such as working conditions, women's suffrage, land reform and calling for an eight-hours per day, five-day working week. He went on to found the *Labour Leader* newspaper, for which he wrote prodigiously. The current Cynon Valley local newspaper covering Aberdare, is called the *Cynon Valley* **Leader**.

In 1886, working again as a miners' agent, he witnessed both the State's use of violence against striking miners and lost faith in the ability of the Liberal Party to represent simultaneously the interests of the workers and their employers. Hardie began visiting London and other parts of England, meeting Friedrich Engels and Karl Marx's daughter, Eleanor. Soon after, in 1888, he stood for Parliament for the first time in a by-election for Mid-Lanark and was heavily defeated. Despite this setback, through his union activism, journalism and a seemingly endless amount of public speaking engagements throughout the country, Hardie was developing a national persona, an appetite for electoral combat and a sense for defiant public relations, all of which he was to deploy in the future.

From the early stages, Hardie was instrumental in the formation of the Labour Party. In 1888 he helped form the Scottish Labour Party, whose

programme reads like a roll call of the reforms of future Labour governments. The year 1888 was also a formative year in the development of
Hardie's internationalism. He had held rather xenophobic attitudes towards
foreign workers until he attended his first international conference –
the TUC Parliamentary Committee's International Workers Congress in
London. Here Hardie had a three-pronged Damascan conversion: in real-
ising that, unlike the British representatives, all the foreign trade unionists
were socialists; in becoming involved in the suffragette movement following
a meeting with the Pankhursts; and in his realisation that working people
were similarly oppressed wherever they lived in the world. From then on,
Hardie had a deep interest in travelling abroad, and in engaging with
working, or oppressed, people. He was by now a famous left-wing public
speaker and politician on the national and international stage.

A genuine and early internationalist, Hardie went on several world tours,
lectured many times in the USA and was a prominent British delegate to
the Second Workers' International Conference in Paris. During a visit to
India, Hardie provoked outrage in the British press by calling for Indian
independence, deploying the irrefutable, but in those days treasonable, logic
that if Britons ruled Britain, so Indians should rule India. Hardie's *Times*
obituary invokes the imperialist mindset of the age, in referring to his Indian
speeches as 'mischievous'. Hardie was viewed by many in the establishment
as a dangerous revolutionary, and was often viciously attacked by the tabloid
press, which continually pilloried him on several fronts and delved, unsuccessfully, into his financial background in an attempt to discredit him as a
politician who could be bought.

MPs received no parliamentary salary, which particularly exposed
working-class MPs to the potential dangers of needing to secure money not
merely for campaigning, but also with which to live and pay staff. Hardie
was not immune to these perils, although was never compromised politically by his financial dealings. The vitriolic attacks on early Labour MPs by
an almost exclusively right-wing press were a foretaste of the onslaught that
was to hit the Labour Party in the 1980s, and which still has to be guarded
against today.

In South Africa, he spoke on behalf of black African rights in Johannes-
burg, at a time when many British radicals sympathised with the Boers, and
while abroad many of his public meetings were broken up by opponents.
The Times noted disparagingly that 'no speaker has had more meetings broken
up in more continents than he'.

During his victorious campaign for the seat of West Ham South in 1892,
he stood as 'an independent supporter of the Liberal Party', who would put
'the claims of Labour above party', indicating the growing tensions generated as the Liberal Party sought to outmanoeuvre nascent Labour politicians,
who themselves suffered from the lack of a formal party structure in the
Labour movement. Hardie was increasingly convinced that such a structure
was essential and, having won the West Ham South seat, was highly active
in bringing this about. He arrived at Parliament in a hired carriage,
surrounded by a large crowd of supporters, accompanied by a cornet player
(although legend has transformed this into a brass band), and dressed partly
in home-made clothes. This caused a minor scandal in 1892, but the legend
that he arrived wearing a cloth cap and tweed suit is perhaps overstated.
The manner of his arrival, in defiantly disregarding the parliamentary dress
code of top hats and long black coats, showed that his purpose was to bring
the interests, concerns, suffering, and even dress sense, of working people
into the corridors of power.

Hardie was portrayed in cartoons as carrying an unemployed man into Parliament over his shoulder; he relished the gibe that he was the 'Member for the unemployed'. He would address colleagues in the House as 'men', which infuriated other MPs, though he failed to see why he should address fellow parliamentarians any differently to his constituents. When entering the House of Commons an attendant asked, 'Are you working here, mate?' Hardie answered, 'I am,' to which the attendant enquired, 'Where, on the roof?' Hardie replied, 'No, on the floor!'

Moves to structure Labour representation formally in the House of Commons continued at the 1892 Trades Union Congress (TUC), where Hardie and his allies' motion setting up the Independent Labour Party (ILP) was passed. Hardie was elected its Chair, and a year later became President.

In Parliament, Hardie was radical, but also intensely practical in his demands of the government, focussing for example on the case of working conditions in government dockyards and arsenals. He was a thorn in the side of an establishment who did not see this as worthy of parliamentary scrutiny. On 28 June 1894, 231 men had died in the Albion Colliery disaster in South Wales, yet the House spent an entire day congratulating the Duchess of York on the birth of her son (the later King Edward VIII). There was a minor scandal when Hardie tabled an amendment offering the condolences of the House of Commons to the families of those killed. He wrote later that 'the life of one Welsh miner is of greater commercial and moral value to the British nation than the whole Royal crowd put together'. Hardie used his position as an MP to bring subjects such as working conditions, arbitrary police power, low wages, ill-health, denial of the right to assemble, and tragedies such as Albion, which would hitherto have been ignored, directly into the chamber of the House of Commons, where they could no longer be swept under the carpet.

Along with all his ILP colleagues, Hardie lost his seat in the 1895 General Election, but this allowed him to embark on a long tour of the South Wales coalfields during the six-month miners' strike. Hardie readily took to the Welsh, stating that 'all Celts . . . are socialist by instinct', something which, electorally speaking, remains the case today. The strike failed, but awoke the Welsh miners' political consciousness, and there was an almost instantaneous huge increase in the number of ILP branches formed in Wales.

In 1900, the formation of a Labour Party came ever closer when the TUC-sponsored conference created the Labour Representation Committee (LRC). This suited Hardie, for whom independence from other parties was crucial to securing working-class representation in Parliament. Hardie now stood for the Merthyr Tydfil parliamentary seat. His strong religious beliefs and the contacts built up during his tour of Wales during the six-month miners' strike of 1898 helped him to become MP for Merthyr Tydfil. At this time, the Merthyr constituency included much of the present-day constituency of Cynon Valley.

He developed friendships with many people in his Merthyr constituency, including a particularly close bond with Agnes (Aggie) Hughes, daughter of the Reverend Hughes, of the English Methodists in Abercynon, Aberdare, whose family had greatly assisted Hardie locally in the 1910 General Election. Hardie corresponded with Aggie regularly, and became particularly fond of pine-flavoured lozenges bought by her from a chemist in Abercynon. In one letter he writes to Aggie that the lozenges are 'all gone, but not forgotten! They are now awaiting a pleasant resurrection – or should I say reincarnation. Either name will taste as good.' In another, he writes fondly, 'our wee Mountain Ash dog is turning out a beauty and as sly as a couple of Philadelphia lawyers. I'm sure he can talk Welsh — at least he understands Scotch.'

As MP for Merthyr Tydfil, Hardie tabled the first motion mentioning 'socialism' in the British Parliament, urging 'the common ownership of land and capital for use and not profit'. Support for the LRC was growing among the unions, which were coming to the conclusion that legislative change was necessary.

In the 1906 Election, 29 LRC MPs were elected. Hardie was not widely liked by Ramsay MacDonald and others and only just won the poll to lead the group. From February 1906 onwards and still today, this group has been known as the Parliamentary Labour Party (PLP). The Labour Party was born. However, Hardie disliked his role as Chair of the PLP, describing it as 'a seat of misery'. Various commentators point out that Hardie was an ineffective leader of the PLP due to being unable to manage diverse opinion. It was perhaps the strength of his views that conflicted with a Chairman's role, as in 1908 he stated to a colleague, 'my strongest reason for deciding to get out of the chair is that I may be free to speak out'. He was ill at ease with the wielding of any kind of political power, or the compromises this entailed — a telling metaphor for the compromises with which all elected politicians must battle in representing their party, their constituents and their own conscience in the face of much lobbying and ever-changing political ebbs and flows.

Hardie's final years as an MP were not happy ones. As an implacable opponent of the militarism and diplomatic failures of the European political elites, he was heartbroken by the outbreak of the First World War. He had agitated for a general strike and hoped that working-class collective action might have prevented conflict. He was, according to the *Aberdare Leader's* obituary, a man who 'declared war against war at all times and under all circumstances'. The *Aberdare Leader* referred to an anti-war meeting held in Aberdare Market Hall, at which Hardie was 'howled down'. It was at this meeting that the pro-war union leader C.B. Stanton, who would succeed Hardie in the Merthyr seat, waved a revolver in the air. Emotions concerning the war were running high and the issue split the Labour Party at all levels (in much the same way as the Iraq war would this century). His health increasingly declined and he rarely spoke in further parliamentary debates. He died on 26 September 1915. The official cause of death was given as pneumonia.

Many people, commenting on Keir Hardie's life, question whether society has changed so radically from Hardie's day that reference to his ongoing influence on the Labour Party and socialism is redundant? Hardie's chief biographer — the historian Kenneth O. Morgan — addressed this question in the 1970s. The current Labour government is governing in a radically different world to that of the 1970s, and certainly the 1890s. Many of the key problems that exercised Hardie are no longer major causes of concern.

However, while the conditions in which people now live are incomparably better than those Hardie endured and campaigned to improve, poverty, inequality, international instability and war have not disappeared. Hardie's legacy can be felt in the fact that it has been successive *Labour* governments that have driven forward progressive democratic socialist ideals, and made them into a tangible and life-changing reality for the people of Britain. Keir Hardie and the generation of 1906 laid the foundations for this.

Hardie's attitude to life; his style; his demeanour; his tireless focus on the poor, the disadvantaged, the disenfranchised and the voiceless; his moral vision for a more just world obtainable not through revolution, but through well-organised political activism; and the quasi-religious zeal with which his working life was imbued are an inspiration for democratic socialists today. Under the surface, inequality, injustice and inequalities of opportunity still exist and are often tenacious enemies despite the reforms of the current Labour government. Hardie's memory implores us not to rest on our laurels, but to retain our sense of outrage about the suffering of our fellow human beings, and to act politically to improve these conditions. For that, for his central role in the forging of our Labour Party and for much more, we have Keir Hardie to thank. Words from the *Aberdare Leader's* obituary provide an appropriate epitaph:

> Even his enemies could not help being impressed by the sincerity of the man, his loyalty to his mission and his enthusiasm for the cause to which he gave his life. No longer is heard the voice of the stern, austere prophet with his plain living and high thinking, denouncing the vices of plutocracy, declaring woe unto warmongers, and laying the axe at the upas tree of capitalism.

Ann Clwyd
MP for Cynon Valley

Ann Clwyd

Arthur Henderson: Labour MP for Barnard Castle, 1903–18, for Widnes, 1919–22, for Newcastle East, January–December 1923, for Burnley 1924–31, and for Clay Cross, 1933–35

ARTHUR HENDERSON. M. P.
COPYRIGHT PHOTO ELLIOTT & FRY.

Chapter 9
Arthur Henderson
1863–1935

NEIL KINNOCK was Leader for nine years. Tony Blair if he retires in 2007 will have been Leader for at least 13 years. Harold Wilson was Leader for 12 years. Clem Attlee was Leader for 20 years. Arthur Henderson was in very senior positions of leadership from 1908 to 1932, 24 years out of his 32 years as a Member of Parliament. If the Labour Party 'owes more to Methodism than Marx', Arthur Henderson must claim much of the credit or blame! He was MP for Barnard Castle from 1903 to 1918, winning a famous by-election by 47 votes. During the campaign, 'Barney' was besieged by the national press for the first – and probably the last – time in its political history.

Henderson was three times Leader of the Labour Party: from 1908–10, from 1914–17 and finally from 1931–32. He was a member of Lloyd George's War Cabinet in 1915, Home Secretary in the 1924 Labour government, and Foreign Secretary in the 1929–31 Labour government. He was awarded the Nobel Peace Prize for his support for the League of Nations and his Presidency of the Disarmament Conference, whilst being a real power in Labour politics for over 27 years.

Henderson spent all his formative years in the North East. He was a prominent North East Methodist local preacher. He rose to pre-eminence in North East trade unionism, and he represented Barnard Castle for 15 years in the House of Commons.

Barnard Castle is a delightful rural market town. In 1903 the constituency consisted of the whole of Teesdale and Weardale, about one-third of the geographical area of County Durham, covering some 1,200 square miles. Farming was crucial to employment and prosperity, but so were lead-mining, coal-mining and quarrying, accounting for Henderson's strong working-class support. Nonconformity was very strong in both dales. Consequently the Liberals were also strong. Indeed Arthur Henderson was the agent for Sir Joseph Pease, the Liberal MP, from 1895. The National Liberal Party was very keen for Henderson to succeed Pease, being keen to recruit working-class candidates. For some time there was genuine doubt as to whether Henderson would remain with the Liberals. He, however, had come to national politics from trade unionism. So, as a strong trade unionist who attended the early meetings of the Labour Representation Committee, Henderson followed his union instincts into the newly born Labour Party. Despite the national Liberals' enthusiasm for Henderson, the local Liberals insisted on fielding their own candidate, fighting a bitter campaign and splitting the anti-Tory vote. This explains Henderson's very narrow victory of 47 votes over the Tory.

There were two drivers in Arthur Henderson's life. The first was Methodism. At 16 he was converted in Newcastle-upon-Tyne in a street meeting under Gipsy Smith, a 21-year-old Captain in the Salvation Army. In the words of his elder brother: 'For Arthur, life began with his conversion. Before that, he was just the ordinary boy.' He was soon involved in all the activities of the chapel including becoming a Sunday school teacher, and visiting the sick and needy of one of the poorest parts of Newcastle. It was in the chapel that his leadership qualities were first revealed. From his faith arose his life-long fundamental belief in conciliation and arbitration rather than confrontation in industrial relations and international affairs. However, he was a 'centralist' and even brutal from time to time as General Secretary of the Labour Party. His faith did not prevent him from fully supporting the First World War as soon as it became inevitable, in contrast to Ramsay MacDonald. Henderson became a notable regional and national 'local preacher'. His religious speaking was frequently passionate, challenging and moving, whereas his political speaking was solid, although highly competent and frequently persuasive.

Henderson established himself as the leading Labour man in the nonconformist world. He was not alone in the Parliamentary Labour Party (PLP). Out of its 30 members in 1906, 18 claimed to be nonconformists. Henderson and the nonconformists were crucial in attracting support away from the Liberals to Labour, especially amongst the 'respectable' working class.

The other driver in Henderson's life was trade unionism. His youth was spent in the iron industry. He was apprenticed at 12 as an iron moulder. It was when he worked for Robert Stephenson and Sons that he became a leading figure in branch meetings and an eager recruiter to the union. Before long, he was Branch Secretary, later becoming the district delegate for Northumberland, Durham and Lancashire. The post was onerous and unpaid. No wonder he was the only nominee! The iron founders' dispute of March to September 1894 brought Henderson to prominence, enabling him to be elected as one of his union's delegates to the 1894 Trades Union Congress (TUC), an important step in his political education. He was soon 'the coming man' among working-class Liberals. Even before his election to Parliament, the Iron Founders were proud to have Henderson as their star speaker at national Labour rallies. When he moved to Darlington, he still worked for the union, using his home as his office. After his election to Parliament, he became the union's President in 1910 and continued as full-time organiser until 1911.

Throughout his long parliamentary career, whether as a Member of Parliament, a Cabinet Minister or as Chairman, Leader or Chief Whip, Henderson kept close to the unions and the TUC. He was always an excellent point of contact between the PLP leadership and both union and Labour Party members, which lead to enormous strains, especially when he joined Lloyd George's War Cabinet and when the Labour Party was in minority governments.

As a Liberal, although a labour candidate within the Liberal broad church and one who advocated municipal socialism, he was elected to the Newcastle Council, where he served with distinction. In 1895 he became the agent to Sir Joseph Pease, the MP for Barnard Castle, at £250 a year providing he moved nearer to the constituency. This led him and the family to move to Darlington, where he was elected to Darlington Council and Durham County Council. Later, as a newly elected Labour MP, he was appointed

Mayor of Darlington. His eight years as agent gave him crucial experience of political organisation and electoral law. This, combined with his wide experience of trade union organisation, equipped Henderson to organise training nationally within the Labour Party and the trade union movement. Moreover in 1903, as victor in a famous by-election (the first won in a three-way contest), he became one of only five Labour MPs so was in great demand as a national speaker. Consequently he quickly grew in authority and stature within the movement.

Henderson was always happiest when he had his hands on the levers of power although not as the Leader. The Chief Whip's position, which he first took on from 1908–10, suited him well. He was prepared to work long hours in the Commons and he was firm with his colleagues. John Hodge told one of Henderson's sons towards the end of the First World War: 'Your father is a dictator. He has to have his own way.' Both as a trade union official and Chief Whip, Henderson was prone to display intolerance of dissent.

He had three periods as Chairman or Leader of the Labour Party. When he took the Chairmanship for the first time in January 1908 the policy of working with the Liberals and extracting legislative concession was already beginning to look like failure. He was soon criticised by leading Independent Labour Party (ILP) figures such as Bruce Glasier for 'playing the Liberal game'. He lacked Hardie's charisma and socialist fervour but he acted much more as the spokesman of the Parliamentary Party than Hardie. During this term, Henderson frequently pressed the government on unemployment, but he lacked the fire of Victor Grayson who caused a scene in the Commons and was suspended. To the dismay of the leadership, Grayson's activities were warmly received by socialists in the country. Henderson's stance, meanwhile, was often indistinguishable from advanced Radicals; for example, he warmly praised Lloyd George's 1909 budget, as similar to the policy approved at Labour's 1909 conference. He saw taxation changes as the major means of redistribution of wealth. He also supported Lloyd George and Winston Churchill's Lords reforms. Little wonder that Beatrice Webb reported in November 1910 that Lloyd George and Winston Churchill had taken the limelight, overshadowing the Labour Party.

In the next two years Henderson pressed MacDonald to take the Leadership. He was responding to the need to fill the vacuum at the top with a capable colleague. He found MacDonald to be a moderate ILP man whose political views were similar to his own, although their personal relationship fluctuated from extremely bad to quite good and was to do so for the rest of their lives. As well as admiring MacDonald's abilities, Henderson saw him as able to control the excesses of the ILP and so maintain the balance between the trade union and socialist wings of the party.

Although Henderson was often the spokesman of the craft unions, he always urged on them a wider view. After the reversal of the Taff Vale decision, he wrote:

> There is a great gulf between those who have and those who have not. To narrow and if possible remove this gulf is the work [to] which we as trade unionists, should devote our best energies. No instrument can assist . . . a highly organised, well equipped independent Labour Party, caring for the social and industrial needs of the wage earners. Seeking to so alter our commercial organisations as to give a fuller and more complete opportunity to the many as well as the few.

He argued for Labour policies of nationalisation. The First World War demonstrated that wide-ranging state control and direction of industry was possible. Henderson was to be involved in oiling the industrial war machine.

Like all leading Labour politicians, Henderson was working nationally and internationally for peace. However, as soon as war was declared, he and the majority of the Parliamentary Party decided that it had to be supported. Indeed this was the decision of the National Executive Committee (NEC), with Henderson as General Secretary. MacDonald along with Keir Hardie and most of the ILP were against supporting Asquith's government and so forfeited the support of the majority of the PLP. Henderson, therefore, temporarily became Chairman in 1914 whilst retaining the Chief Whip's position. Henderson chaired the new War Emergency Workers' National Committee set up under the NEC. This did much to establish Labour as the champion of working people generally. It raised issues of unemployment, high food prices and lack of coal on which Henderson made strong representations to Asquith. In May 1915, Henderson joined Asquith's coalition government. He continually encouraged MacDonald to resume the Leadership, but, when MacDonald declined, Henderson retained the Chairmanship of the PLP. He was involved in recruiting campaigns and the government's efforts to ease labour supply problems in the munitions industries. His involvement in the government's munitions policies and his eventual support for the Military Services Bills brought him into conflict with the Labour movement. In July 1916 he wrote to Asquith: 'Through my associations with you I believe I have permanently forfeited the confidence of certain sections of the organised workers. I am now faced with a much more serious consequence . . . of losing a greater measure of the support of the Labour Party.' These problems were exacerbated when Henderson joined Lloyd George's War Cabinet in December 1916, mostly because the Labour movement was deeply suspicious of Lloyd George. Henderson's attempts to serve both Lloyd George and the Labour movement finally failed in the summer of 1917.

Henderson's enforced departure from the government gave him much more time to devote his powerful organising abilities to the Labour Party and to assist in establishing it as the main opposition to Lloyd George. He saw that Labour needed machinery appropriate to its increased political and economic strength resulting from the war and the enlarged franchise after the 1918 Reform Act. Henderson stated that he did not want to take office again 'in any government, whether in war or peace, that was not controlled by the Labour Party'. He proposed to maintain the existing 'political federation of trades unions, socialist bodies and cooperative societies . . . but to graft on . . . a form of constituency organisation linked up with the local Labour parties or trades councils'. In order to achieve this, Henderson gave up the Leadership of the Parliamentary Party in mid-October 1917.

He had spoken at the TUC in September 1917 of an international movement of workers. It 'would be the finest expression of a League of Nations . . . a League of the Common Peoples throughout the whole civilised world'. This gave rise to cooperation between the Parliamentary Committee of the TUC and the NEC. Their programme stated that 'there shall be henceforth on earth no more war'. Not surprisingly the Labour Party warmly approved of President Woodrow Wilson's 'Fourteen Points'.

Labour increased its representation in the Commons from 42 to 57. With its new constitution and its new programme *Labour and the New Social Order*, Labour had emerged as a national party and the main alternative to Lloyd George's coalition. Henderson continued to concentrate on the Labour Party's organisation and its international activities until he again became Chief Whip in 1921. Labour increased its seats in the Commons to 142 in

1922 and to 191 in 1923. By the autumn of 1923 the character of the Labour Party owed much to Henderson and he was the dominant figure within it. Even so he smoothed the way for Ramsay MacDonald's return as the charismatic Leader in 1922 and Labour emerged as the second largest party in December 1923.

The period of the first Labour government from January to November 1924, according to Wrigley, was not Henderson's finest hour. In spite of his close contact with the party machine and the trade union leadership, he was at times surprisingly insensitive to the views of the Labour movement. The Home Secretary's role suited his own tendency to move forward with great caution, seeking compromise rather than confrontation. While Henderson was not under the thumb of departmental officials, he was far too susceptible to 'nothing can be done' arguments, especially on such controversial issues as the reinstatement of the 1919 police strikers. The Labour movement was very keen on reinstatement yet Henderson recommended against to the Cabinet. He was later to back down, but only after great damage to himself and the government.

After the first Labour government's fall, Henderson rallied the movement behind the Geneva Protocol. For him, the aims of the Protocol, including its commitment to an international disarmament conference, remained a central cause for the rest of his life. Despite their awkward relationship during the government, Henderson continued to support MacDonald as Leader, even though many in the trade unions wanted Henderson. He thought that MacDonald's charisma and platform oratory made a bigger impact on the electorate. MacDonald represented moderation and had a better chance of maintaining party unity than anyone else. Henderson's control over the party machine and his resumption of the Chief Whip's post until 1927 boosted MacDonald's power. However, Henderson was the driving force behind the 1928 Labour conference adoption of *Labour and the Nation*. This bore the stamp of his speeches and moderate policies. Henderson was also involved in widening Labour's appeal to rural workers, co-operators and women, whilst working hard to exclude the communists from the party and the trade unions. Having failed to prevent the General Strike, Henderson and MacDonald acted as political advisers to the General Council of the TUC.

Henderson continued his considerable interest in foreign policy. He was President of the Labour and Socialist International. Throughout the 1920s Henderson was one of the major architects of Labour foreign policy. With Labour's victory in the summer of 1929, Henderson was the most obvious choice as Foreign Secretary. Yet MacDonald would have preferred J.H. Thomas who was more likely to be congenial and acquiescent. Nevertheless, Henderson was appointed and greatly enhanced his reputation. Indeed, Henderson has been recognised as the most successful member of the second Labour government. His conduct of foreign affairs was widely admired by Labour figures, such as Hugh Dalton, as well as by the press. Throughout his career, Henderson won respect for his judgement despite not being quick-witted. Hugh Dalton, his Parliamentary Under-Secretary, and Philip Noel Baker, his Private Secretary, confirmed his good 'grasp of the problems he faced and . . . (his) ability to cut to the heart of an issue without burying himself in the minutiae of detail'. Aided by Dalton, he tried to ensure that the Foreign Office did not deviate from the policies laid out in *Labour and the Nation*. His stature in battling to establish the League of Nations grew considerably during his tenure.

In 1931 Henderson became involved in the government's response to the developing economic crisis as a member of the Cabinet Economy Committee. During this series of meetings, the inner ring of the Cabinet considered ways of achieving major savings to gain the confidence of the international money markets. Henderson was prepared to contemplate some cuts rather than to reject all and so let in a Tory government. He was torn between 'loyalty to my Cabinet colleagues and loyalty to the movement outside'. He suggested to the Economy Committee that they should consult the General Council of the TUC and the Labour Party Executive as well as opposition leaders and the Bank of England. When the opposition leaders rejected the Cabinet's savings proposals, Henderson was of the view that the Labour minority government should resign. On 24 August 1931, the Cabinet met for the last time. Henderson was shaken when MacDonald announced that the King had invited him to stay on to form a National Government. Henderson led the majority of the Cabinet into opposition and so became the natural choice for Leader, despite his unwillingness to assume the role. He was 68, he was tired and his health was weakening. Nevertheless, he launched the election campaign at the Scarborough party conference, little foreseeing the severity of the impending fight. Only 52 Labour MPs were returned out of the 287 elected in 1929 – and the 52 did not include Henderson.

He was left to pick up the pieces; after a spell of recuperation he devoted himself to the Disarmament Conference. International events were already undermining his work, and the Conference, which he chaired, went on far longer than he expected. Inevitably he gave up the leadership to Lansbury at the start of the October 1932 session of Parliament.

Following his re-election to Parliament, his international work was crowned when he was awarded the Nobel Peace Prize in the autumn of 1934. He finally agreed to stand down as Labour Party Secretary in May 1934. According to Dalton 'he had practically to be pushed out'. Henderson died in October 1935, having been a Member of Parliament for 32 years. He dominated Labour politics from his first spell as Chairman in 1908 until his death. He, more than any other single individual, shaped the Labour Party in its formative years, prepared it for government following 1917, and finally served with distinction as Foreign Secretary in Labour's second administration. A superb achievement for 'an ordinary boy' who left school at 12 years of age. He was educated by the Labour movement, served it with great distinction and remained loyal to the end.

Lord Foster of Bishop Auckland DL

Lord Foster of Bishop
Auckland DL

Henderson was nominated by Johan Ludwig Mowinckel,
the Norwegian Prime Minister, in 1934, the nomination
reading 'Henderson strongly supported the League of Nations,
and when he was Foreign Secretary he worked to strengthen
the League in order to guarantee international security. He
was chairman of the League of Nations Disarmament
Conference . . . and he actively worked to establish an
armament limitation plan.'

Nobel Peace Prize

GORTON to the Front

TO HELP THE HELPLESS

Vote for HODGE

THE

People's Champion

and OPPONENT OF MONOPOLY.

Printed and Published by ARTHUR STAFFORD & Co., Market Place, Denton.

*John Hodge:
Labour MP for
Manchester Gorton,
1906–23*

Chapter 10
John Hodge
1855–1937

T HE GORTON CONSTITUENCY was formed in 1885. It has continued ever since, with varying boundaries, though in the 1990s the Boundary Commission proposed its abolition. After Labour made a strong case in the subsequent public inquiry, Gorton was reprieved. In 2005, the Boundary Commission proposed the continuation of the Gorton constituency, with its boundaries further extended.

It started as the Gorton division of Lancashire, since Gorton was at that time a separate urban district with its own council. By 1918, it had become the Gorton division of Manchester, but it was not until 1983, when I became the MP upon the amalgamation of most of my former constituency of Ardwick with Gorton and Fallowfield into a redistributed Gorton constituency, that its boundaries were entirely inside the city of Manchester.

In the 98 years until I became its MP, Gorton had nine Members of Parliament. The first three were two Liberals and a Conservative. In 1906 John Hodge won it for Labour, and, apart from the 1931–35 lacuna caused by the huge anti-Labour landslide of the 1931 election, it has returned Labour MPs ever since.

These have included William Wedgwood Benn, who accepted a viscountcy (Stansgate) in 1937, which his son, Anthony, a quarter of a century later, fought successfully to disclaim. The last Gorton MP before myself, Ken Marks, became Parliamentary Private Secretary to the Prime Minister, Harold Wilson, and then a Junior Minister, before retiring when the constituency was split in 1983 subsequent to boundary changes.

Although he was not elected to the House of Commons until he was aged 50, Hodge had a highly successful, even distinguished, parliamentary career. During the period of the Coalition Government of the First World War, he was appointed by David Lloyd George, the Prime Minister, as the first-ever Minister of Labour and then as Minister of Pensions, and became a member of the Privy Council. He did not want to move from Labour to Pensions, but succumbed to persuasion – and flattery – when Lloyd George told him: 'I want a man at Pensions who has a big heart.'

Before he entered the Commons, Hodge played a historic role in the trade union and Labour movement. When only 30 he was instrumental in forming the first steelworkers' trade union, the Steel Smelters' Association (SSA). He was impelled to do so when the employers at Colville Works in Motherwell demanded a 20 per cent wage reduction. The SSA developed initially into the British Iron, Steel and Kindred Trades Association and then the Iron and Steel Trades Confederation, of both of which he became President. He was President of the Glasgow Trades Council, and presided over the Trades Union Congress when it met in Glasgow. When the SSA moved its headquarters from Glasgow to Manchester, he went with it and made its offices there the most efficient and best-equipped administrative trade union machine in the world.

In Manchester he involved himself in party politics, becoming president of the Cheetham Ward Liberal Association, and ward representative on the Executive Committee of the North West Manchester parliamentary division. He was elected to the City Council as a Liberal representative for Cheetham and sat for three years. However, when seeking a parliamentary candidature in Glasgow, he reminisced: 'Liberals converted me to the opinion that they were hopeless.'

He was a delegate from his union at the Conference of Trade Unions and Socialist Societies, which, in 1900, formed the Labour Representation Committee, the forerunner of the Labour Party. He was elected as a member of its Executive Council in its first year, and retained membership until 1916. In 1901 and 1904 he presided at the Labour Party's annual conference.

What he wanted to become, above all, was an MP. He said: 'My highest hope and greatest mundane ambition was to be a Member of Parliament, the honour of which I did attain.' Before becoming MP for Gorton, he had stood in parliamentary elections at Gower, where he was beaten by only 423 votes, and in a by-election at Preston. At a mass meeting in Preston Town Hall, he 'advised the audience not to be frightened at the word "Socialism" as it was used to frighten grown men, just as parents tried to frighten their children with the bogy man', but he still lost by 2,000. He won Gorton in 1906 by 4,225 votes. His majority fell to 473 in the January 1910 General Election, rose slightly to 653 in the December 1910 Election, soared to 8,042 in 1918, but fell back to 2,001 in 1922. In 1915 he was elected as Vice-Chairman of the Parliamentary Labour Party.

These were outstanding achievements by any criterion, but were especially remarkable because Hodge was born into poverty, in Muirkirk, Ayrshire, on 29 October 1855. His father was a puddler in the steel industry. Young John received an elementary education at Motherwell Iron Works School and then went on to Hutcheson Boys' Grammar School in Glasgow.

As a boy he was employed as a clerk to a solicitor for £10 a year, and in a Glasgow boot shop at the age of 10, with a wage of 4s a week.[1] Then he went into the steel industry, serving an apprenticeship as a smelter, working 12 hours a day. He walked two miles to work every day, and two miles back home again.

He involved himself in politics and trade unionism very quickly, becoming Speaker of Coatbridge Parliamentary Debating Society. When he presided over the Glasgow Trades Congress, he encountered the eminent Liberal MP Sir Charles Dilke (who part-way through his political career became notorious for his sexual escapades). Dilke complimented him: 'You are the most successful chairman the Congress has had, so far as my experience goes, but unfortunately you never gave a correct ruling. Your great asset was that pawky mother wit of yours. It carried you triumphantly through all your blunders.'

1   Equivalent to about £42 a week today.

John Hodge's election manifesto

He took on the role of inaugural, unpaid, Secretary of the new Steel Smelters' union. He was admired among the local workers because, as a Motherwell man put it: 'If the men in the works had an excursion [Hodge] made the arrangements with the railway company; for the fishermen amongst the workmen wanting cheap railway fares and facilities from the railway company [he] was the man to do it for them.'

When he was elected trade union Secretary, Hodge pointed out: 'As I have no job, I cannot be sacked for becoming the secretary.' He was full of initiatives, launching housing schemes for his union members, and insisting that there must be a bath in every home.

Behind the achievements lay the man – stout, with a walrus moustache, dressed always formally, though looking as though he had slept in his clothes, which were creased and with items – possibly including the pipe that he smoked habitually – bulging out his jacket pockets. As an MP he wore a frock coat, striped trousers and what he called a tall hat – what we now know as a top hat – in acknowledgement of Denton, in his constituency, being a centre of hat-making: it was the Denton Hatters' Union that nominated me at my own first attempt to become MP for Gorton.

He was blunt and forthright, taking no nonsense from anybody, whether they might be the people he derided as the 'long-haired intellectuals of the Independent Labour Party' or the left-wingers who caused him difficulties in his constituency. He faced problems from his 'pacifist friends of the left wing' in Gorton when he opposed government proposals to reduce the size of the navy; but 'I carried the Trades Council with me, as they agreed with my point of view that it was the wrong time to cast thousands of men upon the labour market'.

At one point the Gorton Trades and Labour Council wrote informing him that they had chosen a candidate to replace him. He refused to give way, and his would-be supplanters caved in. Nevertheless, this episode may have been one of the causes of his decision to stand down, at the age of 68, at the 1923 Election, at which Labour for the first time became the government in which, as one of the few Labour MPs with ministerial experience, he might have expected to serve. After he retired, he made clear that he would have liked a peerage but Ramsay MacDonald, as Prime Minister, resisted the blandishments of the Tory MP Lady Astor and refused to oblige. He died in 1937 at the age of 81.

When the First World War broke out, he denounced Labour leaders such as Keir Hardie and Ramsay MacDonald, who called for a negotiated peace. He strongly condemned unions that went on strike during the war, saying any industrial action in wartime was equal to treason. Later he was to refuse to support the General Strike in 1926.

He was a tough minister. At the Ministry of Labour, he toured labour exchanges in Manchester and, in some of them, rebuked staff for poor service to clients. At Pensions, he fended off the Treasury, refusing to succumb to their demands that the King's Fund for disabled ex-servicemen, which he had set up, be handed over to them.

At the same time he was somewhat vain, boasting of 'my humour and flamboyant eloquence', and something of a snob, perhaps forgivably, considering the origins from which he fought his way up. He called his autobiography *Workman's Cottage to Windsor Castle*, on the strength of having stayed for one night as the guest of King George V at Windsor, where the King took him aside for a private talk. He rejoiced: 'I cannot remember that even in my wildest dreams for future greatness I ever imagined an honour such as this', and made much of any contacts he had with the Royal Family. Nevertheless, it was those contacts that enabled him, as Minister of Pensions, to set up the King's Fund.

Hodge's autobiography, more than 370 pages long, is maddening. Substantial, tedious sections are devoted to minutely detailed descriptions of trips he made abroad, to France, Australia and the United States, though there is an entertaining account of a meeting at the White House with President Theodore Roosevelt:

> The President turned to me and said, 'You are a Scotsman, Mr Hodge', and I acknowledged this soft impeachment. He then said, 'Ah, Scotsmen make the best settlers'. With a naughty little twinkle in my eye, I said, 'I suppose if I had been a German, you would have said exactly the same thing?' The President sat back in his chair and simply roared with laughter, and his reply was, 'I suppose I would, but you are the first man who has ever told me so'.

On the other hand, there is, frustratingly for me as MP for Gorton, almost nothing about the constituency as it was when he represented it, apart from a photograph of Hodge canvassing two Gorton women who, if their clothes were updated, resemble precisely the sort of formidable ladies I have had the privilege to represent for two decades and more.

Nor did he, during his 17 years as an MP, refer to his constituency very much in the Commons. On one occasion he pleaded, unsuccessfully, for a pension to be paid to a Gorton sub-postmistress. Even this was part of his continuing general campaign for workers' rights, which included advocacy of a better deal for taxi-drivers (one of whom, he complained, was prosecuted for being drunk when he had, in fact, suffered an epileptic fit), and greater consideration for deck-chair attendants in the royal parks (who, he claimed, worked a 73.5-hour week). He also complained of alleged persecution of tramps.

Although in the five years remaining to him as an MP after he ceased to be a Minister he seemed to have lost heart and intervened only occasionally in debates or at Question Time, in his early years he was an assiduous parliamentarian, asking questions on a wide range of subjects and moving a considerable number of Private Members' Bills, mainly to enhance workers' rights. During his period as a Minister he was, of course, extremely vocal and, when at the Ministry of Pensions, boasted that the staff at the Department during his period of office had increased from 3,700 to 6,200.

He alleged political discrimination against industrial workers:

> Speaking for my own constituency, I remember that in the first election of 1910 [in which he scraped home], although there had been no overtime worked during the previous week, it seemed on the day of the election as if there was an epidemic of overtime, with the result that it was very difficult to get the electors to the poll before eight o'clock. It is all very well for gentlemen on the other side who have the command of motor vehicles at a general election. But we Labour men are not in that fortunate position, and our supporters consequently have to walk to the poll.

Both before and during the First World War he was an ardent advocate for the armed forces, and had a lot to say about military bands. On one occasion, he complained of a peculiar situation, in which the wife of an ex-serviceman who was incarcerated in a 'lunatic asylum' was treated as a widow, with an adverse impact on the benefits to which she might have been entitled.

As befitted a Labour MP, he was a vocal class-warrior. He said of a Tory MP, Viscount Wolmer, that 'the Noble Lord seldom, if ever, addresses the House without a sneer at the members of the Labour Party' and warned the MP for Plymouth Sutton, Waldorf Astor, husband of the Lady Astor who later advocated a peerage for him, that 'we are not going to be made fools of by gentlemen such as he'. He was angry that unemployed men had meagre benefits while £10 million (a huge sum then) was paid to farmers as compensation for an outbreak of swine fever.

As someone who was active in the temperance movement, he was annoyed at a reduction in the tax on champagne. He had it in for lawyers, saying on one occasion: 'I have never known any body of men to sing their own praises so much as members of the legal profession. The reason we have so many of the legal profession in this House is that they are all after legal preference.'

He had a sharp tongue. After leaving office on the withdrawal of the Labour Party from the wartime Coalition, he denounced the Prime Minister, David Lloyd George, as not so much a 'Welsh wizard' as an 'illusionist': 'the glibness of the tongue deceives the eye'.

There is, regrettably, nothing at all in his autobiography about his historic role in the creation of the Labour Party, or what life was like in the Parliamentary Labour Party during the 17 years in which he was a leading member of it. Yet I can see him so clearly sitting in the Tea Room of the current House of Commons, in a group of colleagues with whom he is chatting, and to whom he is laying down the law with his 'pawky' humour and flamboyant eloquence.

Sir Gerald Kaufman
MP for Manchester Gorton

Sir Gerald Kaufman

WALTER HUDSON. M. P.

COPYRIGHT Photo Ruddock

Walter Hudson: Labour MP for Newcastle upon Tyne, 1906–18

Chapter 11
Walter Hudson
1852–1935

B Y DEFINITION, all 29 of the Labour Members of Parliament elected in 1906 must have been remarkable people. They brought a new political movement into existence and maintained their identity in the complex situation of a Liberal minority government from 1910 to 1914 and the wartime years that followed.

To Walter Hudson, representing independent interests of working people against those of business and landlords was simply a practical necessity. 'It was the bread and butter of the people which they had to protect, and it was becoming more and more necessary every year to have legislation to benefit the workers.'[1]

Walter Hudson was not a touchy-feely politician in the modern style. He did not justify his views by parading the difficult personal circumstances of his early life. But we should be careful not to infer that he was an emotionally closed-down man in a now unfashionable nineteenth-century style. He would have expected that ordinary people would face difficulties in their lives and that they would have to rely on the solidarity of their friends and family to face those difficulties. The need for collective actions, institutions and services built on those solidarities was obvious. The cause of Labour was a fact of life born out of experience.

Walter Hudson was born in the county town of Richmond, North Yorkshire, in 1852. Both his mother and father died while he was very young. His extended family tried to look after him in a time of declining incomes in agricultural communities. During hard times, he was sent to work at the workhouse. Eventually, at the age of 9, he began work on a farm.

But in the 1860s he got a job working on the railways, which were being rapidly expanded. His first job was as a navvy, which was both heavy and dangerous work, building the railway infrastructure. He then graduated to a number of different jobs; for example, under-guard, mineral-line guard and mainline guard. All of these required a sense of duty, purpose, responsibility, and an ability to make decisions.

Hudson joined his local branch of the Amalgamated Society of Railway Servants (ASRS) in Darlington, and later became its Branch Secretary. His

---

1   Walter Hudson addressing a meeting of workmen on Newcastle Quayside, *Evening Chronicle*, 2 December 1910.

activities led to him becoming a full-time official in 1898, and two years later he joined the executive of the ASRS.

His reputation had grown so much within the union that, in 1891, he became President of the ASRS. This was highly unusual as the tradition was to appoint someone who was from outside the union. He remained as President until 1898. He then resigned his office to take over as the ASRS Secretary in Ireland, which was considered to be a difficult task. By 1910 over 116,000 people who worked on the railways were members of a union. Two-thirds of these were members of the ASRS.

When eventually the ASRS joined with the United Pointsmen and General Railway Workers Union to form the National Union of Railwaymen (NUR) in 1913, Hudson became one of four Assistant Secretaries. He continued to serve the union throughout his parliamentary life.

The economy of the North East grew rapidly in the years between the late 1860s and 1914. Better pumping allowed deeper seams to be worked in the expanding coalfields. The discovery of iron ore in the Cleveland Hills led to a cluster of heavy industries around steel, engineering and ship-building. Both exports, and imports of timber and grain from northern Europe, grew. Not only were there imports of goods, but also people.

The city of Newcastle was also growing rapidly. Over 6,000 men were employed in housing construction. It was the main centre for the business interests that dominated the economy of the North East and the services that supported it. Dominating this sector was the North Eastern Railway with its railway works, its large marshalling yards, and its rail links to the quayside docks and shipyards.

The Liberal Party was forced to acknowledge the growing social and class divisions in cities such as Newcastle. At their national conference in Newcastle in 1891 they set out the 'Newcastle Programme' for state compensation for work-related sickness and accidents, for national insurance and for pensions. The failure to carry out the 'Newcastle Programme' by the Liberal Government of 1892 to 1895 was one of the main spurs for independent Labour representation. It was this cause that Walter Hudson took up in the 'railway servants' union after 1891. He became a staunch supporter of *independent* Labour representation. He spoke in favour of the need for a voice to 'raise one common standard for the cause of labour clear and distinct from either of the two political parties' at the ASRS Conference of 1894.

The Taff Vale Railway judgement of 1901 further prompted the need for independent Labour political representation. This judgement, directed at Hudson's own union, made union funds liable for damage or injury said to be caused by union representatives.

Hudson's fellow railwayman, Richard Bell, had been elected as an MP in 1900 and made Chair of the Labour Representation Committee (LRC) in 1902. But his closeness to the Liberals caused an increasing criticism of him from Walter Hudson and others inside the ASRS.

At the conference of the LRC held in Newcastle in February 1903, Bell was forced to stand down as Chair. Strong resolutions for independence were carried. A Parliamentary Fund for central political campaigning was set up. It was the Newcastle Conference that convinced the Liberals that Labour was a political force with which they would have to deal. It is no accident that it was the same city of Newcastle in which Walter Hudson, the railway union leader, decided to stand.

It was this powerful, confident, growing political base that delivered the Labour nomination for the two-member Newcastle City constituency to Hudson at a mass selection on Saturday 19 November 1903. The conference was held at Lovaine Hall, St Mary's Place, Newcastle. (The Lovaine Hall site is now incorporated into Northumbria, one of Newcastle's two thriving universities.)

Hudson's selection majority was over a thousand, demonstrating the enviable scale of political mobilisation of labour in 1903. Within days a letter was sent to Ramsay MacDonald to inform the LRC of Hudson's selection and seeking their endorsement of him as a Labour candidate. Interestingly, a quarter of the women who worked in Newcastle at the time of Hudson's selection were indoor domestic servants: the LRC candidates were committed to 'votes for women'.

The city of Newcastle had narrowly gone to the Tories in 1895, because an Independent Labour Party candidate polled over 2,000 votes. This cost John Morley, a leading Liberal, his seat. Morley afterwards remained hostile to arrangements with Labour. Newcastle, as an imperial city with a strong defence industrial base, went heavily to the Tories in the 'khaki' election of 1900. So Newcastle was a classic two-member city that was good ground for the MacDonald–Gladstone deal of 1903. This allowed the Liberal candidate to run alongside the Labour candidate for one of the two seats.

Hudson himself realised the weakness of the Liberals and the increasingly powerful role that unionised labour was playing. He sturdily maintained his separateness from the Liberals. Hudson was 'refusing to endorse the Liberal'.[2]

Just as today, in 1906 Hudson's campaign was plagued by problems of getting hold of printed leaflets! 'The literature famine is over and I have stopped swearing in consequence. The fools have been tumbling into place one after another this morning, but we are still short of the quantity ordered; I hope there will be no need to resume the swearing between now and the Election.'[3] But it was Walter Hudson for Labour who topped the poll.

The success at the 1906 general election was down to the 'strength of Labour in the city'.[4] Walter Hudson himself was conscious of the importance of the event. 'The election was undoubtedly the turning point in the history of the Labour movement' said Hudson in a speech to his supporters following the declaration of the result.[5]

He was one of three railwaymen elected in that election. But 25 directors of railway companies had seats in either the House of Commons or the House of Lords. Among them was Stanley Baldwin MP, Director of the Great Western Railway (GWR), and later a Conservative Prime Minister.

Following his election, Hudson pursued his previous interests of railways and railway safety. This was alongside the other manifesto commitments of those LRC candidates, to 'one man, one vote'; female suffrage; old age pensions; housing; land valuation tax; and unemployment. 'There was nothing more serious to the population of today than poverty . . . Every worker should have the right to work and the State should be held responsible for his right to live decently and honestly. In sending Labour these things would be remedied.'[6]

2   *Manchester Guardian*, 17 January 1906.
3   A. Wilson Hildreth, Secretary of Hudson's Executive Committee, 6 January 1906.
4   *Newcastle Journal*, 17 January 1906.
5   *Newcastle Journal*, 17 January 1906.
6   Walter Hudson speech, *Evening Chronicle*, 5 January 1906.

It was Walter Hudson, as an MP, who set the new force of Labour on course to reverse the Taff Vale judgement. He immediately used the opportunity of a Private Member's Bill on 30 March 1906, to sponsor a Trade Unions and Trade Disputes Bill. He emphasised that he was a member of the union against which the Taff Vale judgement had been made. He made it clear that he was not a lawyer but 'he did know what representatives of trade unions wanted as representatives of organised workers'. Drawing on his Irish experience, his Bill covered the rights of associations to peaceful picketing. This also covered the organisations of Irish tenant farmers against the Anglo-Irish landlords and gave him the support of the Irish National Party.

In his speech Walter Hudson rightly referred to the city of Newcastle as 'one of the largest industrial constituencies in this country [which] was the pioneer of trade organisation'. This debate was a substantial challenge to the new Liberal majority in the Commons. The Liberal Attorney General had indicated he did not support Hudson's Bill as Keir Hardie pointed out in the debate. Hardie urged the Liberals not to hide behind the House of Lords. 'Leave that to the Labour members' he said. 'Whoever came into conflict with the movement of organised Labour . . . would live to rue the day they ever entered the lists!' The Liberal Prime Minister, Campbell Bannerman, then spoke and urged the House to give Hudson's Bill a second reading, promising that a substantially similar Bill would be brought forward by the government. Hudson's Bill was carried by a majority of over 300. It formed the basis of the later Trade Disputes Act that reversed the Taff Vale judgement.

Hudson continued to try to further both railway safety and railway workers' rights. In 1907 he sought an amendment to a resolution that called for more railway inspectors. This had been agreed by Bell and the Liberal government. Hudson's amendment called for a limit on railway workers' hours. Later, Labour members voted for this amendment against the Liberals. This led to a long difficulty between Bell and Hudson inside the ASRS. Finally, a row came over Bell's favourable attitude to a 1909 North Eastern Railway Bill that did not concede the rights of all railway clerks to join a union. Bell was forced to resign as General Secretary of the ASRS. This was another important event in the break with 'Liberal Labour'.

Hudson then endeavoured to push the Railway Office Bill through in 1912. This dealt not only with office standards, but also with the idea that nobody under the age of 18 should work nights, and that night workers should not work more than three years continuously on nights. It also made provision for public holidays, time off and a working week of 42 hours. Although it failed to become law, many of the ideas in this Bill were taken up in future Bills.

Hudson also vigorously pursued safety issues. He had previously sat on the Royal Commission on Accidents to Railway Servants in 1899. This was one of Hudson's major causes. Parts of the recommendation were taken up in the 1900 Railway Employment (Prevention of Accidents) Act. Many of his parliamentary questions to Churchill and Tennant (both Presidents of the Board of Trade) reflect this concern.

Hudson was concerned about the practical rights of labour. He asked why inquiries into accidents to railway men did not take place in the order in which they had occurred. He also asked why, when railwaymen were asked to attend the inquiries, they were only given notice the night before or the morning of the hearing, despite the inquiry having been set up months before.

One issue taken up by Walter Hudson has a very topical note. He had strong views on alcohol and licensing. In 1907, alongside others such as

Arthur Henderson, himself a product of the Newcastle labour movement, he signed up to 'The Parliamentary Temperance Party and Sunday Closing'. He was not only worried about the effects of alcohol, but also licensing reform. He was concerned about the effects of alcohol on both the workers in pubs and the people who drank in them: 'The Brewer is made secure in his annual licences and wealth built up on the degradation of the people.'[7]

Newcastle in Hudson's day was a city where many of the original landowners had tried to restrict alcohol consumption when housing development took place. This resulted in legal efforts to stop licensed premises and off-licences being built. In April 1907 Hudson raised the matter of an off-licence in West Jesmond. A house, despite not being granted an off-licence, managed to obtain an excise licence, and so was selling alcohol. Not unlike the complaints of today's Jesmond residents!

Like many contemporary Labour politicians, Hudson had an interest in football. With Arthur Balfour, the former Conservative Prime Minister, he travelled to support Newcastle United in the English FA Cup Final in 1908. Newcastle were tipped to win, and had even asked if they could take the team photo with the cup before the match! Many on Tyneside were glad this wish was not granted, when Newcastle were beaten by Wolverhampton Wanderers. Following the defeat, Hudson gave a speech and actually congratulated the Wanderers. Hudson's generosity was based on a period of great success by Newcastle United.

Hudson stood again for Labour in Newcastle in both elections of 1910. These were held because of the conflict between the Liberal government and the House of Lords over the passing of the Finance Bill of 1909. The Bill proposed a land tax to pay for the old age pensions and other benefits for working people. The city of Newcastle again played an important part in these events. Lloyd George gave three speeches there to mass meetings where he sought to provoke the Lords to reject his Budget and make the case for Lords' reform.

Hudson received well-publicised backing from local unions during this difficult time. It showed how highly regarded he had now become not only as a trade unionist but as a Member of Parliament.

The Newcastle District Committee of the Amalgamated Society of Engineers had adopted the following resolution:

> That we urge our members and all other trade unionists and workers, to vote for Mr. Walter Hudson at the forthcoming election for the three following reasons: (1) Because he, having been a worker himself, knows their needs. (2) Because his past record in Parliament shows that he has looked after their interest and will do so again if returned. (3) Because his programme is full of reforms much needed and desired by workers.[8]

Hudson attacked the House of Lords vociferously during the election campaigns:

> The fact of the matter is you cannot mend them, so the only thing to do is end them! The Lords objected to the pension of 5 shillings[9] to the worn-out veteran of industry of 70 years of age because it would

---

7   Hudson's LRC Manifesto.
8   *Evening Chronicle*, 2 December 1910.
9   Perhaps worth £60 today.

be degradation. If that is so, the Lords are past praying for and have been receiving State pensions all along.[10] I ask you all to give the Lords an emphatic answer this time![11]

Hudson again won both 1910 Elections: 'This result will be written indelibly in the memory of all who had taken part in this election as an object lesson of what collective power could do when it was properly welded, organised, and disciplined for a fight to gain right and justice.'[12]

Labour controversially opposed continuing support for the War Cabinet in 1918, so left the wartime Coalition. Hudson supported this view: 'Those who broke the compact were in point of fact, the late Government, hence it would be illogical for (the Labour Party) to now bind themselves to conditions of which they knew absolutely nothing. They must continue free and unfettered, they could not pledge themselves to unformulated and undefined measures.'[13]

Despite his opposition to the Coalition, Hudson was given and accepted an OBE for his services to labour relations on the railways during the First World War.

When Newcastle City was divided into single-member constituencies in 1918 Hudson stood in Newcastle East. This was the so-called 'coupon' General Election. Newcastle East was the location of the main railway depots and workshops in Newcastle. During the campaign, Hudson called for better housing, and employment for both those on the home front and those returning from wartime armed service: 'The most important question at this juncture is housing, and 1,000,000 cottage dwellings are required . . . on demobilisation and transition if remunerative employment was not found immediately full maintenance should be given to every man, woman and child.'[14]

But he was defeated. Most of my present constituency formed part of the North division of Newcastle in 1918. After Walter Hudson, the part of Newcastle that was allocated to the North division never had a Labour representative again until my own election in 1987. After Hudson's parliamentary career, he continued as Assistant Secretary of the NUR until he retired from the union in 1923. He then became a JP in the Juvenile Court, in Lambeth. He died in 1935.

Walter Hudson realised from his early life that the solidarity of workers and their families broke down without collective action, organisation, law and institutions were required to protect workers from the failure of markets and the power of landlords, big business and even the brewers. It was to Parliament he looked for the laws and collective institutions that could give his people protection. Workers and their families still face the failure of markets and the power of great interests. Walter Hudson's project is not over.

Jim Cousins
MP for Newcastle upon Tyne Central

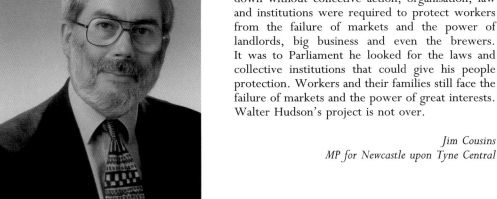

Jim Cousins

10 Hudson speaking at the Elswick shipyard, *Evening Chronicle*, 1 December 1910.
11 *Evening Chronicle*, 2 December 1910.
12 Hudson addressing his supporters after the declaration, *Evening Chronicle*, 6 December 1910.
13 *Newcastle Journal*, 4 December 1918.
14 Speech at Walker Naval Yard, *Newcastle Journal*, 6 December 1918.

John Jenkins:
Labour MP
for Chatham,
1906–10

Chapter 12
John Jenkins
1852–1936

JOHN JENKINS was born in Pembroke on 27 May 1852, the son of a shipwright and preacher. Upon leaving school, he sought to follow in his father's footsteps by seeking employment at the Government Dockyards. He was refused for not being heavy enough but did not let this end his ambition. He eventually gained an apprenticeship as a shipwright before moving to Cardiff where he completed this apprenticeship.

Like his father before him, Jenkins was also a Wesleyan Methodist, teaching in the evenings at the Ragged School in Cardiff where he served as Superintendent. Christian socialism shaped Jenkins' political philosophy and can clearly be seen in evidence throughout his political career.

Jenkins later married the daughter of a shipwright, Sarah Williams, thus further embedding the strong family tradition of shipbuilding (his grandfather had also been a shipwright). Jenkins formed a Shipwrights Society in Cardiff and duly became the organisation's President. He later became President of the TUC in 1895.

Impressively, in addition to the work Jenkins undertook for his own trade union, he was also influential in the formation of several others, such as the Seamen's & Firemen's Union, the Shop Assistants' Union and the Bakers' Society. His passionate interest in trade unionism coupled with his strong Christian socialist tendencies drove his interest in local politics. Elected to Cardiff Town Council in 1890 he later became Mayor (1903–04), which proved to be the last mayoralty before Cardiff Town became Cardiff City.

In 1904 John Jenkins commenced his campaign to win the seat of Chatham in the 1906 General Election. A keen campaigner, a good speaker owing to his preaching background and passionate about the rights of the working classes (particularly those involved in shipbuilding), Jenkins was well equipped to give the Conservative candidate in Chatham a real fight. During this two-year period Jenkins was able to amass a dedicated following and was supported by hundreds wherever he spoke.

A few weeks before the 1906 Election, a very large group of Jenkins' supporters turned up at the local Conservative Party's public hall meeting in Chatham. The *Chatham, Rochester and Gillingham Chronicle* reported: 'Piqued at their inability to gain an entrance to the Conservative meeting, the supporters of Alderman Jenkins became demonstrative.' The police were needed to stop them breaking the door down. Several leaders of the Labour movement made a makeshift platform and began to speak on the political topics of the day, 'amid hearty cheers which were heard by those inside the hall', but the crowd 'seemed to be reserving its energies for the exit of the candidate but in this they were disappointed. They had kept a vigilant watch on the side door but had entirely neglected the main entrance. The result was the hostile crowd kept a fruitless watch for some time after the Major had reached his home. Finding themselves baffled in this matter, the Labour men consoled themselves by singing Rule Britannia' – not a scene likely to be repeated in the twenty-first century!

However, the campaign itself does appear to have been fought with much in common with today's electioneering. The Conservative candidate, Major Jameson, focused strongly on the negative; for example, immigration, of which he said the 'importation of aliens' was a 'danger to the Empire' and a 'grievance to the workers of the UK'. His campaign team also made a number of wholly unjustified and false personal attacks on Jenkins. They were reported to have been telling voters on the doorstep that, if Jenkins were to be elected, the expenses of his election and the continuing maintenance would be paid for out of the local rates. Jenkins said he would give credit to the people of Chatham who knew that 'not a farthing in money could be devoted from the rates for such a purpose' – a dignified response typical of Jenkins' character that was not entirely supported by other members of the Labour movement who angrily demanded an apology from the Major.

Rightly, Jenkins suggested that matters such as this were trivial and should not sidetrack the electorate from the issues of the day – the needs of the workers. At the last public meeting of Labour supporters before the 1906 Election, Jenkins launched a scathing attack on the Major's record, stating that the Tory had disregarded everything of importance to the workers whilst in the House of Commons: 'Major Jameson had not come to represent the aspirations of the workers in Chatham, but simply his own personal aggrandisement.'

The atmosphere after the close of polls in 1906 was magnificently described by the *Chatham, Rochester and Gillingham Chronicle*:

> Easy enough it is to write down the bare facts, but what a different thing to describe the almost unparalleled demonstrations of enthusiasm which took place inside the building when the news – the almost incredible news – of the sensational victory became known. The English language lacks terms sufficiently powerful to convey an adequate idea of the joy of the moment or of the tumultuous excitement which prevailed when Alderman Jenkins MP rose to speak and gazed down upon a veritable sea of faces, as the Member for Chatham. The Labour forces of which Alderman Jenkins was the representative . . . defeated the forces of the Conservatives in overwhelming fashion, the declaration of the poll on Monday night was surprising to even the most sanguine and enthusiastic supporters of Alderman Jenkins.[1]

An enormous crowd had congregated outside the town hall in Military Road where the votes were being counted and cheers and counter cheers for each candidate were frequently made. The crowd was described as wildly excited by the 'startling' result and Jenkins was required to shout at the very top of his voice to make his short speech over the cheers of supporters. Jenkins addressed the crowd:

---

1   *Chatham, Rochester and Gillingham Chronicle*, 20 January 1906.

You have today won one of the greatest battles that will be fought throughout the British Isles. For eight and thirty years you have been tied up in the hands of the classes, but now you have been released and you will be in the hands of the masses. You have won a great victory in the Labour cause.

Let me thank the thousands of electors who voted for me today. I will never betray the confidence you have reposed in me, and I would resign my office rather than forsake your interest.

Farewell! Hip, Hip Hooray!

The number and quality of public meetings held by Labour was instrumental in winning the election, together with the fact Jenkins had been steadily gaining public support over a two-year period via a range of other mechanisms, such as having a very well-organised campaigning machine that ensured the whole borough was systematically canvassed. There was even one street in the Luton area of Chatham that actually succeeded in getting every single voter to the polling station.

Also worthy of note is not only that Jenkins gained the support of those who he sought to represent, namely the working classes, but that he also received the declared support of the Liberals, who did not field a candidate.

Four years later the jubilation of unexpected victory was replaced by the misery of unanticipated defeat. Jenkins was unexpectedly beaten in 1910 by Eton-educated barrister, the Conservative G. Hohler, who served until retiring in 1929. The headlines in the local media were of the 'Surprising Defeat of Alderman Jenkins' but 'surprise' was perhaps an understatement.

A record of a meeting at the town hall a few days before the 1910 Election gives some indication as to just how unexpected was the defeat of such a popular and hard-working MP. The reception Jenkins received was so good, the flowers, letters, gifts and cheers so great, that Jenkins was prompted to say that, although he had never previously feared standing, being an MP or meeting constituents – this reception was 'almost too much to bear'. A few days earlier there had even been an open letter to the *Chatham, Rochester and Gillingham Chronicle* from the previous Tory MP for Chatham, John Gorst, passionately supporting Jenkins, condemning his own party and urging electors to vote for Jenkins.

To add to this general sense of Jenkins' achievements, Chatham Dockyard had never been so successful and the part Jenkins had played in this was widely recognised.

Jenkins had vociferously supported demands for increased pay among the poorest paid dockyard workers as well as pushing for the introduction of a fair compensation system. More jobs were created at Chatham Dockyard, the conditions of work had greatly improved and the pay had also risen significantly. Furthermore, Jenkins had set out his great concern that there was not enough dry and floating dock accommodation, particularly for the Dreadnought type of vessels, and he continued to press passionately for further improvements. Based on this alone it would appear reasonable to expect the dockyard vote to largely have gone Jenkins way. In fact the dockyard workers voted for Jenkins' Tory opponent, Hohler.

Hohler had spoken forcibly and frequently, along with many other Tory candidates across the country, about the urgent need to increase the strength and power of the British navy to match that of the Germans, who were viewed with increasing fear and suspicion. This was dismissed by Labour and Jenkins as 'an absurd scare'; nevertheless it proved immensely powerful with the thousands of dockyard workers as well as the top brass, who took the unusual step of closing the dockyard but ensuring workers received a full day's pay to make sure they had the opportunity to vote. The First Lord of the Admiralty even ordered boats in service to return to the country so that as many naval workers could vote as possible.

Despite all that had been achieved, it would seem that the promise of something more in the future was more alluring than the record of delivery already 'banked'. This is yet another striking example of the power of the 'forward promise'. The defeat of Jenkins highlights once again that as a movement Labour should always be proud of our achievements but focused on delivering more to meet the needs and aspirations of those we represent.

Compare Jenkins' defeat in 1910 with the closure of the dockyard in 1984. The Conservatives under Thatcher closed the dockyard, which resulted in the loss of more than 7,000 jobs and immense hardship for the area. However, at the next election, far from being voted out, the sitting Tory MP increased his majority by more than 2,200 votes! Again, the reality of the loss was not deemed by the electorate to be more significant than what might be delivered in the future. Jenkins clearly failed to appreciate what is now a well-established fact of elections.

The dockyard issue alone was probably sufficient to ensure Chatham lost its first non-Tory MP in almost 40 years but there were a combination of other factors to consider. Issues of the day were strikingly reminiscent of the current political scene; alcohol licensing, education legislation and free trade (of which Jenkins was an enthusiastic supporter) were all hot topics at the time. Another important issue was that of House of Lords reform. Jenkins went so far as to say the House of Lords had mangled one of the finest budgets ever introduced in this country. In contrast, Hohler pointedly refused to discuss the subject at his public meetings – a strategy that clearly helped his success.

The local Conservatives were also buoyed by the victory of the Tory candidate in neighbouring Rochester, an election that took place a couple of days prior to the election in Chatham. Not only did the defeat of Jenkins'

colleague by a victorious Tory candidate have a psychological effect on voters, it also had an effect on the motivation of party activists. The successful Tory campaign team from Rochester moved over to assist Hohler during the final days of his campaign.

On election night a crowd estimated to be in the region of 20,000 had gathered outside the town hall to hear the declaration made at a quarter to midnight. This must have been a deeply disappointing time for Jenkins. Although reported to have been terribly upset at his election defeat, characteristically the upset was not for himself but for the Labour cause. Jenkins very much viewed this loss as a setback for the Labour movement rather than a setback for himself.

In 1910 he returned to Cardiff where he remained an Alderman and a JP as well as becoming a hospital governor. His active membership of the Shipwrights' Society also continued until 1925. He died at home in Cardiff in December 1936.

Jonathan Shaw

Jonathan Shaw
MP for Chatham & Aylesford

F. W. JOWETT. M. P.

COPYRIGHT Photo Henry

Fred Jowett:
Labour MP for
Bradford West,
1906–18, for Bradford
North, 1922–24, and
for Bradford East,
1929–35

Chapter 13
Fred Jowett
1864–1944

THERE ARE MANY colourful figures in the history of the Labour Party – glamorous, flamboyant and controversial. They are often those most popularly remembered. Yet in 1906 a quiet mild-mannered Yorkshireman was among the 29 first Labour MPs elected, a man whose life's work made an enormous impact on the lives of many ordinary people. Fred Willie Jowett of Bradford is not well known, but in researching his background for this piece it was startling how frequently his name appears in books as far apart as consumerism, feminism and even a history of Wales! Knowing even a little about the life of Jowett, it was less surprising that he features in writings about the history of socialism, radical ideology, pacifism, Christian socialism, the first and second Labour governments and the crisis surrounding the national government in 1929. All of these matters were central to his life's work.

Bradford West has a long tradition of trailblazing. Ninety-one years after electing the first Labour MP in the district, the constituency elected its first MP with an Asian background.

Towards the end of his life, Jowett embarked on his autobiography. He died before its completion, but Fenner Brockway took the manuscript and published it as a biography, *Socialism over Sixty Years: The Life of Jowett of Bradford*, with a foreword by Jowett himself.[1] He began by speaking about Bradford's immigrants, contrasting the poverty and squalor of the Irish community with others who had come to Bradford and made their fortunes – the 'millocracy' as he referred to them. He describes the dreadful poverty, 'bad to appalling conditions' in the mills and the 'forgotten monstrosities' that were the ash-pit privy middens serving four to eight households in two-roomed back-to-back houses.

Fred was born in 1864 in such a house, one of eight children, three of whom died in infancy. At 8 years of age he first went to work in the mill, becoming a 'half-timer' and leaving school altogether at 13. His father was West Riding born, but his mother was originally from Devon, coming to Yorkshire at 7 to work in the mills. It was not uncommon for children to be 'sent in consignments by the poor law guardians', although his mother came with two older brothers. Both his parents were passionate advocates

---

1 Fenner Brockway, *Socialism over Sixty Years: The Life of Jowett of Bradford*, G. Allen and Unwin for the National Labour Press, 1946.

of democracy. Jowett's mother inspired him as a boy with stories of hiding under the table at Chartist meetings. His father was a foreman (gaffer) and a political radical. As he walked the moors with his father on Sundays, they often talked politics. When he was 14, three years of trade depression hit: workers were put on short time, mills were closing and people went hungry. These memories stayed with Jowett and helped to shape his political future. Both his parents were active in the co-operative movement, a tradition their son continued. After tabling a successful resolution to reduce shop workers' hours, he was elected Chair of his local branch at the tender age of 24.

Despite leaving school so young, Jowett spent many hours educating himself at evening classes at the Mechanics Institute and Bradford Technical College. As a young man he read Ruskin, William Morris, Edward Carpenter and Robert Blatchford. He rarely had his nose out of a book. But his growing radicalism was far from theoretical; at 22 he joined William Morris's Socialist League, one of less than a dozen members of the Bradford branch. Unlike the London literary and artistic membership, the Bradford members were largely working class, including three German socialists. Sunday lectures, organised by the radical wing of the Liberals, gave him the opportunity to hear his heroes Morris and Carpenter speak in person. He also met Keir Hardie and forged a friendship that lasted until Hardie's death. After the closure of the Bradford branch of the Socialist League in 1889, Jowett was one of the founders and Secretary of the Labour Electoral Association, which lasted for only nine months.

The Manningham Lockout the following year was a catalyst for the next phase in Bradford's radical politics. The strike began just before Christmas 1890, when the mill-owner, Samuel Cunliffe Lister, insisted that workers accept a 30 per cent pay cut. Matters escalated and the strike/lockout lasted for six months during which time the Liberal Council attempted to ban rallies and meetings supporting the strikers. Following the Durham Light Infantry being sent in, a full-scale riot erupted. Within weeks, the strikers were forced back to work as strike funds were exhausted. The Bradford Labour Union was born out of the strike and became the Bradford Independent Labour Party (ILP) in 1891. These two events were significant, marking the emergence of an independent party for Labour breaking with the so-called left wing of the Liberals. Reaction from the nonconformist Liberals was swift and strong. In the midst of controversy Jowett, speaking at a public meeting, threatened that working men would withdraw from the chapels and form their own 'Labour Church'. This came to fruition in 1891 and for many years was a strong force across the North of England.

The same year as Keir Hardie was elected to Parliament, Jowett was elected to Bradford Council for Manningham Ward. In November 1892 he was the first socialist to be elected in Bradford in a contested election, Leonard Robinson having been elected unopposed in Manningham five months earlier. Jowett was to hold the seat for 15 years, during which time he had many significant achievements, but none made without a struggle. He campaigned on housing in 1894 as a member of the Sanitary Committee, urging the Council to take action under the Housing of the Working Classes Act of 1890; he thus began years of battling with the self-interest of property owners. After his election as Chair of the Committee in 1899, he was heavily involved in the conversion of ash-pit 'middens' to water closets. This was initially resisted and a resolution passed that none could be closed and replaced without an inspection by a delegation of councillors. Jowett's tactic for dealing with this was simply to bombard fellow councillors with inspection requests, until they gave up and left him to it.

Housing took longer; he produced report after report detailing the appalling overcrowding and high death rates in parts of the city, pressing for demolition against the interests of the property owners. It was six years before he had some small success, notably in Longlands in 1900, after a three-year struggle. He was elected to the Board of Guardians (Poor Law) in 1901, where he led a fight against the household means test at the same time as George Lansbury was doing so in Poplar.

Following the Boer War, the winter of 1903/04 witnessed severe depression across Bradford highlighted by the plight of underfed and malnourished school children. This again set Jowett against the majority of Liberals and Conservatives on the Council. Resolutions were passed and rescinded but ultimately, joined by Margaret MacMillan, he prevailed and in 1904 Bradford became the first local authority to serve free school meals. The headmaster of Green Lane School, father of J.B. Priestley, proudly served the first meals. Fifty-five years later, Jowett's successor as MP for Bradford West, and the author of this piece, attended that very same school.

We get an insight into Jowett's character in the run up to the 1906 election. He refused to compromise and enter into electoral pacts with the Liberals. He was thus one of only two Labour MPs elected in a three-way contest. (The other was Barnes in the Gorbals, Glasgow.) Brockway reports that, at the first meeting of the Parliamentary Labour Party (PLP) when a name for the new party in Parliament was needed, Fred Jowett proposed the name the Labour Party. Typically, his maiden speech was on the subject of school meals. Sadly, the bill he was supporting failed but in 1911 he was able to take it forward himself. The *Daily Record* reported: 'Mr Jowett, in a delightful little speech very simple and human introduced a bill to enable local authorities to provide feeding for children.'[2]

On arrival in Parliament, Jowett had two immediate concerns. He felt passionately that individual MPs should be free to vote according to their own conscience and that the Cabinet was too powerful. Alongside the extension of the franchise, Parliament had undergone considerable reform during the late nineteenth century, culminating in Balfour's 1902 'parliamentary railway timetable'. This enabled the government to set the business of the House and left private members with control only of Friday afternoons. The character of the Commons was irrevocably altered with power firmly concentrated into the hands of the executive. It was virtually impossible to defeat the Cabinet without effectively having a vote of no confidence in the government. The modern era of politics had been born. Increasingly deals were struck outside the chamber and debates ensued through the media. For Jowett, this was an untenable state of affairs. As well as the independence of individual MPs, he believed that there should be a system of committees with real power to hold ministers to account, similar to that in local government. It is interesting that the pendulum has gone full swing, with recent reforms to local government mimicking national government – the complete opposite of Jowett's proposals. These issues were to return to haunt Jowett later.

Elected Chairman of the ILP in 1909, his first term of office was fraught with controversy after the publication of the so-called 'Green Manifesto', which led to the temporary resignation of key figures including Hardie, MacDonald and Snowden. Jowett become isolated and estranged from both sides. He had not been connected with its publication, but it quoted his criticisms of parliamentary procedure and policy extensively. This was

2 *Daily Record*, April 1911.

followed by acrimonious correspondence between MacDonald and the Bradford party. MacDonald charged him with seeking opinions from other party members going behind the whips; Jowett objected to this sending of private letters 'misrepresenting his actions and impugning his motives'. The Bradford party backed their MP and bluntly rebuked MacDonald. Jowett gave way as Chairman after one year but continued with his proposals to reform parliamentary procedure, bitterly opposed by Hardie and Snowden. Two resolutions were put to the 1912 party conference – known as 'Bradford Resolutions': the first called for MPs to vote on the merits of individual issues; the second proposed the appointment of standing parliamentary committees. The first was heavily defeated, but the second was carried overwhelmingly. At the 1914 conference in Bradford, a further resolution on the 'merits' issue was tabled. At this time, an alliance with the Liberals was being canvassed that MacDonald was rumoured to support (despite his denials). The resolution became an issue of defending working-class issues and was carried by three to one. Jowett was re-elected Chair at the same meeting.

The period leading up to the First World War was difficult for Jowett. Along with Keir Hardie, Ramsay MacDonald, Bruce Glasier and others, he opposed the war. He was not a pacifist, rather his objections were on several grounds. He felt that the war was an imperialist venture and entered into by 'secret diplomacy' without the sanction of Parliament. At that time, the rank and file in Parliament was expected to focus on domestic issues, leaving foreign affairs to the government and the diplomatic services. It was also a capitalist enterprise, and contrary to international socialism. He worked tirelessly throughout the war on behalf of servicemen and their dependants, dealing with over 2,000 cases, which he took up with the War Office and Ministry of Pensions, and raising 166 questions in the House. In 1916 he successfully introduced a motion to grant pensions to servicemen suffering from disease caused or aggravated through war service. He refused to participate in recruitment efforts and was one of only 36 MPs who voted against conscription in 1916. As well as the armed forces, he bitterly opposed the 'conscription' of wealth and the provisions of the Munitions Act, which 'fixes men to the service of one employer as firmly as if they had been branded as serfs'. Wartime sharpened his socialist ideals as he watched profits escalate whilst thousands of young men were sent to their deaths. His analysis of bank lending practices and profiteering became increasingly vitriolic (a subject he was to return to during the Second World War). In those times, when conscientious objectors were imprisoned and deserters shot, it was an unpopular and brave position. Jowett was comparatively lucky and merely lost his seat in 1918. Ironically, Lloyd George won on promises to enforce German reparations, whilst Jowett lost in part due to his stance that this was simply not possible and that the policy would only be to the detriment of the working classes in all the countries concerned. History proved him right in more ways than he could have realised.

Out of Parliament for four years he was far from idle; he became Chairman of the Labour Party in 1921, in a four-year period chairing both the ILP and the Labour Party, and had the opportunity to undertake a number of overseas visits. He visited Hungary, Poland and had narrowly missed visiting Switzerland in 1915 and Russia in 1917. Along with Bruce Glasier he was refused a passport in 1915 on the grounds that it was undesirable for national security; in 1917 he and Ramsay MacDonald were unable to travel to Petrograd because of their anti-war stance, the sailors having been incited to refuse to take ILP delegates. He participated in a fact-finding mission to Ireland in 1920. The delegation (which included

Arthur Henderson and Arthur Greenwood) witnessed first hand the destruction wrought by the infamous 'Black and Tans'; their resulting report
recommended Irish self-determination. In 1921 Eire, the free Irish state,
was born. In 1922 Jowett was returned to Parliament, this time for Bradford
North, when to his amazement he was made Chair of the Public Accounts
Committee, a role that he carried out with his customary diligence.

The rift with MacDonald seems to have healed by the time Jowett was
appointed the first Labour Minister for Works in 1924, a position he
accepted with reluctance given his criticism of the Cabinet procedure.
Together with Wheatley, he refused to wear morning dress and a top hat
to receive their seals of office from the King, turning up at Buckingham
Palace in his ordinary suit and a soft hat. On taking office, he found that
6,000 'temporary' houses for munitions workers still remained following
the war and were by then in a very poor state. Jowett secured £57,000 for
repairs and improvements and £90,000 for roads and drainage. He banned
the use of white lead in paint used in government buildings (ahead of the
bill prohibiting the use altogether). He also supervised the introduction of
public phone boxes, the statues of Edith Cavell and the Rima panel in Hyde
Park (fraught with controversy).

The ILP disaffiliated from the Labour Party in 1932, at a meeting held
in Jowett Hall in Bradford. Jowett played a key part in this, triggered by a
controversy over PLP standing orders. New rules had been introduced by
the Labour Party Executive that bound all those seeking election to agree
to the standing orders and be bound by the Labour Whip. Although this
was completely contrary to Jowett's beliefs in the independence of MPs,
he sought to make compromises to enable a 'free vote' on issues outside
manifesto commitments. After all overtures were rejected, he felt that disaffiliation was the only course open to the ILP. This is documented by
Brockway, including the great sacrifice Jowett made in holding to his principles. Brockway himself was said to regret the disaffiliation, but in 1946
he describes Jowett as 'thoroughly vindicated'. This must have been an
extremely difficult time for Jowett, taking place within a few months of his
wife's death; much of what he held dear was falling to pieces around him.

Jowett also wrote for the *Clarion* for many years until he and its editor,
Blatchford, disagreed over the war. Later, he wrote a regular column for
the ILP news that continued until his death. The ILP archives at LSE include
numerous boxes of his manuscripts and correspondence.

Brockway suggests that there are four contributions towards human
progress that were especially Jowett's. The first was his pioneering work
for the health of children. When he originally persuaded Bradford City
Council to introduce school meals, he could not have imagined that he
would live to see such a policy brought forward by a Conservative minister.

The second point concerned the very foundations of social security.
Jowett believed that the first claim on wealth belonged to children, the
aged, the sick and the working population; their needs could be tackled
whilst the socialist long-term aim of wresting control of capital from
the banks was pursued. He saw many of his principles embodied in the
Beveridge Report although he did not live to see the Labour government
introduce it. The continuing debates about social security would no doubt
have distressed him, but the minimum wage and commitment to end child
poverty would have received his strong support. That these remained issues
to be tackled at the end of the century during which he was first elected
would have been anathema to him.

Jowett's two other main political concerns were not addressed during
his lifetime and seem unlikely to ever be realised. He felt very strongly that

the independence of backbench MPs was crucial to democracy. The Whip system remains a feature of party politics and government. The power of Cabinet and the potential for standing committees were at the heart of his concerns. This debate has moved on with many feeling that the Cabinet itself has become a 'rubber stamp' and power concentrated in the hands of the Prime Minister. The committee system has been virtually abolished in local government. The power of the banks and the economic system was at the heart of his socialism. This thread has now been and gone – much of his thinking was reflected in the Keynesian policies of the 1960s but as capitalism continues to flourish the need for intervention and regulation of markets is now recognised. We can only conjecture what he would have made of the decision to give the Bank of England control of interest rates.

He was a man of principle, yet described as mild mannered, a practical politician and a natural humanitarian: 'He came from the workers, his life was of the workers, and he died a worker' says Brockway. That we know so little about his family life was part of his humility. As Brockway's book was being prepared, Jowett told him that he simply believed that his life outside his politics would be of little interest. He married Emily Foster in 1884; they had one son and three daughters and enjoyed a strong and happy marriage for 47 years. In his later years one of his daughters lived next door and looked after him. Barbara Castle recalled meeting 'the Bradford Pioneer' as a young woman: '[T]he most venerable was Fred Jowett a grey haired but determined little man whose battles on Bradford city council became legendary.' J.B. Priestley described him as 'a modest, short sighted rather frail little Yorkshireman . . . his integrity blazes like a beacon'.

The achievements of Fred Willie Jowett were considerable. A sickly boy whose full-time education ended at 8 years old and ceased altogether at 13. He was truly self-educated, not only elected to public office in local and national government, but also a politician who wrote and published prolifically. His grasp of economics and social affairs was astute and his politics uncompromising. Although not as well known as his friends Snowden and Hardie, he was truly one of the great Yorkshire politicians of his time.

Marsha Singh
MP for Bradford West

Marsha Singh

GEORGE D. KELLEY. M. P.
COPYRIGHT Photo Mc Burney

*George Kelley:
Labour MP for
Manchester South
West, 1906–10*

Chapter 14
George Kelley
1848–1911

GEORGE DAVY KELLEY was born 4 March 1848 in Rushington, Lincolnshire. His father, Thomas, was a cooper. He was educated at the village school where he began to train as a schoolmaster. His parents had planned for him to be a vicar but he only served two and a half years as a pupil teacher before his parents were moved to York. It was there that he obtained an apprenticeship as a lithographer. Once fully trained, he left for London and subsequently went on to live in Birmingham and Leeds before settling for some time in Bradford.

It was there that Kelley became involved in the burgeoning union movement. He managed a small printing establishment and joined the recently re-established Bradford Society of Lithographic Printers. Previously the Society had collapsed but Kelley managed to turn around its fortunes significantly and in 1873 he became its President. The Bradford Society was loosely affiliated with other regional societies through the Central Association of Lithographic Printers of which Kelley also became President. In 1876 he proposed that the regional societies amalgamate. Through his and the Manchester Society's endeavours, several regional lithographers' societies came together to form the Amalgamated Society of Lithographic Printers (ASLP) in 1879. Kelley had been one of the leading forces behind this and became its Secretary. He relocated to 63 Upper Brook Street, Manchester, where the Society's central office was based, and lived there until his death in 1911. The Society under his leadership became one of the most powerful and best managed societies in the UK.

Due to strength of the ASLP, lithographic printers effectively gained a reduction in working hours and wage increases. From an early date, the Society withdrew lithographers from premises that used 'cheap boy' labour, and was able to close shops and achieve results quickly and effectively. It eventually forbade its members from working alongside non-unionised men.

Kelley went on to found the National Printing and Kindred Trades' Federation in 1892, which brought together the various types of printers, and he became its first Secretary. He furthermore pushed for an international association and helped establish the International Secretariat of Lithographic Artists, Designers and Lithographic Printers in 1896 as a forum for the national societies. He inevitably became the Secretary of the association. In this role he travelled as far as the United States and Canada in order to compare the working conditions and pay of the North American comrades, where he found that wages were higher and conditions were significantly better.

Once in Manchester he immediately involved himself in local politics. He became a delegate to the Manchester Trades Council in 1881, and proposed the creation of the Manchester and Salford Trades Council, becoming its first Secretary in 1883. The Council was a combination of trade unions that came together through the Council for advice and cooperation. It was extremely successful and other unions instantly wanted to join. It was initially composed of what were referred to as the 'pompous' trades.[1] Kelley himself was then no socialist and was even described by one contemporary as having 'an aversion to Socialism and Socialists'. Indeed the ASLP under his stewardship acted successfully as a closed shop, but was by no means in the vanguard of an international socialist revolution. The Trades Council during the 1880s was effectively made up of Liberals and there were attempts to keep out lesser-skilled trades people. Unionised railway navvies, gas labourers and ship canal workers requested membership of the Council at the beginning of the 1890s. Kelley, sceptically, did not think that 'the new unionism would last long'. Nevertheless, the attitude of Kelley and the longer standing members of the Council could not stop the growing socialist movement from creeping into the Council and the so-called 'new unionism' did last. As such the Manchester and Salford Trades Council, albeit reluctantly, admitted unskilled members.

Within Manchester Kelley was well respected by both employers and workers; he was not seen as being an antagonist. He generally strove to find a compromise with employers, and preferred negotiation to strike action. He believed that the interests of the employers and the workers were fundamentally compatible. With this in mind, he established the Manchester Joint Board of Conciliation where employers and workers were able to present their views and negotiate. Within the City there was scarcely a trade union movement with which he was not involved, and he was Secretary of various other unions and societies including the Lancashire Federation of Trades Councils.

For many years he was closely associated with the Labour Electoral Association and was, unsurprisingly, its President for some time. The Association attempted to augment working-class participation and power by putting forward working-class candidates into positions on Municipal Councils and school boards. This was an ideal organisation for Kelley as it did not threaten the Liberal presence and in fact gave it a boost by presenting candidates who were more acceptable to the working-class voter. He was not initially supportive of creating a new and independent party to further this cause. In 1891 he was elected onto Manchester City Council as the representative of St Clements Ward. He stood unopposed by the Conservatives, which, according to one author, demonstrated how well respected he was by employers, and that he was non-controversial figure. Although elected as a Liberal, he was the first elected councillor in Manchester who represented labour interests. He made it clear from the outset that while on the Council he stood as a Liberal and would act as a Liberal but when on the Trades Councils he was there to represent labour interests. He was involved in various committees including the Unhealthy Dwellings Committee, the Sanitary Committee and the Cleansing Committee. He stood as a candidate in both the 1894 and 1898 elections but failed to be re-elected.

---

1   E. and R. Frow, *To Make that Future-Now!: A History of the Manchester and Salford Trades Council*, E.J. Morton, 1976, p. 28.

His loyalty to the Liberals was highlighted in 1893 when enthusiasm to create a Manchester branch of the Independent Labour Party (ILP) within the Manchester Trades Council caused controversy. Kelley was the most outspoken critic of this. He felt that the presence of an ILP candidate would only serve to split the workers' vote, usurp a Liberal candidate and, as a consequence, allow in a Tory. In order to convince the Council that this enthusiasm was pure folly, Kelley even offered to provide evidence that money was being donated to the ILP by Tory businessmen; he refused point-blank to permit the Trades Council to be represented at the May Day demonstration organised by the ILP.

Kelley was hostile to other contemporary movements. As the suffragette movement gained support from other unions, Kelley fervently argued against the female vote and against female representation. He did however represent the Manchester and Salford Trades Council at the Founding Conference of the Labour Representation Committee (LRC) at the Memorial Hall in London in 1900. When he reported back to the Trades Council he recommended that it affiliated to the LRC.

It was not until 1904 that Kelley finally announced that he had broken ranks with the Liberal Party, although the Liberals still saw Kelley as their natural ally and continued to give him their full support.[2] When the Manchester LRC was formed, he stood as its candidate for the Manchester South West seat in the 1906 election and comfortably won with a majority of over 1,200. He was helped by the active support of the Liberals and the Free Traders. As a consequence of this victory, he relinquished his position on the Manchester and Salford Trades Council but continued in his post as Secretary to both the ASLP and the International Society of Lithographic Printers. During one parliamentary recess, he travelled to the US to convince the individual unions there to join the International Society.

It is difficult to discover much about Kelley's parliamentary career or ascertain what sort of MP he was. He only served for four years and the record of parliamentary proceedings was not as comprehensive as it is today, with only a few references to him in it. He was described in one obituary as displaying a 'quiet and unobtrusive industry' within Parliament. His speeches and interventions concentrated around labour and labour rights. His longest speech was perhaps that of seconding a resolution tabled by J.R. Clynes in 1908 to shorten the working day to eight hours so as to increase the amount of work available for those who were unemployed. Despite being a member of the opposition he readily backed the Liberal government's stance on labour issues in the voting lobbies. Various people have described him as not being a natural politician but rather an extremely effective organiser. He only served one term in Parliament following advice from his doctor in 1908 to stand down due to the excessive strain on his health that his parliamentary duties were proving to be. He relinquished his seat at the January 1910 election but continued with his union activities.

George Davy Kelley died suddenly at his home in Manchester on 11 December 1911 aged 63, just under two years after standing down as the Member of Parliament for Manchester South West.

Tony Lloyd
MP for Manchester Central

Tony Lloyd

2   Ibid., p. 69.

J. RAMSAY MACDONALD. M. P.
COPYRIGHT HOTO ELLIOTT & FRY.

Ramsay MacDonald:
Labour MP for
Leicester, 1906–18,
Labour MP for
Aberavon, 1922–29,
and MP for Seaham,
1929–35

Chapter 15
Ramsay MacDonald
1866–1937

I F RAMSAY MACDONALD had died at some point in the early 1920s, his reputation as a Labour pioneer, party organiser and socialist philosopher would have been as revered as those of his contemporaries Keir Hardie, Philip Snowden or Arthur Henderson. He would be commemorated on banners and in socialist songs and quoted in politicians' speeches. He helped to build the Labour Party from a disparate collection of local groups and socialist societies into a unified political party capable of forming governments, and he did it in only 25 years. Through his prolific outpouring of books and pamphlets, he gave Labour, along with the Fabians, trade unions, co-operatives and Christian Socialists, a distinctly British brand of ethical socialism. Yet, because of his impotence as Labour Prime Minister in the face of the Great Depression in 1929, and his tragic miscalculation in splitting the Labour government to form the National Government with the Conservatives in 1931, his place in Labour's history is as its greatest traitor: the leader who betrayed us. Even the mild-mannered and taciturn Clement Attlee, who was MacDonald's PPS between 1922 and 1924 and eventually succeeded him as Labour Leader, wrote that he had perpetrated 'the greatest betrayal in the political history of this country'.[1]

The man who built the party also nearly destroyed it, and even today there are those who cannot forgive him. In *Fame is the Spur*, the 1940 political novel by Howard Spring, a thinly veiled MacDonald character rises through the socialist ranks, only to betray his principles, his party, his friends and his class. Ramsay MacDonald is reduced, in some quarters at least, to a kind of political pantomime villain, to be booed and hissed whenever his name is mentioned. MacDonald himself, writing in his diary at the end of his life, said he had come to be viewed as 'the embodiment of wickedness' by his former comrades.

But the real Ramsay MacDonald was a far more complicated public figure, and merits a fairer hearing in the court of history. His career deserves to be viewed in the round. Even within the time of my own association with the City of Leicester, which he represented in Parliament from 1906 to 1918, you could hear those who had known him remembering with pride his commitment to our city and party.

---

1   David Marquand. *Ramsay MacDonald*, Richard Cohen Books, 1997.

MacDonald's story began, like so many of his Labour contemporaries, with great poverty and hardship. He was born on 12 October 1866 in Lossiemouth in Scotland, with the Victorian stigma of illegitimacy hung around his neck. In September 1915, as MP for Leicester, MacDonald was subject to a vicious smear campaign in what today we would call the tabloids. Horatio Bottomley, writing in *John Bull*, accused MacDonald of being 'the illegitimate son of a Scotch servant girl' and reproduced his birth certificate to prove it. The paper called for MacDonald to be taken to the Tower of London and shot as a traitor.

MacDonald lived and worked as a clerk and journalist in Bristol and London, and became involved in the new socialist organisations that sprang up in late Victorian Britain. He worked for a Liberal MP, and in the 1880s and 1890s he was active in the Social Democratic Federation, the Independent Labour Party (ILP) and the Fabian Society, three of the socialist societies that formed, with the trade unions, the Labour Representation Committee (LRC) in 1900.

He became a propagandist for the Fabian Society, giving lectures in the industrial areas of Wales and the Midlands, and was elected onto the Fabian executive in 1894. An early dispute with Beatrice and Sidney Webb is an illuminating example of his priorities. A large legacy had been received by the Society. The Webbs wanted to establish a 'school of economics'. MacDonald wanted at least some of the money to be spent on building up Fabian branches. He wanted to organise, they wanted to educate. MacDonald's defeat meant that the London School of Economics was born.

MacDonald married Margaret Gladstone in 1896, whose private income gave him some security to pursue his political passions, and the couple moved to 3 Lincoln's Inn Fields. This gave him a political base in the heart of London. It was also the first headquarters of the LRC after 1900. We can only imagine the noise and bustle of this home to a growing young family with six children, and political hub, with left-wing journalists, politicians, international visitors and campaigners calling at all hours.

It was natural that Ramsay MacDonald should dominate the new LRC formed in Memorial Hall, Farringdon, in 1900, and the Labour Party after 1906. He was Secretary of the LRC and then the Labour Party for 12 years. He was Treasurer of the Labour Party in 1911 and 1912, and Chairman of the Parliamentary Labour Party (PLP) from 1911 to 1914. These were no honorary positions or sinecures. He threw himself into the organisation of the new party, recruiting members, supporting local branches and raising funds. Keir Hardie was the party's Leader, providing the evangelical zeal and inspiring rhetoric. But MacDonald was the man who booked the rooms, sent out the minutes and rallied the supporters. It is impossible to under-estimate MacDonald's importance in these early years for Labour. Anyone in politics knows that elections and campaigns are not won by lofty ideals or dazzling speeches – they are won by hard work and organisation.

His biographer David Marquand wrote that Labour's rapid growth from pressure group to main opposition party was 'due to the anonymous devotion of thousands of ordinary men and women and to the impersonal pressures of social and economic change. It was also due to MacDonald's drive, organising ability and political flair.'[2]

But there was more to MacDonald than organising brilliance; he was also a skilful negotiator and tactician. In 1903, MacDonald struck an electoral pact with the Liberals, claiming that the LRC could 'directly influence the votes of nearly a million men' and possessed 'a fighting fund of £100,000'.

2   Ibid.

The negotiations were concluded in Leicester, against the backdrop of the
TUC congress in that City, whilst MacDonald was recovering from illness
in Leicester Isolation Hospital. Notwithstanding the veracity of MacDonald's
claim, the electoral pact was a masterstroke for Labour. In the 1906 General
Election, 29 Labour MPs were elected out of 50 candidatures. Of the 29
successful new MPs, 24 had been unopposed by Liberals. This breakthrough
allowed the LRC to rebrand legitimately as the Labour Party. You can
convincingly argue that MacDonald's pact with the Liberals helped to establish Labour as a serious parliamentary force in 1906.

In that same election Ramsay MacDonald was elected as MP for Leicester.
His campaign was fought on a platform of social reform, higher taxes on
unearned wealth, old age pensions, and repeal of the Taff Vale judgement,
which penalised trade unions. His speeches to packed audiences in Leicester
railed against the government's policies in South Africa and for free trade.
The *Leicester Pioneer*, the newspaper of the local ILP, reported on his adoption
meeting in the Temperance Hall:

> [A]s the speaker led them through the many intricate subjects with
> which he dealt they seemed to follow him with an almost breathless
> eagerness. As he added fact to fact, and little by little completed the
> sequence of a practically faultless argument, one could feel the pent-
> up excitement of the audiences: and when the final climax came and
> the speaker had added the last link to his chain, there was such a round
> of cheers as could only have come from the throats of the British
> working men.

Once elected, he brought his considerable organising skill to bear on the
local Leicester political scene. This previously unpublished letter, held by
a current member of my Constituency Labour Party, shows MacDonald's
attention to detail:

> I have been told by various trade union officials that there is some
> resentment amongst certain sections of the trade unionists with some
> of the actions of the ILP and I am trying to remove this feeling. I have
> never believed that it was widespread. We have fallen upon times when
> every mistake is exaggerated and where no mistakes have been made
> they are imagined. There are also mischief makers about and this ought
> to make us all the more wary and careful to bring all sections with us.
> Every party goes through these times so they do not depress me. The
> experience of the Boot and Shoe meeting must not be repeated,
> however and we must set ourselves the task definitely of strengthening
> our grip on <u>workshop</u> opinion. [The underlining is MacDonald's.] That
> is our present weakness. We ought to have a champion in every work-
> shop who will see that every silly statement and every mischief making
> move is contradicted and counteracted.

Ramsay MacDonald was not merely an organiser and politician. He was
a socialist philosopher with an international reputation to rival Karl Kautsky
or Jean Jaures. His intellectual contribution to the development of
British ethical, or evolutionary, socialism was on a par with Sidney Webb
or Richard Tawney. His subsequent fall from grace should not obscure this
aspect of his career. In a dozen books between 1905 and 1921, including
Socialism and Government (1909), *Parliament and Revolution* (1919) and *Socialism Critical and Constructive* (1921), he mapped out a democratic socialism
that was distinct from Marxism, syndicalism and Liberalism, the main *-isms*

on offer. MacDonald's rejection of syndicalism and revolutionary socialism
led him to be detached from the excitement that gripped some of the left
during the Russian Revolution of 1917, and to oppose outright the General
Strike in 1926. His concept of socialism as an evolutionary, gradual and
democratic process was a major influence on Labour's political thought, and
remains so today.

MacDonald opposed Britain's role in the First World War, which Clement
Attlee (who, as an infantry officer in the trenches, took the opposite view)
said 'seemed to mark him as a man of character'. MacDonald resigned as
Leader of the party on this point of principle, a fact his detractors often gloss
over. He was the victim of virulent attacks in the press and Parliament. In
1918, the voters of Leicester rejected him as their Member of Parliament.
He returned at the 1922 General Election as MP for Aberavon.

The breakdown between MacDonald and the Labour Party in Leicester
is suggested by another unpublished letter, which is also a good example of
MacDonald's arrogance and disregard for the work of the rank-and-file.
After attributing his defeat at the 1918 Election to 'jealousies', and declaring
'something had gone wrong with the Party in Leicester', he went on to say:

> [I]t cannot have escaped your notice that the references to the contest
> in the Annual Report of the Lab. Party were most perfunctory and
> there was not a line of thanks in any shape or form. To this day I have
> received from neither the ILP nor the Labour Party a single expres-
> sion which indicates any of those friendly feelings which one naturally
> expects after the work I have done for you all in Leicester.

As any MP can testify, if you wait for your constituents to heap praise and
thanks on an MP they have just ejected, you may be waiting some time.

In 1924, King George V asked MacDonald, elected once more as Labour
Leader, to form a government after the collapse of the Conservatives. For
a few perilous months Ramsay MacDonald was Britain's first Labour Prime
Minister, and the first working-class person to hold that office.

The MacDonald government fell in the 1924 General Election – the
notorious affair of the Zinoviev Letter contributing to the defeat of the
Labour Party. But Labour did win 151 seats and MacDonald became Leader
of the Opposition in the House of Commons. When Labour again formed a
minority government in 1929, MacDonald became Prime Minister for the
second time. In 1929, in perhaps the only positive action of this period of
office, he appointed Margaret Bondfield as the first woman Cabinet Minister
in Britain.

Six months after Labour assumed office, the Wall Street Crash precipitated a world recession, and unemployment rose in the UK from 1 to 3
million. The 1929–31 period was pivotal in MacDonald's career and in
Labour's history. The limitations of both the man and the party he led in the
face of economic depression and rising unemployment were laid bare. The
May Committee, appointed by MacDonald under the chairmanship of
Sir George May to investigate the problems of Britain's economic crisis,
suggested in July 1931 that government expenditure should be reduced
by £97 million. Unfortunately, this sum included a £67 million reduction
in unemployment benefit. The majority of MacDonald's Cabinet rebelled
against this and voted against the May Committee report. This led MacDonald
to offer his resignation to the King. George V, however, persuaded
MacDonald away from this course of action and towards the formation of a
coalition government with the leaders of the Conservatives and Liberals
taking posts as Cabinet ministers as well as Labour MPs.

The formation of the National Government in October 1931 was meant to unite the House of Commons during the economic crisis but instead proved to be extremely divisive. Only three Labour ministers, including Philip Snowden, the Chancellor of the Exchequer, agreed to join the new Cabinet and MacDonald determined to push through the measures proposed by the May Committee. Labour MPs were outraged by MacDonald's actions and he was expelled from the party. George Lansbury was elected Leader in the resulting debacle. At the 1931 General Election, Labour was reduced to 46 seats, no better off than in 1918; it had lost 1,500,000 votes. The National Government had a majority of 500.

MacDonald led the National Government until 1935, when he resigned as Prime Minister, lost his Seaham seat to Manny Shinwell at the General Election, and went into a rapid decline. He died in 1937 on a cruise of the Caribbean.

An assessment of Ramsay MacDonald's career cannot ignore the tragedy of his actions in splitting the Labour Party. It proved a huge error: the National Government was no more able to keep open the factories, foundries and ship works than the short-lived Labour government had been. High unemployment lasted until the Second World War. The resentment MacDonald caused resonates today in a Labour Party always watchful for its leaders' betrayal. Wilson, Callaghan, Kinnock and Blair have all been accused by their critics of being 'the new MacDonald'. He is seen as a terrible warning of what happens to socialists when they get too cosy with the ruling class. MacDonald's fondness for the company of aristocrats did not help his image. David Marquand's (1997) revisionist biography of MacDonald makes the point that Labour has 'a complex about MacDonald – a complex that almost certainly sprang from an unwillingness to face painful truths about its own conduct and record'. Official histories of the Labour Party skip over MacDonald's role. He is the party's embarrassing ancestor, not to be mentioned in company. There are many complex reasons for MacDonald's decision in 1931. The enormity of the economic crisis rattled the entire political class, not just Labour's leadership. On the extreme left it foresaw the collapse of capitalism that Marx had predicted; on the extreme right it heralded the end of democracy and highlighted the need for authoritarianism. For parliamentarians, brought up with the certainties of Empire, Monarchy and Parliament, it was beyond their comprehension or control. We may not forgive MacDonald's actions, but we should try to understand the unprecedented circumstances that led to them. When asked by the King to form a government, the son of a servant and a ploughman did not refuse.

Marquand's biography shows MacDonald as a prisoner both of his times and of events, rather than a deliberate class traitor. Even his contemporaries were capable of some generosity. Manny Shinwell, who defeated him in 1935 by 20,000 votes, magnanimously wrote that:

> To dismiss MacDonald as a traitor to Labour is nonsense. His contri-bution in the early years was of incalculable value. His qualities as a protagonist of Socialism were of a rare standard. There has probably never been an orator with such natural magnetism combined with impeccable technique in speaking in the party's history. Before the First World War his reputation in international Labour circles brooked no comparison.[3]

---

3   Emanuel Shinwell, *Conflict without Malice*, Odhams Press, 1955.

Fenner Brockway wrote: 'Ramsay MacDonald was a born leader, with a commanding personality and a magnificent presence; the most handsome man in public life. He was a great orator whose deep, resonant voice and sweeping gestures added to the force of his words.'[4]

So MacDonald deserves to be understood with a little more sophistication than a cry of 'betrayal'. Without him, Labour would not have grown so fast or so large. His organisational skills helped to build the machine that could win landslide majorities in 1945 and 1997. The structure of Labour Party organisation he introduced, built on branches and constituency parties, remains largely unchanged today. His tactical prowess led to Labour's electoral breakthrough in 1906 and the very formation of a Parliamentary Labour Party, with its own whips and party programme, which we are commemorating in 2006.

His political thought helped us to develop a practical socialism that has outlasted its syndicalist and Marxist rivals, and that has enriched the lives of millions. As Leicester's first Labour MP, he blazed a trail of which those of us lucky enough to follow are proud. As the first Labour Prime Minister, and the first from a poor background, he helped Britain become more meritocratic and democratic. Aneurin Bevan said that socialists must be 'builders as well as dreamers', and MacDonald was both. Despite Ramsay MacDonald's obvious failings, that is how I prefer to remember him.

Patricia Hewitt
MP for Leicester West

Patricia Hewitt

---

4   Fenner Brockway, *Towards Tomorrow*, Hart-Davies MacGibbon, 1977.

JOHN T. MACPHERSON. M. P.

J.T. Macpherson: Labour MP for Preston, 1906–10

Chapter 16
J.T. Macpherson
1872–1921

JOHN THOMAS MACPHERSON was born in Poplar on 10 October 1872, the son of an iron and steel worker, Hugh Macpherson. His father's employer, Millwall's Phoenix Ironworks, closed in 1873 and the family moved first to Sheffield before ending up in Middlesbrough, via Workington. He was educated until the age of 12, when he went to work in the North-Eastern Steel Works in Middlesbrough. At the age of 15 he joined his father at the Dorman, Long and Co. works, where he remained until 18.

Macpherson recounted that growing up 'in the home, round the fireside, the whole of the talk was of steel, iron and trade unionism', and therefore it was not surprising that he became an active trade unionist at Dorman. This led to his dismissal and, he said, 'for a few months I was made to realise the unfairness of the word "agitator". I obtained several jobs in that period, but when my name was known there was no further need for my services.'[1] Unable to find a job in his particular trade locally, he went to sea as a fireman and over the next couple of years visited Europe, India, Burma and the United States.

He returned home to Middlesbrough in the late 1890s and rejoined his old employer Dorman as a steel smelter. In 1899 he married Catherine Ann MacArthur, the daughter of a master mariner turned steel smelter. He was soon engaged in trade union activities once again, and became President of the Middlesbrough branch of the British Steel Smelters' Association (BSSA), a delegate to the Middlesbrough Trades Council and, from early 1899, the BSSA's first Organising Secretary. Within six months, the membership of the union had grown by more than 2,000 and there had been significant expansion in South Wales, organising the tinplate workers. Such was the growth in different parts of the country that more organisers were soon appointed to join Macpherson. He appears to have been appointed Assistant Secretary of the BSSA in 1900, and in 1903 the union sent him for a year's study at what was then called Ruskin Hall.

The BSSA's General Secretary John Hodge had been a strong supporter of the Labour Representation Committee (LRC), and stood unsuccessfully in Gower in the 1900 general election and in the Preston by-election of

---

1 *Pearson's Weekly*, 1 March 1906.

May 1903. The LRC in Preston invited Macpherson to be its parliamentary candidate for the 1906 election, and his union agreed.

Preston was a two-member seat, and had been held safely by the Conservatives for many years. However, in 1906 Macpherson topped the poll with 10,181 votes, with the Liberal Harold Cox being elected for the second seat with 8,538 votes. The two sitting Conservative members, John Kerr (who had been elected in the by-election) and Sir William Tomlinson (who had held the seat since 1882) were both defeated in what was a remarkable achievement for Labour.

Macpherson spokes several times during his time in the House of Commons. The first record of him speaking in the Commons in 1906 was a question undoubtedly close to his heart:

> *Mr Macpherson (Preston):* I beg to ask the Secretary to the Admiralty whether he is aware that certain armour-plate workers in the Sheffield district, engaged upon Government work, are at the present time paying less then the recognised trade union rates, particularly in the melting department; and what action he proposes to take.
>
> *The Secretary to the Admiralty (Mr Edmund Robertson, Dundee):* No complaints have been received on this point.
>
> *Mr Macpherson:* If I supply the right hon. Gentleman with information privately will he inquire into it?
>
> *Mr Edmund Robertson:* Undoubtedly, Sir.[2]

Later that year he raised the issues of a disturbance at Portsmouth Royal Naval Barracks, carpenters employed in the Transvaal, and whether MPs could be given free postage for up to 25 letters a day (given that at the time MPs were not even paid, the answer was unsurprisingly 'no').

However, his first full speech was on a motion put forward by the Liberal government aimed at restricting the power of the House of Lords to amend and reject Bills passed by the Commons. Arthur Henderson put forward an amendment proposing abolition of the Lords, and Macpherson seconded it. Noting that, between them, the Labour MPs and defeated candidates represented half a million voters, he summed up the party's attitude to the Upper House:

> Probably the Labour Members ought to criticise the Lords more kindly because we are the only party of which they have shown any fear. Nevertheless we Labour Members realise that the House of Lords have always been our enemies, and are our enemies to-day. We know that in whatever path we desire to strike out for freedom there they stand blocking the way, and it is time the people of this country took the matter into their own hands and politely put them out of the way of the path of progress.[3]

Financial difficulties in the BSSA meant that they could only afford to fund one candidate for the January 1910 election, and this support went to John Hodge, who by that time was MP for Manchester Gorton. Without financial support, and with attacks on his record in the Commons and sectarian schooling issues causing the Irish Catholics to vote against him,

2   House of Commons Hansard, 29 March 1906, col. 1527.
3   House of Commons Hansard, 25 June 1907, cols 1202–03.

Macpherson lost his seat in 1910, coming third by 1,621 votes behind the two Conservatives George Stanley and Alfred Tobin.

In 1916 the BSSA rearranged its organising work and Macpherson, who had resumed his work with the union, was asked to move from his home base of the North East to take charge of the Northern district, which would cover Workington, Cumberland and Barrow. Macpherson's relations with the union executive were apparently already strained and, not wishing to leave the North East, where he had spent the large part of his life and work, he declined the move and resigned.

Macpherson does not seem to have had any further involvement with the union movement, and in the years following he worked for Armstrong Whitworth as a foreman in the shell shed. He died at the age of 48 on 2 July 1921, at his sister's home in Saltburn-on-Sea.

Macpherson was a committed trade unionist and he once summed up his view of the benefits of collective action:

> I hold – and I realised it almost in my boyhood – that individually human souls are but straws in the wind, but to the aggregation of units all things are possible. And probably one great reason why there are twelve million souls on the verge of starvation in this country is the fact that they have neglected to avail themselves of the principle of combination, and hence they are at the mercy of anyone desirous of buying their services.[4]

Although an MP for only one term, when first elected he had a clear view of his mission, and it is one that would be shared by his Parliamentary Labour Party (PLP) colleagues of 1906, and no doubt successive members of the PLP down the years: 'Today the burden of life presses hardest upon those who are the least fitted and least able to bear it, and my aim and my object will be as far as possible to repay those who helped me by endeavouring to help others.'[5]

Mark Hendrick
MP for Preston

Mark Hendrick

4   *Pearson's Weekly*, 1 March 1906.
5   Ibid.

JAMES O'GRADY. M. P.

James O'Grady:
Labour MP for Leeds
East, 1906–18, and
for Leeds South East,
1918–24

Chapter 17
James O'Grady
1866–1934

J AMES O'GRADY came from humble beginnings to achieve a unique
place in Leeds history as the city's first Labour MP. He ended his career
as Governor of the Falkland Islands. His was a life of contrasts, but one
that revealed a man of great character and determination.

James O'Grady was born on 6 May 1866 in Bristol to Irish parents, John
(a labourer) and Margaret. He attended St Mary's Roman Catholic Primary
School and started work in a mineral water factory when he was 10 years
old. At 15 he was apprenticed to a furniture-maker, which brought him
into the trade union movement. Having spent some years taking his skilled
trade around the country to find work, in 1890 he returned to Bristol and
married Louisa James, a childhood friend, with whom he had two sons and
seven daughters.

He threw himself into union and political activity in the city. In 1892,
at the age of 26, he joined the Social Democratic Federation. Five years
later, he was elected to Bristol City Council, where he successfully introduced a scholarship scheme for elementary children.

As an organiser for the National Furnishing Trades Association, his abilities as a speaker and negotiator soon led to higher office. He assumed the
post of Secretary of the Association, and in 1898 he was President of the
TUC in the year of its Congress in Bristol.[1] His speech on that occasion
was notable for a stinging attack on child labour that invoked the wrath of
The Times. He also argued for the trade unions' own political organisation,
independent from other political parties.

Having moved to London to become the union's full-time organiser, he
attended the 1903 meeting of the Labour Representation Committee (LRC).
But it was a dispute in the furnishing trade that brought him to Leeds, where
the Trades Council had been the first in the country to affiliate to the LRC.
His relations with the employers were later described by the *Weekly Citizen*
– the first socialist Labour paper in Leeds – as 'stormy'. The dispute meant
that he spent some months in the city at a time when the East Leeds Labour
Party was looking for a candidate. He was duly adopted, and in the 1906
General Election he beat his Conservative opponent, H.S. Cautley, by 2,091
votes, giving Leeds its first Labour representative in Parliament.

1   *The Times*, 31 August 1898.

In his maiden speech, during the King's Speech debate, he spoke in favour of Home Rule for Ireland. Hansard recorded that:

> He wanted, as an Irishman, to refer to the constant taunt that only one portion of Ireland was loyal. His answer to this was to be found in the record of Irishmen who had come from the South and West and who had died to maintain the prestige of the British nation. If they wished to get rid of all this bitterness upon Irish questions it would be well to cut out the religious controversy, and look at the subject from a wider and broader point of view.

O'Grady's Social Democratic Federation past, and his membership of the Independent Labour Party, put him on the left of the new Parliamentary Labour Party. He was also the only Roman Catholic Labour member. He spoke often in a range of debates, including on foreign affairs. He combined being an MP with trade union activity, remaining the national organiser of the Furnishing Trades Association until 1912. He later became Secretary of the National Federation of General Workers.

In the January 1910 Election, O'Grady retained his seat with an increased majority (3,065). He held it again in the second election in December that year.

During the First World War he was Vice-President of the patriotic British Workers' League. He paid several visits to the western front and was one of a group of Labour MPs who, together with Will Thorne, went to Russia in 1917 to meet Kerensky, then leader of the provisional government. On the same trip he heard Lenin speak in Petrograd. Two years later, he met representatives of the new Bolshevik government in Copenhagen to negotiate on the exchange of prisoners of war.

In 1918, O'Grady received a commission under the Irish Recruiting Council as a Staff Captain, and went to Dublin to help with the army's recruiting campaign. He complained about the lack of support he got, telling one newspaper that 'I have even had to walk through the streets with a servant-maid carrying my portmanteau'.

When boundary redistribution divided his old seat, he was adopted as the candidate for the new South-East Leeds division in August 1918. His nomination was unanimous, and had the support of the old East Leeds Party plus eight union branches. O'Grady was in Ireland at the time, and wrote to accept the nomination: 'You can assure the conference that I am, as hitherto, a loyal member of the Labour Party, and shall esteem it an honour and privilege again to fight under its banner whenever the general election comes . . . in all my activities since the fateful 4 August 1914, I have had but one thought in my mind – the triumph of democracy over autocracy.'

In the event, and despite not having recovered fully from an attack of pneumonia, he was returned unopposed in the General Election. The *Leeds Weekly Citizen* noted that 'there is no desire to oppose him, even by the pacifist section of the Labour Party'.

In 1923, there was fevered speculation that O'Grady would be appointed as the new Ambassador to Moscow should Labour come to power and formally recognise the new Soviet government. In the event, this did not happen; instead, the first Labour Prime Minister, Ramsay MacDonald, appointed him as Governor of Tasmania in the spring of 1924, a post that also brought him a knighthood.

He accepted the commission, but told the *Leeds Mercury*: 'It is a terrible wrench for me, for I have been with the Leeds people for so many years.' Thus, 18 years after he was first elected, James O'Grady bade farewell to Leeds and his constituents, and sailed off to the other side of the world, taking with him the travelling clock that the members of the local party had given him as a memento of their long association. In the same year, the East Hunslet Ward Labour Party published a book of favourite quotations, and on the very first page was this from James O'Grady: 'Short-sighted is the philosophy that counts on selfishness as the master motive of human action.'

The accounts of the many farewell events in his constituency show the deep affection in which he was held. He undoubtedly made a strong impression on the city as its first Labour MP in a seat that – in its later manifestations – was to claim Denis Healey, Hugh Gaitskell and Merlyn Rees among its representatives.

He served in Tasmania for just over six years, assisted by his daughter Margaret, Lady O'Grady being too ill to travel. In April 1931, he was appointed, again by MacDonald, to succeed Arnold Hodson as Governor of the Falkland Islands. Having served there for two years, he was forced to return to Britain for treatment when he contracted a form of blood poisoning. He died in a London nursing home on 10 December 1934, at the age of 68.

By all accounts, James O'Grady was a much respected constituency MP. Known universally as 'Jim', he was generally softly spoken. A political opponent in Leeds, writing in the *Leeds Mercury* in 1924, described him thus: 'Always he made friends. That is his great gift and the secret of his success. Men went to tackle him, remained silent as listeners, and went away with the feeling that, although his political views might be wrong, at least he was broad-minded. Thus he won respect.'

The *Yorkshire Evening Post* was similarly warm: 'Personally, he is a man who wins the deep and lasting affection of those who know him. He is sincere, outspoken, a fighter for any cause in which he believes, but a man devoid of bitterness and venom, who would find it difficult to make enemies, even if he tried.'

The *Leeds Weekly Citizen* wrote: 'On every industrial question, Mr O'Grady is thoroughly alert, and he has rendered many valuable services to democracy, not in this country alone, but in Ireland and India.'

Three contrasting interests dominated his political life.

The first was trade unionism, as his long career as a union official demonstrated. He believed strongly in workers' organisation, a conviction that he held throughout his time in Parliament. In 1912, having failed to be called in a debate in the House of Commons on the dock strike, he declared it was a 'damned scandal' and walked out of the chamber.

The second was his passionate interest in Russia. He visited several times, on one occasion describing Lenin as a 'great statesman'. He also argued for recognition of the new communist government and against international military attempts to defeat it. His commitment to Russia's cause cost him physically as he contracted smallpox when he went there to help with famine relief in the early 1920s.

Finally, there was his patriotism. He was a strong supporter of the First World War and was attacked by pacifist members of the party for his views. When he agreed to go to Ireland in 1918 to help recruit for the army – a challenge, to say the least, given the history and politics of Britain's presence

– he gave up his position as President of the Board of Management of the National Federation of Trade Unions, which he had held for the previous six years. This showed that, for James O'Grady, the call of his country came first.

His obituary in *The Times* called him the 'First Labour Colonial Governor'.[2] It was a description that fitted an extraordinary political life.

Hilary Benn
MP for Leeds Central

Hilary Benn

2   *The Times*, 11 December 1934.

JAMES PARKER. M. P.

*James Parker:
Labour MP for
Halifax, 1906–18,
and for Cannock
Chase, 1918–23*

Chapter 18
James Parker
1863–1948

JAMES PARKER was elected as the first Labour Member of Parliament for Halifax in the 1906 landslide and took his seat as a member of the first Parliamentary Labour Party. Born at Awthorpe, near Louth, Lincolnshire, on 9 December 1863, the son of a farm labourer, his mother died when he was three. Despite this, he described his childhood as a happy one saying:

> [F]or though I lost my mother at three years of age my sister filled her place with loving care for me, and as I was the youngest member of a family I was petted and spoilt. I was soon able to walk the two miles to the day school, a small one-roomed building where about 30 boys and girls were taught together the three 'R'. When I was ten years old fate took a hand. With my sister we visited the West Riding, coming to Carlton near Yeadon. There she found a lover, and in a few months they were married. I was with them so Yorkshire has sheltered me for about 70 years.[1]

He went to live with his sister at Carlton, near Leeds, where he then had a three-mile walk to Bramhope School.

After leaving school, Parker worked successively as a greengrocer's assistant, doctor's groom, milkman and barman. Throughout all this time he studied science and art at Guiseley and Yeadon's Mechanics Institute where, in his own words, he 'passed out of the elementary stage reasonably well'. When he was 19 he came to Halifax and found work as a labourer with the Halifax Corporation, moving on to work as a packer and warehouseman for Blakey and Emmett, electrical engineers.

It is widely acknowledged that he learned his debating skills when he joined the Brunswick Church Mutual Improvement Society. He later acknowledged that it was at this time that he really began to learn, read extensively and debate with others, particularly on social matters. Not surprisingly, he soon became interested in politics and his first acquaintance with the principles of socialism dated from 1890 when he joined the local branch of the Fabian Society.

---

1   *Halifax Courier*, November 1943.

Parker was an early member of the Independent Labour Party (ILP) and became the paid Secretary of the Halifax branch of the ILP in 1895. So just 12 years after settling in Halifax he had begun to work full-time on organising and recruiting members for the new party. In this he was extremely successful and the party grew beyond expectations. He was later to become a member of the ILP Administration Council and of the Labour Representation Committee.

As an early pioneer of the Labour movement, he had contact with Keir Hardie, Tom Mann, Philip Snowden and others. The *Halifax Courier* reported that he was an experienced election agent helping such pioneers in the Labour movement as Pete Curran in Barnsley, Keir Hardie in a by-election in East Bradford, and Robert Smillie in North East Lanark. He also helped Tom Mann and was election agent to Philip Snowden in a by-election at Wakefield.

However, in Halifax he is remembered for early public service. In 1897, after a few unsuccessful attempts, he was elected to the Halifax Council for the Northern ward. Of the so called 'khaki' general election of 1900 he said: 'Those were the days of fighting the slums. Shall I ever forget them? Days of greater freedom and responsibility sitting lightly on my shoulders. I was well known to the police, but never got locked up though I often broke the law in chalking notices on the pavement.' Parker was adopted as the parliamentary candidate for Halifax in a four-cornered fight in which he not only lost but came bottom of the poll.

Later he was to become the Chairman of the Waterworks Committee, a powerful position. It was during his chairmanship that major progress was made in building some of the beautiful reservoirs that surround Halifax. He was still the Chairman of this Committee when, in 1906, he was elected on his second attempt as the first Labour MP for Halifax. Although not born in Yorkshire, James Parker was an expert on Yorkshire and its industries. Whatever differences that were later to develop between Parker and some of his ILP colleagues, he was widely respected by the general public in Halifax for his commitment to public services in the town.

Interestingly, the local paper reported in 1907 that 'Mr James Parker MP expresses himself as heartily in favour of the scheme for a Channel Tunnel' on the grounds that '[a]nything which helps to facilitate the interchange of commerce, which tends towards bringing closer touch the peoples of Europe, makes for peace and progress'.

Parker served jointly as the Member for Halifax with Mr J.P. Whitley until 1918 when, with the revision of seats, Halifax became a single-member constituency. On his re-election to Parliament in 1910 Parker introduced a Bill to amend the Education (Provision of Meals) Act, the amendment aimed to make provision for poor children during school holidays. This was needed because the Government Auditor had surcharged members of the local council Education Committee for the expenditure on food for children during the holidays.

In 1917 he became Junior Lord of the Treasury (a Whip). It was at this time that the War Savings Certificate came into being and he claimed to have introduced the idea to government. It was also during this period that he became a more establishment figure and left the ILP. Politics entered into this decision as, like a number of Labour MPs, he put party considerations on hold and devoted his energies to recruiting and urging support of the war loans. Along with his colleagues, he had opposed the Military Services Bill at all stages, but unlike them he became an enthusiastic worker for voluntary recruiting. This almost certainly alienated him from some of his local party activists and led to him refusing the nomination for the Halifax seat in 1918. Activists in the party both national and local had not agreed with Parker either on his support for the war, or on his acceptance of ministerial office. This dissatisfaction came to a head locally when the selection committee of the Halifax Trades and Labour Council said they would only nominate him if he signed an undated resignation letter to leave with them when they nominated him. This he refused to do saying 'I hope to find another constituency where Labour can at least trust a man who has always followed the decisions of the majority of his party.' A year earlier the National Administrative Council of the ILP had decided that it would no longer recognise him as an ILP MP. This must have been trying for a past ILP full-timer, and past President both of the Gas Workers and General Labourers' Society, and of the local Trades and Labour Council.

Within his constituency, however, his work was recognised and appreciated. In November 1918 he was presented with the freedom of the borough of Halifax, becoming the last person ever to receive this honour. In the same year his work was recognised nationally and he was made a Companion of Honour.

In 1918 Parker stood as the Labour candidate for Cannock Chase and returned to Parliament. He was for a period the Vice-Chair of the party, and then Chief Whip, acting as Leader when Ramsay MacDonald was in India.

During the war Parker had embarked on a countrywide recruitment campaign for the Labour Party and was held in high esteem by the leadership. It should be remembered that at the outbreak of the First World War the Labour Party's structure was still very weak, with very few individual members. Membership was mainly based on affiliations through trade unions and the socialist societies. This meant that Parker's recruitment drive for members was a great help to a party that needed people on the ground if it was to have any success when organising elections.

The immediate post-war years were difficult for the Labour Party, great ideological differences opened up and it was claimed that, in the end, the party had become all things to all men. In 1923 Parker stood as an Independent against Labour and Liberal opponents; he lost the seat and stood down from public life. It is a measure of his affection for Halifax that he continued to live there, at Chester Road in Boothtown. His marriage had broken down but on retirement he and his wife were reconciled and he was grief-stricken when in 1933 she died.

In his later years he continued to write articles on many subjects for the *Halifax Courier and Guardian*. He was often called upon to take part in civic occasions. A keen bowler, he joined the Akroydon Bowling Club where he had many friends.

On 11 February 1948, the *Halifax Courier and Guardian* reported: 'Mr James Parker, C.H. dies at age of 84. The only surviving Freeman of Halifax, a former member of Halifax Town Council and for many years a Labour MP, died at his home, 14 Chester Road, Halifax. Mr Parker leaves one son.'

Alice Mahon
MP for Halifax, 1987–2005

Alice Mahon

T. Freddie Richards:
Labour MP for
Wolverhampton West,
1906–10

Councillor T. F. RICHARDS.

Chapter 19
T. Freddie Richards
1863–1942

FREDDIE RICHARDS, a man of the Midlands, was born at Russell Street, Wednesbury, Staffordshire on 25 March 1863 and he wrote an account of his early life in *Pearson's Weekly*.[1] His father was a commercial traveller who described himself as a Conservative, although Freddie says he suspected 'he was more of a democrat than a Tory'. When the Board schools started up in Wednesbury his father immediately took him out of the Church school and put him into the state school saying he did not wish Freddie to 'grow up as an aristocratic pauper'. But there was nothing aristocratic about the poverty he subsequently endured.

At 11 he started working half-time at file cutting earning three shillings a week. Within a year his father died leaving his mother and five children unprovided for, and 'against the grain' he left school, where he was a star pupil, to work full-time. He was too young to work in a factory but the Factory Acts did not apply to licensed victuallers so he worked in a public house for five shillings a week and the occasional meal 'of broken meat'. But at home he often wondered why the family was allowed to go half starved.

At 13 he entered a factory making gas piping and, when his mates produced their breakfasts, he made up stories of the splendid breakfast he had enjoyed at home before coming to work. He changed his job and was working in an iron foundry when the struggle to keep the family together finally failed. He went off to Birmingham and got a job as a carter's boy.

His next job was in Aston and then he went to live in at the Birmingham boilermaker factory of Thomas Taylor, as a rivet carrier. He says that when he started he had scarcely a rag on his back and they gave him an old overcoat that was 'miles too big'. He did not want to go about like the Artful Dodger and had the sleeves cut down. But too much was taken off and the effect was even more ridiculous. Eventually he 'burnt the hateful thing'.

He 'seemed no good at foundry work' so went as a pot-boy at the Leopard Inn, Hockley, a public house that brewed its own beer. But he was a 'temperance man' and after saving a few pounds paid his premium and in due course became a boot-laster in Leicester.

---

1   'How I Got On', *Pearson's Weekly*, 26 April 1906.

He joined the Leicester branch of the National Union of Boot and Shoe Operatives (NUBSO) in 1885 and got himself 'heartily disliked by the employers and by the union officials, waging a bitter war against the aggressiveness of the former and the supineness of the latter'.

At that time the bulk of the work was done in workers' homes, 'a disease breeding state of affairs'. He says they succeeded after many reverses in getting factories built but even then he was not content. He recalls how one day he complained to the factory manager that 76 men had been put into a room 'where you wouldn't put 76 pigs'. Soon afterwards he was dismissed. 'The sack,' he says 'was my constant experience but I worried along somehow.'

He became a union permanent official in 1893 and in 1894 Vice-President of the union's Leicester No. 1 branch. In the same year he became the first Labour member of Leicester Town Council representing Wyggeston Ward. He gained a reputation as a vigorous debater and regarded his greatest triumphs as an increase in street sweepers' wages and gaining one day's rest in seven for the local police force. He remained a Town Councillor till 1903 'unconsciously qualifying myself for Parliament which I never dreamed of entering'.

In the *History of the National Union of Boot and Shoe Operatives 1874–1957*, Allan Fox describes how Richards in his early days was a thorn in the side of the union's leadership opposing arbitration, leading unofficial strikes in Leicester, and speaking at the union's National Conference against increasing the General Secretary's salary and allowances. He tried to fight mechanisation in the Leicester factories by instructing union members to restrict output to that previously achieved by hand work. When the employers introduced piecework to frustrate this restrictive practice, Richards was the driving force behind piecework calculations that sought to deprive employers of any advantages from new machinery.

Richards was a keen supporter of the co-operative principle and used £1,000 of the Leicester branches' funds to set up the St Crispin Productive Society. Sadly the venture was not a success and was succeeded by the Leicester Self-Help Boot Society under Richards' presidency.

As time went by and in the face of mechanisation and a declining membership Richards adopted a more moderate approach, yet still successfully opposed the centralisation of all union funds and the standardisation of benefits. Branches retained their funds and the right to decide sickness and other benefits locally. Despite this moderation he was often seen at Penrhyn during the bitter slate quarrymen's strike that lasted from 1900 to 1903.

After the turn of the century the relentless attacks on the working classes turned many unions, including the NUBSO, towards political action and socialism. It was in this context that in 1903 Richards was adopted by the Wolverhampton Trades Council as the Labour Representation Committee candidate for West Wolverhampton. He was backed financially by his union. The *Express and Star*, the very powerful and popular local paper still published today, reports that he immediately set about wooing the constituency with great energy, soon building up 'with his attractive personality, pleasing voice, great fairness and moderation a considerable degree of support'. His programme was Free Trade, nationalisation of coal and the railways, old age pensions, and a land increment tax. His slogan was 'Labour First and Always'. He toured the constituency tirelessly addressing street corner and factory gate meetings.

West Wolverhampton was a Conservative seat represented by Sir Alfred Hickman, a powerful local Iron Master who had been returned unopposed in 1900. It was not a safe seat, however, and the Liberals had won it by 123 votes in 1886, but the intervention of a Labour candidate would make it difficult for the Liberals. Shortly before the 1906 election Richards had private discussions with the Wolverhampton Liberals, and at a large Liberal gathering at the Temperance Hall on 11 December 1905 they decided to stand down and back the Labour candidate.

Straightaway Richards launched attacks on Sir Alfred's poor voting record in the House of Commons saying he was either absent on votes concerning working-class interests or voted against them. Sir Alfred responded by saying that out of about 250 Leicester Town Council meetings each year Richards was absent for about 100 of them.

A huge Labour meeting was held at the Agricultural Hall on 9 January 1906. People were in the iron rafters and on top of the organ. Doors were closed 20 minutes before the meeting was due to start and Richards made a rousing speech favouring Free Trade and opposing Protectionism. He spoke of the 'worst villain unhung' but it is unclear whether he was referring to Sir Alfred or Joseph Chamberlain.

Echoing some of the features of later political campaigning, Labour's opponents spread rumours that Richards had been in prison and had separated from his wife. Printed cards were distributed outside churches saying he was an agnostic. When it was announced from the Town Hall that Richards had won by 171 votes (1.6 per cent of the poll) there was a crescendo of tumultuous cheers and a shocked silence from Sir Alfred's supporters.

The *Express and Star* observed:

> [W]hen Mr Richards first entered upon the campaign his appearance was not seriously regarded. Every opportunity was seized upon to taunt him and decry his candidature and not until we were in measurable distance of the election did Sir Alfred face the evidence that he would have to fight every inch of the ground. The Tories rode the high horse and now were in sackcloth and ashes. They forgot that the war would not be waged on personal grounds and that Labour had been hard at work in Wolverhampton for a considerable period. We can see in Wolverhampton the wakening of the workers to the consciousness of their power.

The campaign had left Richards exhausted. One of his first votes in the House was against Chinese indentured labour in South Africa and he then travelled to Wolverhampton to a social gathering on the 24 February 1906 of the Wolverhampton branch of the Boot and Shoe Union at the Co-op Hall, where he welcomed the King's speech and spoke in favour of women's suffrage.

In Parliament Richards asked a continuous stream of questions on labour issues, particularly on wages and conditions in government-owned factories. One question revealed the existence of a government-owned factory in Deptford making chocolate for the navy. Another secured a shilling rise in weekly pay for bricklayers at Chatham Dockyard. He asked about wages and conditions for postmen, bus drivers, painters, cutters in the Pimlico Army Clothing Factory and, of course, his members in the boot and shoe factories. Another issue he pursued was the right for people to conscientiously object to smallpox vaccination, which by law was compulsory. His first speech was against an amendment to the Education Bill that would have made evening or technical school attendance compulsory up to the age of 17. It was too much to compel children to attend evening school after a day's work and a far better policy to benefit the working classes would be to raise the school leaving age to 15 or 16.

He became a Junior Whip and absorbed himself in the detail of a number of parliamentary bills including the Miners' Eight-Hours Bill, The Feeding of Children (Scotland) Bill, an Anti-Sweating Bill, and a Bill to give local authorities powers to acquire land.

Again echoing a later pattern, within 12 months of entering the House, left-wing socialists in the union were condemning the Parliamentary Labour Party and Richards for failing to adopt a definite socialist programme and accommodating themselves to the conventions and rituals of the House of Commons. Allan Fox, however, in his history of the union (1958), suggests that the rank and file membership was content with Richards' performances in the House.

At the first of the two general elections in 1910 the issue was reform of the House of Lords. Richards opened his campaign at the Co-operative Hall where he said, 'I am not a revolutionary of the violent type but of the ballot box . . . The House of Lords are a bunch of anarchists and labour wants nothing less than abolition.'

Richards received strong support from the *Express and Star*. Each day the paper carried the national election news under the headline 'Lords *v* The People' and announcements of the virtues of the Liberal government and the dangers of Protectionism if the Conservatives won. They described Richards as the champion of the people. Once again he was touring the factory gates and so many people could not get into a meeting at Dudley Road School that 'the popular member for Wolverhampton West' had to address an extra overflow meeting in the playground. The campaign again took some toll on his health and at a meeting addressed by clergymen at the Wolverhampton Empire it was explained that Richards could not be present through indisposition. The Rev. J.A. Shaw expressed disgust at the repeated allegations that Richards was an atheist.

On the eve of poll Richards toured the constituency and there were cheers for 'Good Old Freddie' wherever he went, but early results were ominous. Of the first 92 declarations there were 18 Tory gains and the swing of the pendulum was taking marginal seats such as West Wolverhampton. Freddie lost his seat by 592 votes.

The union's monthly report said that Richards had done 'all that was possible to secure election. He had worked very hard and assiduously in the House of Commons to further the interests of the workers. The result shows still more education is needed if we are to make permanent headway. The reverse must only serve us to greater efforts to secure future victory.' Richards blamed his defeat on bad health and corrupt 'treating' practices by his Conservative opponent, Alfred Bird, who was chairman of A. Bird & Sons, Manufacturing Chemists.

Although he had lost, the swing against him as a Labour candidate had been only 1.6 per cent compared with a swing against the Liberals in Wolverhampton South of 2.8 per cent and 6.5 per cent in Wolverhampton East. He was anxious to stand again. The union, however, professed nervousness over the implications of the House of Lords Osborne judgement, which had declared that a trade union had no right to spend money financing the Labour Party or any form of political activity. Some unions had already been restrained by injunction from contributing money to political activities.

Richards was convinced that this was an excuse used by certain union Council members to damn his political chances. This may be true for there were some who felt that Richards was too enthusiastic in wooing political fame. He cherished this grievance for the rest of his life.

Soon after his defeat in Wolverhampton he was offered the Labour candidature in Northamptonshire East and he stood there at the December 1910 election without union support. He came a poor third behind the Liberal and Conservative and he asserted that the withholding of union funds lost him the seat. This seems unlikely. He polled less than 10 per cent of the vote and any increase in support would have been at the Liberals' expense and could have put the Conservatives in. So that was the end of Freddie Richards' parliamentary career, though he served the Labour movement for another 29 years.

In 1910 he became President of the union. Allan Fox writes that a study of Richards' actions and utterances reveal two important characteristics: an exceptionally strong will to power, expressed in a tendency to identify himself with popular causes, and restless sniping at those above him in status and authority. The other was an ability to rationalise his motives and invest them with an emotional passion and vehemence, which gave them an air of a disinterested crusade.

Despite this apparent ambition he refused a CBE offered by Lloyd George in recognition of his services during the First World War on national and governmental departmental committees. Just after the war he went with a delegation from the union to Czechoslovakia to investigate labour conditions.

By the time he became President of the union he had changed from an extreme 'anti-arbitrationist' to a moderate. Allan Fox feels no criticism should be attached to this: 'The workshop hothead of today is often the sound loyal Union officer of tomorrow.'

Richards mellowed in more senses than one. Early photographs show him neat and conventional. Later he was among the first dandies of the Labour movement and a few sneered at the 'Beau Brummell' of the trade unions. Bow tie and white spats and an 'anarchist hat' were the keynote. James Crawford in his 1945 presidential address remembered as a boy attending a meeting addressed by Richards outside a factory around 1911: 'The most elegant figure that ever mounted a soapbox . . . He had personality and great ability, but wore white spats, a white waistcoat and a straw hat. The meeting unanimously rejected his advice.' Perhaps Richards was reacting against the Artful Dodger overcoat he wore in Birmingham that had so shamed him.

Soon after becoming President in 1910 Richards had persuaded the union to adopt the idea of a 'Union Stamp' on footwear made under union conditions. The public were urged to buy no footwear that did not carry the stamp. This was an attempt to boycott non-union goods to compel employers to come into line. It was adopted by a few manufacturers – mainly Co-ops – yet Richards often complained that even his own union members failed to buy stamped footwear.

Another Richards' initiative was the 'anti-shoddy campaign'. This was a response to post-First World War competitive pressures that were lowering standards of construction and materials. Lower standards damaged the union members' interests as cheaper, less skilled labour was employed. Cheaper footwear undercut quality goods and obliged more manufacturers to follow suit or seek cost reductions, often at the expense of the workforce. By 1924 the employers were partners in the campaign against goods that 'endangered the health and well-being of the wearers'. Both the 'Union

Stamp' scheme and the 'anti-shoddy campaign' came to nothing but con- tinued throughout the inter-war period. The problem of course was that low priced goods were popular; they looked what they were and the public did not feel deceived.

Between 1927 and 1930 Richards and the union leadership fought off attempts by the Communist-led Leather Workers Minority Movement (LWMM) to gain control of the union. This was achieved by a decision in 1928 banning any member of the Communist Party or the LWMM from holding office at branch or national level. The LWMM hit back by accusing the leadership of taking away the rights of branches (an argument Richards had used in his early clashes with the leadership in the 1890s). The LWMM failed to attract any sizable support among the rank and file but many members were unhappy with the 1928 decision and attempts to have it reversed were made at the national conferences up to 1936. The fact that Conservatives could hold office while Communists could not was a source of uneasiness to many.

Another development during Richard's reign as President was greater co-operation with the employers and he held the presidency of the Joint Industrial Council of the shoe trade. It was in the interests of the Employers' Federation and the union to protect the industry from cut-throat competi- tion from small non-union firms and there was a 'black list' of unscrupulous firms recognised by both sides. Foreign competition was also a danger and in 1927 Richards led a successful application, supported by the Employers' Federation, under the Merchandise Marks Act for all imported footwear to be marked 'Of Foreign Manufacture'.

Although the national union gained benefits for its members during the 1920s, it lacked the resources to mount a determined onslaught against unscrupulous manufacturers although plenty of funds were held by branches. Richards and Poulton, the union's General Secretary, never seemed to have considered recasting the union's machinery to provide funds for bolder campaigns, remaining convinced by their earlier experiences that the branch empires would never permit centralisation.

In 1929, at the age of 66, Richards retired from the presidency. His con- siderable abilities were recognised by those who knew him. One colleague described him as 'full of activity and a born fighter'. He was capable of 'biting sarcasm and stinging satire that was a terror to his opponents'. He also received tributes from the Employers' Federation for his great services to the shoe trade. The Federation's Vice-President said: 'He has engendered in us – the opposition – the greatest amount of admiration.'

But Richards was not finished yet. He was back on the Leicester City Council for Newton Ward from 1929 to 1939, and served on numerous committees as a minority-party member, including the 'City Farms Com- mittee' of which he was Vice-Chairman. From beginnings steeped in poverty he served the Labour movement as a trade unionist, a Member of Parlia- ment and a local councillor for 54 years.

Freddie Richards died at Birstall in Leicestershire on 4 October 1942 and was survived by two children from his first marriage, an adopted son, and by his second wife Miss M.J. Bell, a former Secretary and President of the Leicester Women's branch of the Boot and Shoe Union.

It was in this same year, 1942, that I was born – in Bilston just 2 miles away from his Wednesbury birthplace. His Wolverhampton West parlia- mentary seat comprised part of the Black country which was such a ferment of political and trade union insurrection – despite the dire threats of retribution by the Tory candidate, Sir Alfred Hickman, one of the constituency's largest employers. As a fellow Black country native, I am proud and humbled to have served as MP the same community of people whose forbears gave the Labour Representation Committee an historic victory in Wolverhampton, thus beginning the great march of progress for working people, on a journey which continues the political and social advance through our present Labour Government one hundred years later.

Dennis Turner
MP for Wolverhampton South East

Dennis Turner

George Roberts:
Labour, Independent
then Conservative MP
for Norwich, 1906–23

Chapter 20
George Roberts
1868–1928

1868–1906: THE EARLY YEARS

GEORGE ROBERTS was born in Chedgrave on 27 July 1868. His parents, George Henry Roberts, butcher and shoemaker, and Ann Larkman, had married in Chedgrave church on Christmas Day 1867. By 1870, the family had moved to nearby Thurton where Roberts was baptised on 15 May.[1] Soon after, Roberts' father set up as a shoemaker in Norwich. In 1871 the family were living in Armes Street but they soon moved to Eagle Walk. Roberts went to the nearby National School in St Stephen's. He was a bright pupil and became a monitor before leaving school at 13, as was customary, when he was lucky enough to be apprenticed at J.C. Pentney, a printing firm in St Benedict's. His first wage was just 1s 6d a week.[2] While an apprentice he attended evening classes at higher grade and technical schools.

After completing his apprenticeship, Roberts worked as a printer in London from 1889 until 1892 when he returned to Norwich, becoming foreman of the printing works at Coleman and Co., the soft drinks manufacturers. He soon became a leading trade union man in the city. He was a member of the Typographical Association and soon became President and Secretary of the local branch. In 1898 he was elected President of the Norwich Trades Council.

On 8 November 1895, Roberts married Anne, daughter of Horace Marshall, at the Octagon Chapel in Norwich. Their first son, George, was born on 23 December 1902. They had three other children – Violet, Sidney and Jack.

Roberts began his political career as a radical Liberal, belonging to the Norwich Gladstone Club. He joined the Independent Labour Party (ILP) in 1896; three years later he was President of the local branch and stood for the Norwich School Board for the ILP. His was a deliberately radical programme, which attracted the support of both the ILP and the Social Democratic Federation. He campaigned for the raising of the school leaving age to 16, free maintenance for all school children, and for class sizes to be

1   Norfolk Record Office (hereafter NRO), PD 604/2.
2   About £6 a week in today's money.

restricted to a maximum of 30 — and also for a purely secular education. There were 19 candidates for the 15 seats on the Board. Roberts came sixth with 11,387 votes: the first Labour victory in Norwich at any level.

The ILP suggested to Roberts that he stand in the 1900 General Election, but he declined. The election was held during the Boer War and the mood of the country was extremely jingoistic; Roberts was probably shrewd enough to realise that any Labour candidate would have no chance of success. The Liberal Party no doubt took the same view. The two Conservatives — Samuel Hoare and Harry Bullard — were elected unopposed.

The September 1903 agreement between Labour and the Liberals not to oppose each other in certain constituencies covered Norwich. However, things were not to work out so smoothly. Sir Harry Bullard died at the end of 1903. As Hoare continued as an MP, this meant a by-election at which the voters had just one vote apiece, although both the Liberals and Labour fielded a candidate. Many people, including some on the Labour Representation Committee, thought this broke the spirit of the agreement with the Liberals. In the event, it made little difference. The Liberal candidate, Louis Tillett, had a majority of almost 2,000 over the Conservative, with Roberts trailing a poor third. Roberts then took on a full-time union job as the southern organiser of the Typographical Association. One of his first acts was to speak at the 1904 TUC in favour of free school meals.

Under the agreement, Labour and the Liberals each put up one candidate for the 1906 General Election — Roberts and Tillett. The Conservatives also fielded just one candidate, so that there were only three candidates for the two seats. Roberts' election manifesto included a commitment to adult suffrage for both men and women. He was strongly in favour of Free Trade. As a trade unionist he thought unemployment would be the key issue at the election and so he distributed an article he had written on this, which called for a maximum working day of eight hours, which would 'modify the terrible modern paradox of some working inordinately long hours whilst others are denied work'. He also advocated raising the school leaving age, and recommended a system of education to develop 'each child's particular aptitudes'. The result was a triumph for the candidates of the left, and especially for George Roberts. He topped the poll with 11,059 votes. Tillett was just 87 votes behind, with the Conservative a distant third.

1906–14: PARLIAMENT

The Labour MPs elected Keir Hardie as their Leader. He appointed Roberts and Fred Jowett as his parliamentary secretaries. Hardie very soon came to appreciate Roberts' qualities as an organiser. He sent him a copy of the poems of Robert Burns as a Christmas present in 1906, his accompanying letter acknowledging: 'I should have found the duties of my position much more irksome but for your assistance. If circumstances so ordain that I again occupy the position of chairman next session I sh[oul]d like nothing better than to again have your services.'[3] The following year Roberts became Whip of the Parliamentary Labour Party and in 1912 Chief Whip — his stepping stone to high office.

Roberts was an active parliamentarian, especially concerned with employment and trade unions. In his first speech, on 26 February 1906, he

3   NRO, MC 655/1; Kenneth O. Morgan, *Keir Hardie*, Weidenfeld & Nicolson, 1975, p. 155.

addressed labour issues, asking the government to move further in the direction of the eight-hour day and saying that his party was 'keenly alive' to the problem of unemployment. He showed his background by speaking in praise of the Liberal Cabinet Minister John Burns, proclaiming that working men were proud of Burns as coming from the working classes and of being worthy of a seat in the Cabinet.

In March 1909 Roberts spoke in a debate on the Trade Boards Bill, which proposed Boards be set up in various trades, on which both employers and employed would be represented, and which would fix minimum wages within the trade. Roberts remained loyal to his union roots, asserting that 'no clause will ever be perfectly satisfactory unless it is based on strict trade union principles'.

In 1910 there were two general elections. The Liberal-Labour pact still held in Norwich. Tillett decided not to stand again, but the Liberals put up a strong candidate, the barrister Sir Frederick Low. There was a small swing to the Conservatives but they were still well behind the Radical candidates. However, this time the Liberal was elected the senior member, by 138 votes. The second election was an almost exact repeat of the first.

Roberts was beginning to diverge from the official Labour Party over defence. Despite his position as Chief Whip, he was one of eight Labour MPs who rebelled against the party line by voting against a reduction of the money spent on re-arming the navy in July 1912.

However, Roberts was still campaigning eloquently for radical policies on most issues. In February 1912, in a keynote speech in Parliament, he argued for a minimum wage, rejected the idea of tariff reform, and urged nationalisation of coal mines and railways. In June 1913, he spoke at an open-air rally at Briston organised by both railway and farm workers' unions. He pointed out that he had introduced a Bill demanding a minimum wage for farm workers. The Bill would also introduce a maximum working week for farm labourers of 50 hours, including a statutory half day's holiday each week.[4]

1914–18: THE FIRST WORLD WAR

The August 1914 outbreak of war took people by surprise. Most were in favour of it, especially after Germany invaded Belgium – the defence of 'gallant little Belgium' was a popular rallying call. Roberts was strongly in favour of the war, unlike most of the ILP. By coincidence, the ILP held its annual conference in Norwich in 1915, with its two main speakers being Keir Hardie and Ramsay MacDonald. The April 1915 conference issued a statement: 'In each of the countries at war, the Militarist Jingoes declare that they will not rest content short of smashing and dismembering enemy countries.'

In May, Asquith was forced to bring Conservative and Labour members into a Coalition government. Arthur Henderson, the Leader of the Labour Party, entered the Cabinet. Other Labour MPs joined the government in lesser positions, including Roberts, who became a Junior Lord of the Treasury. Roberts did valuable work in the government as a pro-war trade unionist and was involved in the negotiations that ended the South Wales miners' strike in July 1915. He was part of a parliamentary committee that inspected the camps of German prisoners of war and interned enemy civilians and paid several visits to France where he made contact with

3   NRO, MC 655/1; Kenneth O. Morgan, *Keir Hardie*, 1975, p. 155.

pro-war French working-class groups. On one occasion he visited the Western Front, and went so close as to put himself in danger. In August, Roberts moved to a new department, becoming Parliamentary Secretary to the Labour Adviser.

In December 1916 a plot by the Conservatives and some Liberals replaced Asquith with Lloyd George, who was seen as a more charismatic leader. The Labour Party was a minor player, but it still had to be represented in the government. Roberts was again one of their ministers, becoming Parliamentary Secretary to the Board of Trade. Arthur Henderson represented Labour in the War Cabinet but was sacked in 1917 and replaced by the Minister of Labour, George Barnes. Prime Minister Lloyd George then replaced Barnes with Roberts as the Minister of Labour in August 1917. This was to be the pinnacle of Roberts' career: the son of a village shoemaker had achieved the rank of a Minister in His Majesty's government.

Traditionally, when an MP was appointed to such a post, he submitted himself to a by-election to secure the approval of his constituents. There were some precedents for not doing so, but Roberts went ahead and a by-election was announced. The Conservative and Liberal Parties, as part of the Coalition, said that they would not run candidates. The question was whether the Norwich Labour Party would put up a man against him. In the event no 'peace' candidate came forward so Roberts was returned unopposed. However, in October 1917 he was asked to leave the local branch of the ILP. The Secretary, W. Maxey, wrote to him: 'Doubtless you are aware that a vast amount of difference has existed between the local branch and yourself for some time past and the climax to such difference was made manifest a short time ago when the Local Movement repudiated your candidature at the recent Bye-election at Norwich.'

In his reply, Roberts said that he was being asked to resign 'owing to differences on war questions between some members of the branch and myself'. He pointed out that he had been a member of the branch for 'about 22 years', and he doubted if the majority of the ILP branch members would agree with the decision. However, he accepted his dismissal with good grace.[5]

Norwich as a city loved Roberts. As one of the few Norwich MPs to achieve high government office, he was presented with the freedom of the city on 10 May 1918.

In the summer of 1918 the Labour Party withdrew its support for Lloyd George's Coalition. This was a crisis for the Labour ministers in the government. They had a straightforward choice: stay in government and leave the Labour Party, or leave the government and stay in the party. Four ministers decided to break with the Labour Party and stay in the government. They were George Barnes, James Parker, George Wardle — and George Roberts.

After the war, Lloyd George called a snap election in December 1918. His supporters were awarded a coupon and this was given to both Roberts and Edward Hilton Young, a Liberal who had been elected MP for Norwich at a by-election in 1915. They were opposed by two members of the anti-war section of the Labour Party in Norwich: Herbert Witard and Fred Johnson. The result was an enormous victory for the two coupon candidates.

5   The new *Oxford Dictionary of National Biography* says that Roberts left the ILP in 1914. My information comes from original letters at the Norfolk Record Office (NRO, MC 655). Roberts' wartime career is discussed in Frank Meeres, *Norfolk in the First World War*, Phillimore, 2004.

1919–28: THE LATER YEARS

George Roberts was one of a tiny group of former Labour Party men who preferred power in the Coalition government to the opposition benches. He was appointed Minister of Food, or Food Controller as he was commonly called, in January 1919. The job had been of key importance in the war, responsible for the voluntary (and, in the last months of the war, compulsory) control and rationing of the nation's food supplies. However, these problems did not disappear as soon as the war ended. At first Roberts declined Lloyd George's offer of this post, but the Prime Minister was not used to being thwarted and persuaded him to take the job.[6]

During 1919, Roberts' views moved decisively to the right. There was a great deal of discontent as soldiers returned to find high prices and few jobs. There were many strikes and a good many reasonable people feared that revolution would break, there being some suspicion that Russian Bolsheviks were behind the unrest. Roberts took this line; he was still a convinced trade unionist, but thought the unions were in danger of being taken over by people who favoured revolution. In a speech at the Savage Club on 1 April 1919, he linked these revolutionaries with anti-war leaders:

> Some professed to be ready for a great revolution. Many of those who describe themselves as pacifists and whose conscience was so alive that it would not allow them to take part in shedding blood, were those who now talked most freely of manning barricades and turning machine guns on men of their own race who happened to belong to a different class from themselves.[7]

In any event, the role of ex-Labour men in the Coalition government soon ran its course. When George Barnes resigned in January 1920, Roberts followed, resigning as Minister of Food in February. Roberts' career as a Minister was over, but there were many other opportunities. As an MP, he took an interest in the blind, becoming President of a Special Committee appointed by the government to enquire into blindness among babies.

In the General Election of 1922, Roberts once more stood for Norwich, but this time as an Independent. The Liberals put up one candidate, and the Labour Party two. Once more it was an easy victory for Roberts and Young: their personalities had imprinted themselves on Norwich. Although technically an Independent, Roberts was associated in many people's minds with the Lloyd George Liberals. Young and Roberts celebrated victory together in the Liberal Club: his political career had moved full circle.

However, Roberts was to go one step further and complete his political journey to the right; in October 1923 he joined the Conservative Party. Why did he do this? He gave a typically honest answer: after sitting in the Commons as an Independent he realised that it 'was impossible to act as an individual'. So he looked at each party, deciding which one to join. First he thought about the Labour Party: 'A lengthy experience with the Labour Party made it impossible for me to entertain the idea of a return to that party. In fact, my main reason for remaining in politics is to assist in combating the new brand of Socialism now impressed on that party.'

6   NRO, MC 655/8: letter from Lloyd George to Roberts offering him the post, 9 January 1919; Roberts' letter of refusal, 10 January 1919.
7   *Eastern Daily Press*, 2 April 1919.

He rejected the Liberals too, so there was only one choice:

> To help to free my fellow trade unionists, to uphold the national consti-
> tution, to assist in restoring the trade of the world, and to help forward
> ordered progress and wise reform, objects which I believe the party
> now in power is best designed and inspired to accomplish, are the
> reasons why I have decided to throw in my lot with the Conservative
> Party.[8]

Roberts formally crossed the floor of the House to join the Conservative
benches, one of a very small number of people to have served as a Labour
MP, as an Independent and as a Conservative. The Norwich Conservative
Party was delighted to have such a famous recruit. They immediately
adopted him as one of their candidates for the next general election. Roberts
did not have long to wait. Baldwin had decided in favour of tariff reform,
but felt obliged to honour Bonar Law's pledge that this would not be introduced before a further general election. It was held on 6 December 1923.

This election was bitterly fought in Norwich. The Labour, Conservative
and Liberal parties each put up two candidates, the only time this happened
between the wars. The Conservatives nominated H.D. Swan, a former
cricketer, alongside Roberts. The Labour Party fielded two strong local
candidates, Walter Smith, a trade unionist and formerly Roberts' agent, and
Dorothea Jewson, a former suffragette and a women's union worker in the
war. The Liberals put up Hilton Young once more along with Henry
Copeman, leader of the Liberals on the city council. The two Labour candidates topped the poll. Roberts finished fourth but, with over 2,000 more
votes than his Conservative partner, suggesting that he retained strong
personal support in the city.

Roberts never stood for public office again, although he had offers from
at least one Conservative constituency organisation. He plunged into the
world of business with as much enthusiasm as he had given to politics.
Among his many interests were British Sugar and Coalite. His health had
never been good – he was an inveterate smoker. He had in fact
collapsed in the House of Commons in 1912. He lived to see
the vote being given to all women in April 1928, a cause he
had strongly advocated throughout his life. He died, aged 59,
on 25 April 1928 at Edenhurst, Sevenoaks, a hotel where he
had been staying on his doctor's advice.

Charles Clarke
MP for Norwich South

Charles Clarke

8   *Evening Standard*, 2 August 1923.

JAMES A. SEDDON. M. P.
COPYRIGHT ROWLAND KING EARLESTOWN.

James Seddon:
Labour MP for
Newton, 1906–10,
and MP for Hanley,
Stoke-on-Trent,
1918–22

Chapter 21

James Seddon

1868–1939

J AMES ANDREW SEDDON was born in Prescot, Lancashire, on 7 May 1868, the eldest son of Thomas Seddon and Marion Seddon (née Heggie). His father was born in St Helens around 1844 and his mother in Scotland about 1842. His father was a nail-maker, as was his paternal grandfather (also James). He had two sisters, Ellen and Annie, and a brother, George.

The Seddon family were committed nonconformists. James' father was a deacon, and his brother became a Congregational minister; the 1901 census shows Charles Davie, of the same occupation, visiting from Ansty, Leicestershire. The family's active involvement in their religion influenced James; he served in Sunday School and was an active worker on behalf of the YMCA. He took a prominent part in the formation of the Pleasant Sunday Afternoon Movement, occupying every office from Secretary to President. He was also a member of the Rechabites, an order of teetotallers.

His father offered James an example of self-improvement. Thomas had followed his own father into the nail-making trade but by 1871 he had expanded his business and was employing one man. By 1881, Thomas had changed from a manual job to become a collector in the service of the Local Government Board under the Prescot Board of Guardians. Each census shows James' family at a new address; they did not move far – always in Prescot but each time the accommodation improved. James Seddon was born in a poor two-up, two-down terraced property at 4a Victoria Place but moved during his school years to a better terraced house at 19 Kemble Street. After he left home, James' parents moved to 40 St Helens Road and when James took his own family to a generous semi-detached property at 27 Station Road his parents were living at number 22.

In early 1890 he married Ellen Brown and set up home at 53 Eccleston Road, Prescot, where his daughter Marion was born. Unfortunately she died, aged 5, early in 1896. He had two other daughters, Annie and Ethel. He followed the family tradition of moving to better houses and by the 1906 General Election was living in a newly built, three-bedroomed property at 48 Lingholme Road, St Helens, overlooking Queens Park.

In a letter to W.T. Stead in 1906, James Seddon spoke of his early influences as 'a boyhood in a strong Radical and Nonconformist home'. Books available to him in his formative years included the Bible, Carlyle and Chartist literature. Through a book club he got many ideas and was particularly influenced by Kidd's *Social Evolution*. James' formal education was at Prescot and Huyton. He left school at 12 and became a grocer's assistant, working behind the counter for 16 years. In early manhood he began to study social questions that brought him into contact with the Labour Party.

He moved into organised socialism when he entered the trade union world in St Helens as an organiser of shop assistants who were then working as many as 12, even 14, hours a day, six days a week. He was President of an 'early-closing' organisation in St Helens and, when the National Union of Shop Assistants formed, he was instrumental in inducing affiliation to it. In 1893 the National Union of Shop Assistants became the National Union of Shop Assistants, Warehousemen and Clerks (NUSAW&C) and five years later joined forces with United Shop Assistants' Union to form the National Amalgamated Union of Shop Assistants, Warehousemen and Clerks. In the same year Seddon became a member of its executive committee and by 1902 was its President. Trade unions were originally non-political bodies. In 1885 Thomas Glover, then Secretary of the Trades Union Council of St Helens and later the borough's first Labour MP, wrote to the editor of the *St Helens Newspaper and Advertiser* assuring readers that politics had never been allowed in its meetings. In 1890 the Trades Council was replaced by the St Helens and District Trades Council. In 1904, with Seddon as its President, it held a meeting in the St Helens Hippodrome on Chinese indentured labour being imported into Africa, showing that unions were now involved in politics.

At this time Seddon belonged to the Independent Labour Party and was becoming involved in its attempt to take a greater part in government, both local and national. The earliest reference to political activity was his bid to be chosen to stand as an MP in the 1900 General Election. Despite being unsuccessful he worked to support other candidates and in 1904 was Registration Agent for Eccles. By 1905 he had been accepted as a parliamentary candidate to fight the Newton seat. At the same time he was nominated to serve on the Prescot Board of Guardians but withdrew owing to the pressure of his parliamentary candidacy.

The borough of Newton had been returning two MPs since 1559. In 1832 it was disenfranchised and became part of the new Southern Division of the County of Lancaster, which contained the Hundreds of West Derby and Salford, roughly south of a line from Southport, through Wigan, Chorley and Haslingden. In 1868 the county was further divided, Newton being within the new South West Division, which was divided from the South East Division by a line roughly from Wigan through Hindley, Atherton, Astley and Culcheth to Hollinfare. The Southern Division had been represented by both Conservative and Liberal MPs, including W.E. Gladstone (1865–68). In 1885 the Southern Division was split into the Parliamentary Borough of St Helens and the Newton Division, each returning one MP. The Newton seat was won at each subsequent general election by the Conservative candidate and in 1899, when Lord Newton went to the Upper House, the Liberals did not even contest the seat, leaving Colonel Richard Pilkington (of Pilkington Glass) to take his place unopposed.

The Labour movement was growing rapidly meanwhile and the Newton Division of South Lancashire was one of the seats planning to put forward a Labour candidate. In 1885 John Cross had intended to stand but had withdrawn. The first candidate proposed for 1906 was Sam Woods but he stood down owing to ill health. The Labour Representation Committee then tried to get Thomas Greenall from Accrington as the candidate but failed and so James Seddon was unanimously selected to stand. His financial status was an issue and there was some concern that someone with 'a full election exchequer' would be better able to reach the scattered electorate of a division that covered some 70 square miles. However, the electorate included nearly 5,000 miners, who knew Seddon from his work for the Miners' Federation, and the problem was overcome when they, and other union workers, met his election expenses through a voluntary levy.

What he lacked in wealth Seddon made up for in physical stamina and determination. When Churchill visited St Helens in November 1905, he congratulated Seddon for attending despite a broken ankle. During the 1906 campaign, he addressed over 100 meetings, many in the open air, and on the eve of the Newton poll he began at 11 a.m. and was 'footing and motoring' until late that night. Following his 1910 defeat, the London correspondent of the *Manchester Guardian* referred to him as 'one of the most active members of his party'. His campaign was aimed at workers, trade unionists and non-organised alike, promising he would try to change the law on the duration of the working day, a minimum wage, workmen's compensation, unemployment benefit and old age pensions. He also supported free trade, the abolition of Chinese slavery under the British flag, Irish self-government and a co-ordinated free educational system.

At the 1906 General Election, despite having been third choice as candidate, James Seddon polled 6,434 votes and took the seat with a 541 majority. This success was the greater first because he succeeded where the Liberals had so often failed before, and second because he had defeated a Pilkington. The Pilkington family owned the world's biggest glassworks and were the major local employer. Their factories in St Helens employed 17,000, with up to 4,000 of these living in the Newton Division. The local belief was that to speak, act or even think in opposition to a member of the family would be most ill-advised. Many voted for Colonel Pilkington, notwithstanding the secrecy of the ballot, because they feared that to do otherwise would imperil their daily bread. Seddon recognised this dilemma and advised working electors to 'keep their mouths shut when their bread and butter was in danger, but to vote right at the ballot box'.

At this time Labour was very under-represented on St Helens Council holding only eight of the 36 seats. The major problem for party members who would have liked to serve as councillors was that meetings were held during the day so working men would have to lose time to attend them. James Seddon MP stood for election as councillor for the West Sutton ward of St Helens borough but was defeated by 'Fighting Jim' Grace (Conservative). He said the reason for his defeat was that 'all the Tory machinery and money were brought against us'. Certainly the Labour Party was young and inexperienced in electioneering, but the local Conservatives were thirsting to avenge their defeat in the Newton parliamentary election by the 'presumptuous Mr Seddon MP'; some felt so strongly about this that they would have rather conceded all of the other six wards that had Labour candidates than see him take the seventh.

James Seddon was a charismatic man with the gift of oratory. His speeches were rousing and impassioned, and as a working man from humble beginnings he knew exactly which issues concerned his supporters. The Conservatives attacked his personal integrity in their electioneering, accusing him of atheism, wife-beating and debt to the point of bankruptcy: all untrue. He had strong principles and criticised his old friend Joe Turner for 'partaking of the flesh pots of Egypt' by becoming advertising agent to Beecham's. He listed reading as his hobby in *Who's Who*, his books including poetry, which he often quoted and paraphrased. He also had a sense of humour. Speaking against 'the idea that women would vote as their

husbands, fathers or sweethearts dictated', he said 'anyone who held that
view had obviously never been married'.

Despite this jest he supported the emancipation of women. At a meeting
in St Helens Town Hall called by the National Union of Women's Suffrage
to form a local branch, he refuted ideas that women were intellectually infe-
rior or would be unable to use their votes effectively. His wife and daughters
sometimes accompanied him to meetings.

As an MP, Seddon supported many socialist policies, one of which was
old age pensions. Typical was his address on 9 January 1907 to a crowded
meeting at Crewe. He referred sympathetically to the discharge of old men
from the railway works and said it was one of the tragedies of modern life:
'Their old industrial soldiers when their days work was done were cast out
with less ceremony than scrap iron was sent to the breaker.' It was the duty
of the nation, he added, to see that aged workers were not allowed to end
their days in the modern Bastille. If a Labour man was made Chancellor of
the Exchequer he would find funds for old age pensions in 12 months. The
year 1909 saw the introduction of old age pensions. At a meeting with his
constituents at Burtonwood during the January 1910 election campaign,
Seddon's speech was interrupted by an old man who rose from his seat to
say: 'It was one of the best things ever done. I have got a pension and I
thank you, Sir, for it.' The importance of the issue is reflected on one of
James Seddon's election handbills which reminded voters that:

Some day you will be old, but remember that in all England
ONLY TWELVE TORIES VOTED FOR OLD AGE PENSIONS

The 'modern Bastille' he referred to was the workhouse, and the impact
of the old age pension on this dreaded institution was profound. In January
1910 the Prescot Board of Guardians saw 60 of their 1,319 inmates leave
because they had been awarded a pension.

Seddon contested the Newton seat again in January 1910, this time against
the Conservative Lord Wolmer, son of Lord Selborne. Lord Wolmer was
adopted on the recommendation of Lord Newton and while in Newton he
took up residency in Lord Newton's manor house. The contest was fiercely
fought and on polling day missiles were thrown, one of which struck Lord
Wolmer's chauffeur on the side of the head. Other people were also hit
by potatoes. One major difference between the two campaigns was that
James Seddon spoke at public meetings while admission to Lord Wolmer's
meetings was by ticket. Seddon polled 7,256 votes and took the seat by a
majority of 752. In the December 1910 General Election, the contest
between the two men was repeated, but this time Viscount Wolmer turned
the tables, polling 6,706 to win with a majority of 144. Seddon identified
two main reasons for his failure. First, his supporters had been overconfi-
dent and some 300 of them had failed to go to the polls. Second, he cited
the more general problems that the trade union movement and Labour Party
were experiencing.

After his 1910 defeat, Seddon was out of Parliament for some years and,
although he was still the Labour candidate for the Newton division in 1912,
he concentrated on his union career. He was chosen to represent the trade
union workers of Great Britain in America. He believed that, whatever their
nationality, the workers' problem was the same the world over: the same
struggle was going on between capital and labour. Interestingly he included
Germany in the countries he cited to illustrate this point when speaking in
Haydock in October 1912. In the same address he mentioned the rising war

cloud in the Balkans, which might mean a great deal to civilisation even though only small states were involved. He reminded his audience that international capital was interested in the small as well as the big states, and that the men who manipulated international finances could influence the event of war according to whether it suited their pockets.

He had been a member of the TUC Parliamentary Committee since 1908 and by 1913 he was acting as its Chairman, a post he held until 1915. It was in this capacity that he helped dependants left starving by the Dublin dockers' strike of 1913. A plea for help was sent from the striking dockers to the Manchester TUC. Seddon went with Harry Gosling (first President of the national Transport Workers' Federation in 1910 and later the first President of the Transport and General Workers Union) and Charles Bowerman (Secretary to TUC) to the directors of the Co-operative Whole-sale Society who agreed to supply 60 packages of food. The three persuaded dockers striking in Salford to break their action and load the packages onto a boat which then made a perilously speedy journey to Ireland.

His association with food supply continued, and during the war he worked at the Ministry of Food in its temporary headquarters at the Grafton Hotel on Tottenham Court Road, London. The People's Museum, Manchester, has a letter to him from the Co-operative Wholesale Society in Manchester concerning the significant rise in the cost of basic foodstuffs.

In September 1915 he gave the presidential address at the TUC in Bristol, speaking of the need to pursue victory. He took the same message to workers in America. When the British Workers' League was formed in 1916 he was Chairman of its organisation committee. The League's mani-festo called for an all-out effort to win the war. On 22 January 1918, the King made him a Companion of Honour 'for services in connection with the War'.

At the time of his investiture, Seddon was living at 'Fernleigh', Wood-berry Gardens, North Finchley, London; it was from this address that he wrote to the *St Helens Reporter* to answer the newspaper's complaint about 'the inexplicable manner in which St Helens is ignored when honours are being awarded'. He endorsed the complaint, expressed the wish that honour would be given to the town's men and women in the future and thanked all of those who had sent him congratulations. This was typical of a man who never failed to acknowledge and thank those who supported him and worked on his behalf.

His work in the British Workers' League led Seddon outside the Labour Party and he joined the National Democratic Party at its formation in 1918. As an offshoot of the British Workers' League, it received financial support from the Conservatives and Lloyd George's Coalition Liberals. In 1917 he was selected as its candidate for the Hanley Division of Stoke-on-Trent, and, with £500 from British Commonwealth Unions for his campaign fund, he fought the 1918 General Election successfully, polling a majority of 336. His opponents were Harper Parker (Labour), L.L. Grimwade (Liberal) and R.L. Outhwaite (Independent Liberal). In 1922 he fought the seat as an Independent with National Liberal support but lost to Harper Parker. In 1923 he stood as a Conservative and, having failed again, went into political obscurity.

He changed his religious affiliation as he had changed his political one. In 1929 he was appointed Secretary of the Church Association, a body formed in 1865 to maintain the Protestant ideal of faith and worship in the Church of England. In 1950 it joined with the National Church League to form the Church Society.

The stamina that James Seddon showed as a young man continued and he was still working in 1936 as Secretary of St Pancras Chamber of Commerce.

He died, on 31 May 1939 aged 71, from a heart attack while taking a bath at his home, 17 Western Parade, New Barnet. He left a wife and two daughters. Obituaries were placed in *The Times* (which gave an incorrect date for his marriage) on 1 June 1939, and in *The Earlestown Guardian*. No record was found of a will.

Dave Watts
MP for St Helens North

Dave Watts

DAVID JAMES SHACKLETON. M. P.

*David Shackleton:
Labour MP for
Clitheroe, 1902–10*

DAVID JAMES SHACKLETON was born in Clough Fold, a tiny community in Rossendale Valley, in November 1863. The brooding presence of Hall Carr Mill, a great weaving mill, dominated Clough Fold, and its community of weavers, much as a feudal castle towered over the vassals and serfs. Cotton was king, but in 1863 the great cotton famine was at its height. The mills of Lancashire had been cut off from their supplies by the American Civil War. Like other families dependent on cotton, the lives of the Shackleton family were blighted. Both his parents had been weavers. David Shackleton was the second of four children and the only survivor; his elder brother died at the age of six months. Both of his sisters and his mother died when he was four – in a scarlet fever epidemic. His father later re-married.

At the age of 9 he started in the mill, as a half-time weaver. This meant a working week that was nominally 30 hours, but in practice 36. He worked six days a week from 6 a.m. until noon; and on weekday afternoons, he then went to school. Shackleton later boasted that at the age of 12 he had had charge of three looms, 'a record likely to last for all time' in the weaving industry. The family moved to Haslingden, and later to Accrington. At 13 he was put to full-time weaving, though he attended night-classes. Shortly after the Shackletons' arrival in Accrington, one of that era's greatest industrial struggles took place: the 1878 cotton strike, in opposition to a 10 per cent wage-rate cut. It lasted over two months and ended in total defeat. Violence accompanied the bitter struggle, with extra police and troops called in. Shackleton's lasting memory was of the 'employment of English soldiers against Englishmen' and the poor organisation and feeble resources of the strikers. It stimulated his interest in industrial problems. He would eat his dinner whilst at the mill, so as to spend his dinner hour in a reading-room 'devouring the Manchester Guardian'. He was excited by the General Election of 1880 and, aged 17, joined a Liberal Club.

His father and stepmother were teetotal and he enrolled in the Band of Hope – and never touched strong drink. At 19, he married the 18-year-old Sarah Broadbent who also worked in the mill. They lied about their age (parental consent being required but not sought) claiming to be 21, and married in a Wesleyan Chapel, well away from both families.

He soon joined the local union – the Accrington Power Loom Weavers' Association, the largest in the town. Fifteen months later he was elected to the management committee, just short of his twenty-first birthday. Shortly after he was sacked, and quickly found that he had been blacklisted. It was a disheartening period. Over 17 months he 'wore out his boots' trying to get work, both of them surviving on Sarah's income. He eventually got a job through a friendly overlooker, in a mill owned by someone from outside Accrington who tolerated his union activities. By the time he left in 1893 he had been promoted to overlooker.

Shackleton became active in the Weavers' Amalgamation (Northern Counties Amalgamated Weavers' Association) as well as the local union, of which he became President. In 1890 he attended his first TUC as an Accrington Weavers' delegate. He was Secretary of a Liberal Ward Association, prominent in the temperance and friendly society movement and, in 1892, became a JP – gaining some satisfaction from sitting on the same Bench as his former employer. This was a significant honour. The first working-class magistrates had only been created in 1885. The Conservatives opposed his appointment on the grounds that if the weavers were entitled to a representative then what about the miners and other working men? Chimney sweeps and scavengers and lamplighters? 'It is tending to make a burlesque of the Bench.'

However, his more significant achievement was mastering the extraordinary complexity of piece-work in the weaving industry, enabling him to calculate 'sorts' and thus dispute the wages paid to weavers. He could therefore protect and enhance the earnings of the weavers, the majority of whom were women. It was this skill that helped him be appointed Secretary of the Ramsbottom Weavers' Association in 1893.

The following year he was appointed Secretary of the Darwen Weavers, Winders and Warpers' Association, which had over 5,000 members. It entailed a significant pay rise – to £2 per week. In 1894 the Shackletons moved with their three children to a union-owned house in Darwen, next door to the office.

Shackleton missed the 1893 TUC as the Ramsbottom Weavers were too impoverished to send a delegate. In his first years in Darwen, such representation was highly controversial so he did not attend a further TUC until 1897. Thereafter, he attended every Congress for the next 13 years, sometimes representing the Weavers' Amalgamation, but mostly the Darwen Weavers. Shackleton was not content just to appear on the attendance list. In 1897 he moved two resolutions. In 1898 he was elected a teller, moved a resolution, seconded another and spoke in the debate on half-timers. Similar involvement in each Congress followed and in 1901 he was elected to the General Purposes Committee and would have had a seat on the TUC's executive, the Parliamentary Committee, had his way not been blocked by the President of the Weavers' Amalgamation, David Holmes, a prominent Liberal.

Union activities took Shackleton away from home a great deal. By 1902 he was said to have been a member of every cotton union deputation that had 'waited upon the Home Secretary' in the preceding four years. In 1902, he accompanied six Lancashire cotton employers to the USA to investigate the textile industry, and especially the new Northrop loom.

Shackleton had ended his formal connection with the Liberals when he moved to Darwen and could therefore stand for the local council, on the nomination of the Trades Council, when a vacancy occurred in 1895 – as a representative of Labour. The issue of Labour representation – direct representation – on elected bodies was highly controversial, especially in the cotton unions where long-established Liberal and Conservative loyalties died hard. In Darwen, the issue was debated, and rejected, on three occasions during the 1890s. In 1899 the Darwen Weavers voted not to be represented at the 1900 Conference that gave birth to the Labour Representation Committee (LRC). The tide turned with the Taff Vale Judgement. Only legislation could remedy the decision of the Law Lords, and only parliamentary activity could bring that about. In January 1902 the Weavers' Amalgamation reversed its policy and instructed its leadership 'to take the necessary steps to secure direct representation in Parliament'.

They had still not actually agreed to affiliate to the LRC by that summer when two major events occurred: the elevation to the Lords of Sir Ughtred Kay-Shuttleworth, Liberal MP for Clitheroe; and the decision that David Shackleton would contest the by-election as the independent Labour candidate. The 1902 by-election was one of the most remarkable of the last century. When the nominations closed, the Returning Officer waited for a full half an hour – perhaps not quite believing what was happening – before declaring there were no other nominations. He then waited another hour for any objections before announcing that David Shackleton had been duly elected.

Shackleton had also been chosen unopposed as the candidate by the Clitheroe Division of the LRC. He had not been the only person interested in standing, but by the eve of the selection conference there were only two names left in the frame – his and Philip Snowden's. The future Chancellor of the Exchequer was well known in Lancashire as a brilliant orator and Independent Labour Party (ILP) organiser. At the last moment, he withdrew, writing to the selection meeting: 'Although I should appreciate very highly the position of parliamentary representative for . . . Clitheroe . . . I think Mr Shackleton, as a trades union official and one so thoroughly associated with the staple trade and with the labour conditions of the district, has a far better claim, and would make a more useful representative.'

The socialists in the Clitheroe Social Democratic Federation (SDF) were disappointed, since Shackleton was not a socialist and had a well-known past as a Liberal. The Liberals, on the other hand, in their own stronghold, were in a fractious state. Twice they had chosen a candidate and twice the candidate had declined the nomination.

The Clitheroe Conservatives, who sometimes did not contest the seat (Kay-Shuttleworth had more than once been re-elected unopposed in this Liberal stronghold), reacted to the goings-on in the Liberal Party by announcing that they would not contest the seat unless the Liberals did. In the end the Liberals failed to nominate a candidate, the Tories were hoist by their own petard and 'Labour' won its first by-election, with its candidate having a walk-over.

In Parliament Shackleton joined the two LRC MPs elected in 1900 – Keir Hardie and Richard Bell – both of whom depended on Liberal support in their two-member constituencies.

The significance of the strange turn of events should not be underestimated. It propelled Ramsay MacDonald into secret discussions with the Liberal Party leadership. Whilst MacDonald's thinking about an entente with the Liberals grew from his experience in Leicester in 1900 (he split the Liberal vote in a two-member constituency and let a Tory in), the discussions did not start until after Clitheroe. They received additional impetus from the further by-election victories in 1903 at Woolwich (Crooks) and Barnard Castle (Henderson). The resultant entente paved the way for the LRC's triumph in 1906.

Shackleton took his seat in Parliament just before the Summer Recess of 1902. He was soon busy making speeches and tabling questions. His very first question was about conditions in cotton weaving sheds, but his maiden

speech was devoted to opposing the Conservative government's Education
Bill. Within months he had charge of a private member's bill – the TUC's
first, modest attempt to counter the Taff Vale Judgement. He attracted
great attention. The *Cotton Factory Times* predicted a battle royal between
the forces of capital and labour in the Commons, while the *Manchester
Guardian* praised his second reading speech.

By the start of the 1904 session, the five-strong LRC Group in Parliament
was completely riven. There were problems with Richard Bell, who would
not attend Group meetings, would not sign 'the pledge' (the LRC constitution) and who, despite his LRC-sponsorship in 1900, still operated as a
Lib-Lab member. There were problems with Keir Hardie, who had been
in Parliament off and on for a decade and who was too used to going about
things in his own sweet way.

The Group was also subject to strident criticism in the pages of *Labour
Leader* for their shortcomings. And there were problems in the relations
with the nine Lib-Lab MPs. Some of these grievances spilled over into the
wider movement. There was a contretemps at the 1904 TUC between
Shackleton and John Burns, the Lib-Lab MP who was nominally Chairman
of the Grouping in Parliament of both bodies. This was occasioned by Burns'
parliamentary tactics, which Shackleton saw as 'wrecking' his resolution on
wage rates in state factories and shipyards. Conservatives sneered that it
showed what happened 'when men of immature judgment were entrusted
with legislative responsibilities, which rightly belonged to men of education'. The *Cotton Factory Times* opined that 'providing sport for the Philistines
ought to be strictly tabooed'.

At the same Congress Shackleton was finally elected to the Parliamentary
Committee of the TUC, defeating David Holmes. For the next five months
Shackleton was the only person to be simultaneously a member of the
Labour movement's two major executive bodies – the Parliamentary Committee and the LRC Executive. It put him in an uncomfortable position that
was resolved by not seeking re-election to the LRC Executive in 1905. His
last duty as an LRC office holder was to preside over its fifth Annual
Conference, when he used his presidential address to argue against two key
motions – to weaken the principle of independence from the Liberal Party
and to restrict conference representation to trade unionists – and so helped
secure their defeat.

Shortly after the LRC Conference, a meeting of the Executives of the
LRC, the TUC and the General Federation of Trades Unions was held, at
Caxton Hall, to work out a plan of action for the approaching General
Election. Under the Caxton Hall Agreement, the TUC undertook to endorse
all the LRC's candidates and the LRC accepted the TUC's right to endorse Lib-Lab candidates. It was also agreed to form a consultative body
– the tripartite Joint Board. Shackleton was on the TUC's three-man delegation that drew up the constitution of the Joint Board, and was a member
when it sat for the first time in November 1905. Attempts were made
to patch-up the relations in Parliament between the LRC members and the
Lib-Labs, with some success. The foundations of the Parliamentary Labour
Party (PLP) were being laid, with Shackleton playing a critical role.

In 1906, Shackleton almost had a second walk-over. Clitheroe had been
uncontested for 14 years, but at the last moment a candidate entered the
field, ostensibly as an Independent, to be greeted by disbelief. The opponent, a Mr Belton from Surrey, was a brewer, a tariff reformer and a Roman
Catholic. There was Catholic hostility to Shackleton on education from his
maiden speech and because he supported secular education and repeal of
the Conservative's 1902 Education Act. However, the challenge did not

amount to much and Shackleton's majority was over 8,000 on a 77 per cent turnout. The great moment was soured by the car in which Shackleton toured the constituency on election day striking and killing a young father of two small children.

When all 29 newly elected LRC members met for the first time on 12 February 1906 – in Committee Room 12 at the House of Commons – Shackleton was nominated for the position of Chairman of the expanded group. Arthur Henderson, Chair of the LRC, took the Chair. Prior to the meeting there had been private discussion about the Chairmanship. Many believed that Shackleton was the natural choice. The only possible rival was Keir Hardie who had serious reservations about accepting the Chairmanship. He was aware of his limitations as a unifying force, and preferred his old role as a 'socialist pioneer' – out and about making speeches and rousing the masses, rather than attending to tedious parliamentary activity. It was hoped that he would not be nominated, or, if he was, would decline the nomination. However, Barnes nominated Hardie, and Hardie did not decline. Shackleton was nominated by Crooks. The vote, on a show of hands, was 13–13. The minutes then refer to a second vote, by secret ballot. Hardie won this 15–14. Contemporaneous accounts suggest that the decider was at the third attempt, but the official minutes, hand-written by J. Scott Lindsay, do not confirm that. Shackleton accepted the position of Vice-Chairman; Henderson and MacDonald were elected as Whips. Three days later, the Annual Conference of the LRC agreed to change the name to the Labour Party.

Although Keir Hardie served as nominal Chairman of the PLP for two years, almost from the start Shackleton was de facto Chairman. Hardie did not have the temperament to work collegially, and was often absent. Much of that first year was taken up by the Trades Disputes Bill, on which Shackleton took the lead. On the evening the Trades Disputes Act received Royal Assent, a celebratory dinner was held, under the joint auspices of the TUC, the Labour Party and the GFTU, at which he was the guest of honour. Although widely expected to take over from Hardie as the PLP's next Chairman, he declined to let his name go forward, even after Keir Hardie's threat at the party's Belfast Conference to resign from the PLP following a resolution demanding the total and immediate enfranchisement of women. Hardie supported a gradual approach and had backed a more limited Bill to this end. This incident caused consternation within the movement and the PLP, and Hardie's re-election in 1907 was far from guaranteed. However, Hardie smoothed things over by indicating that if re-elected for a second year he would not stand again. For most of the year he was absent from Parliament, and took a long cruise, for the sake of his health.

Shackleton, notwithstanding his duties in Parliament, increasingly concentrated on his work in the union movement and was appointed as one of two union representatives on a Home Office committee of inquiry into artificial humidity in cotton-weaving factories – the 'Humidity Committee'. This move confounded his parliamentary colleagues but was wholly in character as he prioritised the interests of the cotton weavers. He also regarded this as a signal as to where the party ought to concentrate its efforts – on amelioration of workers' conditions. It thus represented a repudiation of the socialist wing of the Parliamentary Party. The ILP, through the pages of *Labour Leader*, gave Shackleton an increasingly rough ride. The inherent conflict between trade unionism and socialism – evident in the PLP from its first moment – increasingly came to the fore.

Shackleton was clear about his priorities and increasingly angry at what he saw as unjustified criticism by the ILP. In 1907 he accepted the TUC

Chairmanship, effectively ruling himself out of succeeding Hardie as Chairman of the PLP in 1908.

Until 1906 Hardie had been the only socialist in the LRC Group in Parliament. After 1906, the balance of the PLP changed considerably. Although only seven of the now 30-strong group were officially sponsored by the ILP, probably 18 were members and one other was a member of the SDF. A Group with such a pronounced socialist majority was bound to be uncomfortable for Shackleton, who had a keen awareness of the disparate character of the Labour Party, which he described as a 'federation', 'alliance' or a 'combination' of the union element and the ILP. He worked hard to maintain this uneasy, even contentious, alliance. He did not regard the ILP as acting with the same motives but as seeking to advance its own position, often with wilful disregard of the possible consequences, given the fragile nature of the alliance that was the Labour Party. This peaked in 1907 with the Colne Valley by-election and the unexpected (to the Labour Party as well as the Liberal Party), and unwelcome, victory of Victor Grayson. Shackleton nonetheless believed that the party, if it conducted itself properly, could make great strides at the next election – anticipating the return of 100 Labour MPs.

His increasing disaffection with the socialist wing propelled him to concentrate on his work on the TUC Parliamentary Committee, which he chaired, and which was not bedeviled by the ideological friction of the PLP. His ascendancy in the TUC is underlined by the extraordinary decision at the 1908 Nottingham Congress that he should continue as Chairman for a further 12 months (though noting that this should not set a precedent). Nobody since the 1870s had held the TUC Chairmanship for more than one year, nor has anyone since. The TUC may have felt that they had no better protector against the fashionable view within the ILP (and to some extent the party) that the TUC was redundant 'now that the Labour Party has become the political organ of trade unionism'. Shackleton proved to be a doughty fighter for the TUC position: whilst it wished to work closely with the party, it wanted to continue to make direct and independent representations to government on matters close to its heart. These issues dominated discussions in 1909 – the year that saw the Miners' Federation finally join the Labour Party with the resultant disintegration of the Lib-Labs as a separate political force as the majority accepted the Labour Whip.

Meanwhile, the next election – and the anticipated breakthrough – loomed. At one point Shackleton feared an SDF candidate standing against him in Clitheroe – especially after the SDF brought Ben Tillett to the constituency to make a vituperative speech against him. However, neither that nor a Liberal challenge emerged. The local Liberals had still not recovered from the post-1902 recriminations. The Tories fielded an official candidate, a rather more serious figure than the half-hearted Belton, and a vigorous two-month campaign took place leading up to the General Election of 1910. Shackleton stormed home with a 7,000-plus majority over his Tory opponent. It was again a hugely popular victory. Scenes of enthusiasm outside Clitheroe Weavers' Institute were 'beyond description' according to a Conservative newspaper, with similar scenes repeated in Nelson and Colne.

In his victory speech, Shackleton said that he 'was only a young lad yet' and that he appreciated the voters' renewal of their confidence. But the hoped-for breakthrough of 100 seats had not materialised. Indeed the PLP was smaller in January 1910 (with just 40 seats) than prior to the election. Before the year was out and the second General Election, Shackleton had retired from Parliament. Thus ended, as spectacularly as it had begun eight years previously, a remarkable political career. At the very centre of the

Labour and trade union movement in the founding years of the Labour
Party, Shackleton suddenly removed himself from the fray.

He received and accepted an overture from Winston Churchill to
become, as a civil servant, the Labour Adviser at the Home Office – a position specially created for him and at a salary more than commensurate with
this post. He consulted with the Weavers' Amalgamation, which gave its
blessing and defended him vigorously against criticism that he had betrayed
the movement in accepting such a post.

His last engagements within the union movement were at the 1910
September TUC Congress, in Sheffield. Here he was as active as ever, but
the clouds were darkening. In an acrimonious debate about Labour
Exchanges, Ben Tillett again attacked Shackleton allegedly describing him
as a 'traitor to the cause of Labour'. This was probably the last straw.

The Congress ended, not with the usual few remarks from the President,
but with a lengthy statement by C.W. Bowerman, the acting Secretary,
describing Tillett's speech as a vicious and uncalled for attack 'on our good
friend Shackleton, which he has taken much to heart'. Will Thorne defended
the absent Tillett. Bowerman demanded an apology, or a denial about the
words allegedly used. Shackleton made a short speech saying that Tillett's
assertion, that he had to choose between the employing class and his own
class, was to make a most unwarrantable statement; his life's work showed
which side he had chosen – and he knew that he had the confidence of the
Parliamentary Committee and its delegates. It was sour note on which to
make his exit from the movement and the party.

It was not the last the country heard of David Shackleton, as he embarked
on a new career within the civil service. After frequent changes and various
promotions he emerged, during the wartime Coalition government under
Lloyd George, at the very top of the tree – the first Permanent Secretary
at the newly created Ministry of Labour, in December 1916.

Lloyd George had struck a wartime bargain with the Labour Party, one
item of which was the formation of a Ministry of Labour. The first Minister
of Labour was John Hodge MP, then Acting Chairman of the PLP; and
he wanted the civil servant heading his ministry to be someone who understood Labour. He chose Shackleton – who thus became the first working-
class man to reach such a dizzy height. The higher echelons of the civil
service were reserved for university graduates – generally Oxbridge graduates and the products of public schools. That a 'poorly educated', former
half-time weaver should have risen so far was miraculous. He was spectacularly the odd man out. The protests were considerable, the first and most
direct coming from William (later Lord) Beveridge, who was effectively
passed over for the post that he believed should have been his. Whitehall
was seething about interloping amateurs breaking through the class
barrier. Questions were asked in Parliament and Hodge was put under great
pressure. Shackleton offered to stand down, but Hodge would have none
of it. With Lloyd George's authority for them both to stick to their guns,
they met the challenge of the 'caste difficulty', within the mandarinate, by
securing a knighthood for Shackleton, thereby demonstrating his equal
social status with the other Permanent Secretaries. This was conferred in
June 1917. Shackleton was thus arguably the first working-class man ever
to be knighted – 'the first Labour knight' as he was dubbed – another breakthrough, like his twice-Chairmanship of the TUC. In more than one way,
this 'Lancashire lad' was unique.

Sir David Shackleton retired from the civil service in 1925 and lived
with his wife (by then Lady) Sarah in St Anne's-on-Sea, on the Lancashire
coast. Apart from his life-long commitment to the Independent Order of

Rechabites and his continuing work as a JP in Preston, he entirely disappeared from public view. He died in 1938, aged 74.

Shackleton's approach to politics is best summed up in the advice he gave to the rising generation: 'Use your opportunities. Don't waste time and breath crying for the moon. When you have got a certain amount of power, don't bother your head about how you are to get more. If you rightly use the power that you have, more will come to you at the proper time.'[1]

Alan Haworth
Former PLP Secretary

Alan Haworth

1   *Pearson's Weekly*, 15 March 1906.

*Philip Snowden:
Labour MP for
Blackburn, 1906–18,
and for Colne Valley,
1923–31*

PHILLIP SNOWDEN. M. P.

C PYRIGHT   Photo Shawcross

Chapter 23
Philip Snowden
1864–1937

PHILIP SNOWDEN had quite an effect on Blackburn when he first campaigned in the town, then the capital of the textile industry, in 1900. According to the journalist A.G. Gardiner, the young Snowden, 'a pallid and hatchet-faced young man', caused such a stir that his 'name was on every lip, his sayings ran like rumour through the weaving sheds and the street'.

Gardiner warmed to his theme: 'Men in their greasy caps, and carrying their "kits", hurried from the mills to his meetings, and sat as if hypnotised under the spell of revelation. He fought the battle absolutely single-handed, and he fought it with a dignity of spirit rare in politics.'

It was not, however, enough. Snowden lost the poll, but, having 'touched the lost chord in the heart of Blackburn', recorded just over 7,000 votes, the largest by a socialist candidate in the 1900 'khaki' election. Gardiner describes him as having 'shaken the Gibraltar of Toryism to its foundations'.[1] Six years later, the Tory foundations crumbled further, and Snowden became Blackburn's first Labour MP.

Looking back at his life in 1934, Snowden appears almost ambivalent about the merits of a political career, hesitating to recommend such a course to others, and questioning whether he should have instead confined himself to what he saw as the 'missionary work' he conducted outside Parliament.[2] Had he done so, the Labour movement would have been deprived of a substantial contribution from one its early pioneers, a man who was one of the party's most significant figures in the early twentieth century. But it would also have meant that Snowden's name would not be inextricably linked with that of Ramsay MacDonald for his role in the end of the second Labour government in 1931 – what Clement Attlee called 'the greatest betrayal in the political history of this country'.

That controversy inevitably casts a shadow over consideration of Snowden's life. Snowden himself records only 'jeers and ironical cheers from a small section of the Labour Party' when he took his place opposite his former colleagues for the first time in the House of Commons Chamber

1   A.G. Gardiner, *Prophets, Priests and Kings*, Dent and Sons, 1914.
2   Viscount Philip Snowden, *An Autobiography*, Ivor Nicholson and Watson Ltd, 1934.

as a member of the new National Government. That is to downplay the
fury that the actions of Snowden and the others caused, as well as the sense
of betrayal, described by Attlee, which lingers to this day. But to see
Snowden's contribution to the Labour movement purely through the events
of 1931 – which he described as 'the most painful experience of my life' –
would be to overlook his hugely significant contribution to building the
party.

Philip Snowden's childhood was founded on a Liberal Nonconformist
community in the West Riding of Yorkshire. Born in the village of Cowling,
near Keighley, on 18 July 1864, his parents were cotton and worsted
weavers at the local mill. Brought up as a strict Wesleyan Methodist, he
also followed his father's example and never drank alcohol (a subject about
which he wrote regularly during his early years in Parliament).

When the mill closed in 1879, the family moved east across the Pennines
to Nelson. Snowden left school at 15 and began work as a clerk in an insurance office before passing the entrance exam for the civil service and
becoming a revenue officer in the Customs and Excise Service. He was
posted to Liverpool, Aberdeen, the Orkneys and Redruth. However, a bone
deformity caused by illness or a cycling accident – which meant that
Snowden walked with the aid of a stick throughout his life – forced him to
return to Cowling, where his mother had returned after the death of his
father.

By this time, the young Snowden's political awakening was well established. He devoured Fabian essays, collected radical books, read the leaders
of the Chartist movement and wrote for local papers, notably as editor of
the *Keighley Labour Journal*. Snowden first joined the Liberal Party but
switched to the Independent Labour Party (ILP) in 1895. He represented
the party at parish council, school board and town council level in the
West Riding before his unsuccessful attempt to enter Parliament in 1900
in Blackburn. By then in his thirties, he had developed a reputation as an
accomplished public speaker, drawing crowds large enough to rival those
of Keir Hardie (with whom he wrote a pamphlet about their shared Christian
Socialism).

Blackburn might have seemed an unlikely stamping ground for Snowden.
It had generally returned Tory members to Parliament since becoming a
two-seat constituency in the 1832 Reform Act. In 1900 the MPs were Sir
Harry Hornby – said to have never made a speech in 23 years in the House
– and Sir William Coddington. The Liberals failed to put up a candidate in
1900. Paternalistic Toryism had much of the working class in Blackburn in
thrall. The Fabians had tried to set up a branch but failed. The more Marxist
Social Democratic Federation (SDF) had only a few hundred members. The
Weavers' Association had many more members, but was wary of socialism.

Snowden, however, 'wrought a miracle' in his first attempt to win a
Blackburn seat. 'That election will never be forgotten by those who
witnessed it' wrote Gardiner, a journalist then working in Blackburn and
later editor of the *Daily News*. 'It was like a sudden wind stirring the leaves
of the forest. It was a revival movement gathering momentum with each
hour. It may be that Philip Snowden is only the comet of the season, a
meteor flashing across the dark sky of Blackburn Toryism, but for the
moment he is the most striking personality in Blackburn.'

Opposing the Boer war – and answering criticism for his stance with the
words 'what are empire and glory to a weaver with a pound a week?' –
Snowden terrified the Tories, prompting posters declaring 'Down with
Atheism, Socialism and Anarchy'. Another declared: 'Vote for men who
have known you all their lifetime, and have contributed to almost every-

thing in the town, from the boys' football and cricket clubs to bazaars of all denominations, and not for a youth of the romancing socialist type.'

Snowden did not do enough to win in Blackburn in 1900. However, despite undertaking no personal canvassing – 'I never in all the elections I have fought, ever made a personal appeal to a voter to give me his vote' – he built the foundations for his success in 1906 and boosted the town's Labour movement. The ILP opened its own club, joining the already established SDF club.

In 1903, having lost another parliamentary battle in Wakefield a year earlier, Snowden became Chairman of the ILP. It was the first of two spells in this position, the second being between 1917 and 1920. He resigned from the ILP in favour of Labour proper in 1927, in part because of what he said was a drift into revolutionary socialism.

Snowden came to the 1906 election campaign in Blackburn shortly after his marriage to Ethel Annakin, a prominent suffragette who won her husband's support for the cause. Facing opposition from two Tories and one Liberal, he spoke at two meetings a night during the campaign, on 8 January being joined at the Town Hall and the Exchange by Keir Hardie. Fighting the campaign against protectionism – a lifelong commitment – and against the expansion of the Empire, he polled 10,281 votes, enough to come second and win one of the two seats, on a turnout of 95 per cent. Returning to his home village of Cowling to visit his mother a few days later, he was welcomed by a brass band, with local schoolchildren given the day off in honour of their local hero. It seemed that socialists had moved on from being regarded as 'hare-brained curiosities', he commented in his autobiography.

Snowden represented Blackburn for 12 years, being returned twice in 1910, polling 11,916 votes in the first election and then topping the poll with 10,762 votes in the second. That election was called when Snowden was on a lecture tour of America; the *Blackburn Weekly Telegraph* reported that, on his return to the town, an open carriage took him from the station to the market square accompanied by a torchlight procession. Such was the chanting and cheering of the 40,000 crowd in the square that all Snowden could say was 'I am here to celebrate a certain victory.'

In Parliament, Snowden was one of only two Labour MPs, suggests Gardiner, who could be described as socialists first and foremost, the other being Keir Hardie:

> Others subscribe to the economic theories of Socialism. They alone live for them and for nothing else. Others join in the political fray; they stand aloof from what they regard as idle trifling: their eyes fixed on the ultimate goal. To them the House of Commons is not a place for petty skirmishes and paltry triumphs. It is a platform from whence to preach the Social Revolution. They will not prune the tree: they will uproot it.[3]

In 1907, the *Weekly Sun* newspaper also considered the new MP for Blackburn in a sketch, which, with the headline 'The Bogey-Man', gives another vivid sense of how the Labour contingent in Parliament was regarded in the early twentieth century. Comparing him to Robespierre – 'if he cannot cut aristocratic heads off, he can make bourgeois flesh creep' – the article suggests that Snowden was a ghostly presence who inspired

---

3   Gardiner, op. cit.

'the feeling which Macbeth must have had when he first met the Weird Sisters upon the blasted heath'. It was, said Snowden later as he reproduced the column in full in his memoirs, one of the 'cleverest and most amusing' articles written about him.

During the First World War, Snowden was part of the pacifist minority in the House of Commons. He refused to take part in the recruiting campaign in Blackburn and spoke in the Commons against conscription, a stance that led in part to him losing his parliamentary seat in another 'khaki' election in 1918. He described the campaign, during which he was supported by Siegfried Sassoon, as the 'most strenuous contest that I ever waged' and, although defeated, polled his highest ever vote in the constituency: 15,274.

Indeed, such was his reputation in Blackburn that he was invited by the party to stand again at the next election. Optimistic about his chances of success, he accepted, but in 1921 switched his attentions to nearby Colne Valley. 'My colleagues were anxious to make a certainty of my return to Parliament at the next election,' he wrote, 'and they did not share my optimism about my prospects at Blackburn.' The party in Blackburn were reluctant to let him go, and there followed a meeting with the executive that was 'a very painful ordeal'. When agreement was reached, a resolution was passed stating:

> It was with the greatest reluctance and regret that the Blackburn Labour Party agrees in deference to the advice and wishes of the National Council of the ILP to release Mr Snowden. They never had a representative in the House of Commons who gave more time and service to them than Mr Snowden did during his period of membership from 1906 to 1918.

As MP for Colne Valley, Snowden became Labour's first Chancellor of the Exchequer in its first government in 1924. 'Few of us who had toiled through the years to achieve this object had expected to see it realised in our lifetime,' he wrote. He presented his first budget on 29 April 1924 with 'boyhood mates' in the Strangers' Gallery and his wife – 'suffering from a state of nervous tension from which I was happily free' – in the Speaker's Gallery. Snowden had long had a reputation as an economic expert and was regarded as a Chancellor with a commitment to returning to the Gold Standard, free trade and balancing the budget. But this economic orthodoxy and his failure to introduce socialist measures brought him criticism among Labour MPs.

He won support, however, by refusing to accept a reduction in the British share of German reparations in the Young Plan in 1929, but his policies floundered as the Wall Street Crash sent shockwaves around the world over the following 18 months. In 1931, faced with a huge deficit, Snowden advocated 10 per cent cuts in unemployment benefit and increased taxation for the middle classes, a move described as 'equality of sacrifice'. With the tax increases later abandoned, the cuts caused deep division in the party and, after an indecisive vote, ultimately led to the resignation of the second Labour government and the creation of the National Government.

At this point Snowden, having been returned in four elections in Colne Valley, joined the House of Lords as Lord Snowden of Ickornshaw and became Lord Privy Seal in the National Government, campaigning against his former party (which had expelled him) and accusing it of adopting policies that amounted to 'Bolshevism gone mad'. He subsequently resigned from the government in 1932 over what he saw as the rise of protectionism.

In his autobiography, Snowden attacked MacDonald and was pessimistic about Labour's future, arguing that the party had 'lost much of its idealistic quality and spiritual fervour . . . it has become an ordinary political party, with little to distinguish it from the quality of other parties'. He predicted a long period before 'unwise leadership and bad political judgement' would make way for the 'wiser counsels' who would help the party gain a majority.

Echoing his opposition to the First World War, he closed his autobiography by writing darkly of the threat of a fresh conflict, describing it as 'criminal madness to talk about and prepare for the next war'. He died two years before the outbreak of the Second World War, suffering a heart attack after a long illness, on 15 May 1937.

Snowden will always be one of those Labour figures who inspires mixed emotions. Our movement owes a great debt to those like him who fought with such determination for the common cause of their fellow men and women.

The Blackburn in which Snowden campaigned was very different to that which I represent today, and yet one only needs to know a little of its history to understand more about the conditions in which he framed the great cause that he espoused. Here was a man, his very being founded in the lives of northern textile workers, his life blighted by illness, fighting for those people, against the odds and against Tory complacency.

In his autobiography, Snowden reflects on his beliefs during a final chapter that has a melancholic air. He talks about his belief in 'gradualism in social progress . . . But I do insist and have done so from my earliest days of my Socialist teaching, that every step forward must carry with it the approval of public opinion, and that every change must be consolidated before the next step is taken.' Although expelled from the Labour Party, he had not lost faith with his core beliefs: 'After forty years of the advocacy of Socialist principles, I am more than ever convinced of their rightness and that society will inevitably if gradually evolve into that stage.'

Snowden believed in a socialism that 'will not destroy individual enterprise and initiative but will actually encourage these things in a larger number of people by restricting the power of the exploiter. Competition would be raised to a sphere where the success of one would not mean the impoverishment of the many – the realm of the intellect and the spirit from which no soul need be shut out.'

Although pessimistic about the future of Labour, he had no doubts about the importance of the movement. 'I have devoted a lifetime to the advocacy of this principle and to the building up of a party to give practical political application to it,' he wrote. 'I do not regret this. The Labour Party has profoundly influenced political thought and given a new interest in politics and sound reforms to millions of electors who were formerly indifferent.'

Yet Snowden's role as Ramsay MacDonald's number two in a great betrayal, a man who turned on his party, is an indelible stain on his reputation. He can also be accused of lack of foresight, of sticking too rigidly to economic orthodoxy and, as Chancellor, of missing the opportunity to underpin his beliefs through reform. But that is not to write off Snowden's huge significance. He himself believed he had helped in the creation of something important with the ability to change the lives of those who were so mesmerised by him in Blackburn in 1900 and 1906.

Reflecting on his split from the party, he wrote: 'The incidents of the last few years have alienated me from the Labour Party, but they have not

robbed me of my memories of the past, nor of the satisfaction of having
helped to create this great instrument which, intelligently used, may yet be
potent in advancing social progress.'[4] In that, Snowden was right. He was
a fundamental part of the creation of a truly great instrument of change.
For that we owe him an immense debt of gratitude.

Jack Straw
MP for Blackburn

Jack Straw

4   Snowden, op. cit.

THOMAS SUMMERBELL. M. P.

*Thomas Summerbell:
Labour MP for
Sunderland,
1906–10*

Chapter 24
Thomas Summerbell
1861–1910

THOMAS SUMMERBELL was one of the more obscure members of the 1906 intake. Unlike some of his famous contemporaries featured in this collection – Keir Hardie, Ramsay MacDonald, Arthur Henderson, Philip Snowden, Will Thorne – he made only the merest ripple on the national consciousness.

In Sunderland, however, he was a substantial figure. So much so that, when he died, special trains were laid on to bring mourners to his funeral and the cortege stretched for more than a mile.

The contemporary photograph shows a balding, solid, respectable citizen with a walrus moustache and the de rigueur stiff collar. His origins, however, were humble. Summerbell was born in 1861 in Seaham Harbour, son of a coal trimmer. He left school at the age of 12 and, after working first for a hairdresser and then as a grocer's errand boy, he was apprenticed to a printer on the *Seaham Weekly News*. After serving a seven-year apprenticeship, he found work as a journeyman printer in Felling and later in Jarrow, leaving because his employer did not keep trade union hours.

After working briefly in South Shields, Hartlepool and Newcastle, he finally settled in Sunderland, working first for a local newspaper and eventually establishing his own printing business.

Summerbell's political awakening was gradual. In his youth he was briefly attracted by the smooth-talking Disraeli and later by Gladstone (on account of his commitment to Home Rule for Ireland). Eventually, however, Summerbell came under the spell of a Newcastle radical, Joseph Cowen, and joined the Independent Labour Party (ILP), which set the direction for the rest of his life. By 1888 he was Secretary of Sunderland Trades Council and helping to unionise the unskilled.

In 1892 he was elected to the town council of which he remained a member until his death. As a councillor, he was a keen advocate of municipalisation and was instrumental in persuading the local authority to buy out the old tramways company and to install a system of electric trams that remained in service until after the Second World War.

In 1906 Summerbell was elected to Parliament and thus became one of the 29 founding members of the Parliamentary Labour Party. Until that time Sunderland had been represented by a succession of wealthy local businessmen, standing either as Liberals or Conservatives, mainly from the big ship-building or coal-owning families. Summerbell was the first to break their grip and he paved the way for what would become, in due course, two safe Labour seats.

In Parliament, his preoccupation was almost entirely with the dreadful condition of the labouring classes, not merely in Sunderland, but throughout the country. A glance through Hansard shows him asking questions about the education of paupers, deaths by starvation in Whitechapel, the wages of labourers at Kew Gardens and the incidence of TB (tuberculosis) in the army.

At a public meeting in the East End of London in April 1906, Summerbell was reported as saying that 'the Labour Party in the House of Commons recognised that they had been returned by the workers to do something for them and the government would have to do something, otherwise the Labour men would want to know the reason why', adding that 'He was afraid that matters would not go smoothly with the House in the future as they had in the past'. There was talk of organising a demonstration of unemployed men and women to march through the West End on a week day 'so they could cause a good deal of inconvenience'.

A report in *The Times* has him taking part in a delegation, led by Arthur Henderson and Keir Hardie, to Prime Minister Asquith to ask for more powers to help local authorities relieve unemployment.

His maiden speech, however, was devoted not to unemployment but to coastal erosion, an issue of some relevance to his constituency where the mining of sand and shingle from the foreshore was causing the disappearance of beaches and coastline and the destruction of sewers. He was later appointed a member of the Royal Commission on Coastal Erosion.

During the summer recess of 1907 Summerbell, along with other ILP MPs, embarked on a nationwide schedule of public meetings, described in *The Times* as 'a missionary tour' (a forerunner, no doubt, of the Big Conversation). *The Times* gives a flavour of the subject matter: 'Their tours will extend from Cornwall to Scotland, and from Kent to Wales. The theory and practice of Socialism from the Independent Labour Party's point of view in politics will be dealt with at all the meetings and special prominence will be given to questions of old age pensions and unemployment.'

All this activity took a toll on Summerbell's health. *The Times* of September 1908 reports him as having to withdraw from a meeting in Leicester, 'owing to illness induced by over-exertion'.

In September 1909, he drew the attention of the Prime Minister to the fact that the nearly 1,000 of his constituents in Sunderland had been struck off the electoral register as a result of having to seek poor relief and being put to work breaking stones. (It is forgotten now, but until well into the last century those on benefit were disenfranchised.) What plans, asked Summerbell, did the Prime Minister have to end this penalisation of poverty? The reply he received was non-committal.

This disenfranchisement of the poor was of more than academic interest to Summerbell since the impoverished represented a significant section of his potential voters. Sure enough, five months later, in the general election of January 1910, Summerbell and his Liberal colleague were defeated by two Conservatives. A month later, aged just 48, he was dead.

Had he lived, Summerbell might have gone on to become as well known as some of his contemporaries. He would certainly have been re-elected to Parliament in the December 1910 election and might eventually have served in the first Labour government, though probably only in a junior capacity. He was at heart a local man, firmly rooted in his community.

For a while his name lived on through his son, also called Thomas, who followed his father onto the council and in 1935 became the first Labour

Mayor of Sunderland. Today, however, Summerbell is a virtually forgotten figure, even in his home town. His house, in Vincent Street, Hendon (about 100 yards from my own), still stands although there is no clue that he ever lived there. His only memorial is a stone cross above his grave in Bishopwearmouth cemetery. If the day ever comes when trams are reintroduced to Sunderland, we could do worse than name the first one after Thomas Summerbell.

Chris Mullin
MP for Sunderland South

Chris Mullin

WILL THORNE, M. P.

*Will Thorne:
Labour MP for West
Ham, 1906–45*

Chapter 25
Will Thorne
1857–1946

WILL THORNE'S life (1857–1946) stretched from before the dawn of democratic politics to the election of the first majority Labour government. The rise of the working-class movement that followed the widening of the franchise owed much to Thorne.[1]

Without a doubt he was amongst the two or three leading trade unionists of his generation. He was outstanding in two ways. Though there were other trade union leaders who supported the principles of 'new unionism', Thorne was unique in his combination of aggressiveness and perseverance. Whereas Tom Mann and Ben Tillett shared Thorne's belief in militant trade unionism and socialism, neither of them had quite Thorne's organisational ability or the single-minded determination necessary to sustain and develop a major union.

Thorne was also extraordinary in the sheer breadth of his achievement. Not only did he, a completely uneducated labourer who had been sent out to work at the age of 6, create an entirely new union, the Gasworkers; but he also carried it through the difficult years until 1910, and expanded it, both through an astonishing growth in membership and by amalgamation, into the great General and Municipal Workers' Union of 1924. He was also a convinced internationalist (attending more Socialist Internationals than any other trade union leader before the 1914 war), was prominent in the first Labour-controlled local authority in Britain, and, most important of all, played a vital part in the creation of the Labour Party. First elected for West Ham in 1906, he combined the General Secretaryship of his union with a seat in Parliament for nearly 30 of his 40 years in the House. Stimulated by Thorne, union members and officials were exceptionally active in politics at all levels, and the union's President, J.R. Clynes, and Chief Woman Officer, Margaret Bondfield, were ministers in both minority Labour governments of the 1920s.

From the beginning, the Gasworkers' Union had definite political and social aims. Thorne's membership of the Social Democratic Federation (SDF) was an important influence on the character of the new union. The

---

1   This chapter is based on E.A. and G.H. Radice, *Will Thorne: Constructive Militant*, George Allen and Unwin, 1974.

previous generation of trade union leaders had been Lib-Labbers, content to work through the existing political system, and their objectives had, therefore, been limited. As a result of his political commitment, Thorne always saw industrial problems in a wider context. He was convinced that it was impossible to make radical improvements in the living standards of his members without changing the political and social system. It was Thorne whom Engels had in mind when, surveying the British trade union scene, he wrote to Laura Lafargue, daughter of Karl Marx: 'These new trade unions of unskilled men are totally different from the old organisations of the working class aristocracy and cannot fall into the same conservative ways . . . they are organised under quite different circumstances . . . In them I see the real beginning of the movement here.'[2]

In one sense, Engels was right. For the logical consequence of Thorne's socialism was trade union participation in politics – an involvement that, by the end of the 1890s, because of the employers' counterattack against the unions, both directly and through the courts, had become even more necessary. Thorne realised that the only hope of change was for the workers to set up their own independent party – preferably one committed to a socialist programme. In the years after 1894, part of his energy was, therefore, concentrated on the creation of a new political force.

The Gasworkers' contribution under Will Thorne to the Labour Party, both locally and nationally, cannot be overestimated. Thorne, who served for many years as a West Ham councillor, was an innovator in local government. Nationally, the role of Thorne as the vital linkman between the trade unions and the socialist groups in the negotiations leading up to the formation of the Labour Representation Committee (LRC) in 1900 has not been sufficiently emphasised by historians.

The Gasworkers played a key role in the development of the LRC. The major unions (the miners, engineers, textile workers and carpenters) did not join at once; the Gasworkers' Union, after the Railway Servants, was the second largest union to affiliate. The union was represented on the Executive of the new body by Pete Curran, who in 1904 was joined by Clynes. Thorne became involved in national politics from early on, and stood unsuccessfully as the parliamentary candidate for West Ham South in the General Election of 1900.

In the run up to the 1906 Election, Thorne had difficulties in his constituency, mainly because of his membership of the SDF. However, he thought that the time had come when the unions ought to support a Socialist and Labour Party of their own. At West Ham he decided to run, as he had in 1900, as a 'Socialist and Labour' candidate. The LRC refused to allow him to do so. A row ensued: Thorne declared that he would stand down, as his own West Ham party, which had a majority of SDF members, wanted him to stand as a Socialist candidate. Clynes attempted to save the situation and a resolution was passed at the Gasworkers' Biennial Congress in 1904, asking the representatives promoting Thorne's candidature in South West Ham to assent to his running under the common title imposed on all candidates supported by the LRC. As Thorne's local party was made up largely of members of the Gasworkers, Clynes thought that they would be amenable to a union directive. However, a special joint delegate meeting representing

---

2   Emile Bottigelli (ed.), translated by Yvonne Kapp, *Frederick Engels, Paul and Laura Lafargue*, vol. 2, Foreign Languages Publishing House, 1959, p. 330, Engels to Laura Lafargue, 17 October 1889.

the unions, the Independent Labour Party (ILP) and SDF in South West Ham declared that they would conduct the election in their own way. Thorne agreed to this saying: 'I cannot very well see my way clear to overthrow the decision of about eighty *bona-fide* workmen, who are prepared to pull off their coats and do everything that lays in their power to secure my return.' An impasse appeared to have been reached. However the union again intervened, and this time was successful in persuading the local party to allow Thorne to stand as a Labour candidate.

Had the union not won the day, Thorne might have had difficulties in winning the seat. The secret pact that MacDonald made with the Liberals in 1903, by which most LRC candidates did not have to face Liberal opposition, meant that the LRC ticket became very valuable. In the end, Thorne had a straight fight and received strong 'non-conformist' support. Though running as a LRC candidate, he issued an unashamedly Socialist manifesto. The electors of West Ham South were exhorted that a vote for Thorne was:

> a vote on behalf of the down trodden and oppressed, a vote on behalf of the famished children in our schools, and of the disinherited in our pauper bastilles; it is a word of hope to the struggling masses in all parts of Great Britain, and of encouragement to all who suffer under the heel of Capitalism; a blow struck for the workers in that war between Capitalism and Labour which must be waged relentlessly until the emancipation of the workers is achieved by the abolition of the Capitalist system.

And the Countess of Warwick, arriving in a red motor car to help in the election, told the electors of West Ham that 'they had a man in Mr Will Thorne who was the envy of the constituency'.[3] The voters responded and Thorne was returned to Parliament with a majority over his Conservative opponent of 5,237. It was the start of a parliamentary career that was to last till 1945.

Fittingly, Thorne's maiden speech in May 1906 was on unemployment. In it, he spoke up for the unemployed of West Ham. Though there is a convention that maiden speeches are non-controversial, Thorne was unable to check his passionate concern for the plight of the unemployed. He said that he was willing 'if the government did not do anything, to advise the unemployed . . . to go and help themselves'.[4] Stirring words indeed! In fact, Thorne had had stage fright just before he began to speak. 'I felt,' he wrote later, 'as though I was chloroformed. Every eye in the House seemed to be fixed upon me. I imagined that everyone's ears were three or four times their normal size and that all were reaching out to catch the words I felt I could never get out of my mouth.'[5]

A year later he again brought up the subject of unemployment, suggesting that the Liberals ought not only to introduce an eight-hour Bill but should bring forward a Bill 'so as to have at hand some machinery by which when a man dropped out of employment he could be picked out at once, because in most cases when men were out of work for a week they were, vulgarly speaking, on their beams ends and had to pawn something to find food

3   *Daily Chronicle*, 13 January 1906.
4   Hansard, 30 May 1906.
5   Will Thorne, *My Life's Battles*, George Newnes, 1925, p. 206.

for their wives, and children'.[6] He spoke with the voice of experience, for
West Ham had, in 1905, gone through the worst unemployment year within
living memory.

By no stroke of the imagination could Thorne be called a conventional
Member of Parliament. Though a great user of Question Time, he was not a
parliamentary orator. When speaking, he resembled 'a boy's clockwork
engine fitted with a good spring wound to capacity and then released before
the engine is placed on the rails. The wheels dash round at amazing speed and
stop when the spring has run down.'[7] He was also given to interruptions and
loud exclamations, and even to whistle-blowing. At times, he expressed
himself in unparliamentary language. One of the best examples of this was in
1909 over the state visit of Tsar Nicholas II of Russia to Britain. Thorne asked
whether the visit would be official, and, on the Foreign Secretary's admission that it was, the following exchange took place:

> *Mr W. Thorne:* I hope he will get his deserts when he gets here. The
> British do not want him.
> *Major Anstruther-Gray:* May I, Sir, call attention to the fact that an Hon
> Member said that when the Tsar of Russia came here he would get
> his deserts? Is that in order?
> *Mr W. Thorne:* I said I hope he would . . . He is an inhuman beast.[8]

An equally controversial exchange took place during the committee stage
of the Finance Bill on 14 July 1909. The debate was heated and Thorne,
sitting next to the Labour MP for Gorton, John Hodge, who was continuously interrupting, suggested to Hodge that 'he had better shut up, for
there's going to be trouble'. No sooner said than Thorne himself was
accused by a Conservative MP of being in no fit state to take part in the
debate. This was too much for the MP for West Ham who, springing to
his feet, shouted: 'I am as sober as you are, my young friend'.[9] Immediately
there were cries of 'withdraw', and Lord Winterton, who had made the
remark, did so grudgingly. Thorne accused him of being a liar, and refused
to take back his remark unless the Tory was prepared to withdraw properly. Whereupon Thorne was asked to leave the Chamber by the Chairman
for using unparliamentary language. It was Thorne who had the last word,
for the episode had a curious sequel. Most Members agreed that Thorne
had been slandered by Winterton, and the Prime Minister, Asquith, therefore asked that the entry of the suspension in the House Journal should be
expunged from the Minutes, making this only the third time that the records
had thus been erased.

If Thorne appeared controversial to his opponents, he also managed, at
times, to have the same effect on members of his own party. One occasion
on which they were aroused, in particular the ILP members, was his introduction of the Citizen's Army Bill in 1908. The SDF believed, in view of
the unsettled state of Europe, that expenditure on defence was a justifiable
outlay of public funds. They also considered that the sooner all citizens
were trained in the use of arms, the quicker their goal of Socialism
would be reached. For only when the workers were armed would there

6   Hansard, 20 February 1907.
7   *Graphic*, 23 May 1925.
8   Hansard, 15 June 1909.
9   Will Thorne, op. cit., p. 207.

be 'a guarantee of individual liberty, of social freedom and of national independence'.[10] Thorne's Bill was in answer to the government's Territorial and Reserve Forces Act, setting up volunteer units in association with, and supplementary to, the Regular Army, which was seen by the SDF as a form of conscription. The Bill's main provisions were that every male between the ages of 18 and 29 would have annual military training in camps, and then pass into the reserves. The citizen soldiers would elect their officers and have full democratic control over them; they were not to be called out to act in any case of civil disturbance or to be mobilised in any emergency other than an actual or threatened invasion. The authority for enforcing and administering the Act would be the city or borough council. Such a revolutionary concept naturally had no support from the government. The ILP, however, were even more vicious in their attack on the Bill, announcing that it was only because the air was full of war-mongering rumours that Thorne had the audacity to 'unbag his little abortion to the public gaze'. His manner 'shows that he rightly appreciates the ungainly character of the nursling committed to his charge'.[11] The Bill made no progress.

In the period before the war, though the Gasworkers played a part in shaping some of the reforms passed by the Liberal government, Thorne was often impatient with the progress being made by the Labour Party in Parliament. In part, it was the frustration of being a member of a small group that was, by force of circumstances, dependent on the Liberals for any success with parliamentary legislation. Thorne's own Bills on the Minimum Wage and the Nationalisation of the Railways did not get far. In part, it was because Thorne's views were more radical than those of many of his colleagues. For example, he opposed the insurance principle of the National Health Insurance Scheme of 1911 because he felt that low-paid workers would not be able to afford the contributions; he also supported George Lansbury when he resigned as a Labour MP and stood as an Independent on the issue of votes for women.

Will Thorne was, and remained, a good constituency MP. But he saw himself primarily as a workers' representative, raising trade union questions and bringing up in Parliament resolutions passed at the TUC Congress. To Thorne, Parliament was an important extension of his trade union activities but it could never be more than that. His trade union came first.

Thorne's whole life was devoted to the struggle to achieve rights for the workers. In the deeply divided and unequal society of his time, it was natural that he should see industrial relations and politics primarily as a class struggle. But, at the start of the 1914–18 war, he was faced with an agonising dilemma. Were there any circumstances in which, despite their deprivation, the workers should give their obligations to the community as high a priority as their battle for their own rights? Although he was an active participant in the international working-class movement, Thorne believed the war did provide such a set of circumstances. Of course, during the war, his union was able to win some very important gains for its members. But Thorne never disguised his view that, to protect Britain from German militarism, workers had also to accept their obligations to their country. During

10 Chushichi Tsuzuki, in Henry Pelling (ed.), *H.M. Hyndman and British Socialism*, Oxford University Press, 1961, p. 203; Harry Quelch, *Social-Democracy and the Armed Nation*, Twentieth Century Press, 1907.
11 *Labour Leader*, 4 September 1908.

the war, he became Colonel of a volunteer regiment, provoking criticism from the pacifist wing of the party, especially Philip Snowden. However, he always believed that, without far-reaching social changes, there could never be lasting industrial peace. As he said in 1915, he did not see how it was possible to harmonise fully the interests of employers and employees under 'our present system of production', by which wealth was so unfairly distributed. He lived just long enough to see the formation of the first majority Labour government in 1945, committed to radical, egalitarian reform.

Tony Banks
MP for West Ham, 1997–2005
(and for Newham North West, 1983–97)
and
Giles Radice
MP for Chester-le-Street, then North
Durham, 1973–2001

Tony Banks   *Giles Radice*

STEPHEN WALSH. M. P.

COPYRIGHT Photo Hill

Stephen Walsh:
Labour MP for Ince,
1906–29

STEPHEN WALSH was born to Irish immigrants on 26 August 1859. His father died shortly before he was born and his mother died before he was a toddler. His first memory was being picked up by a policeman from the steps of St Nicolas Church, Liverpool, and carried off on his shoulders to a home for waifs and strays.

In 1868, the year the TUC was founded, Stephen was admitted to Kirkdale Industrial School where he was lucky enough to receive an elementary education. Now living with an uncle, he excelled in his studies and developed a passion for literature that never left him. He was greatly influenced by Twain, Carlyle, John Stuart Mill, Victor Hugo and above all the works of Dickens, which he described as an 'inexhaustible banquet'.

When he completed his studies at the age of 13 he applied to become a teacher. However the school worried that he lacked the physical stature needed to control the pupils. He left Kirkdale and moved in with his brother who lived in Ashton in Makerfield. There he worked in the pits for 18 years as a ponyboy, a miner and eventually a checkweighman at Garswood Hall Colliery.

He began his working life in the Pewfall Pit, Haydock, St Helens. The wages were meagre, only 10d for a ten-hour working day, and the conditions were unimaginably dangerous. In the Ince Moss Colliery nearby a series of horrific explosions had left dozens of workers dead. Walsh proved an immensely popular figure with his fellow miners. Standing fully grown at 5 feet 1 inch, he became universally known as 'Little Stee'. Many miners were illiterate and poorly equipped to represent themselves against ruthless employers. Stephen Walsh's education, his quick wit and his gift for oratory developed as he regaled his fellow miners with stories he had read. His talents were instantly recognised by his fellow workers and he became a spokesperson for them.

With other activists he founded the Wigan and Makerfield branch of the Lancashire and Cheshire Miners' Federation. In years to come, the founding of this branch would be significant in both industrial and political terms. In 1890 he was elected district officer for the fledgling union and by 1901 he was a full-time officer for the Lancashire and Cheshire Miners' Federation.

His interest in politics grew. He was first elected to the Ashton District Council in 1894, sat on the Co-operative Society Committee and presided over the influential Wigan Trades Council. As a youth he had been an admirer of Gladstone but Liberalism could not satisfy the urgency of the working-class cause as he saw it. Like so many trade unionists of the period, Walsh was coming to the realisation that independent Labour representation was needed to effect the kind of fundamental change that was required.

The Lancashire Federation, unlike other sections of the national Miners' Federation, had been unsuccessful in electing working men through the Liberal Party. After the establishment of the Labour Representation Committee in 1900, the Lancashire and Cheshire Miners' Federation was the first miners' branch to affiliate (in 1903). Frustrated by the local pit conditions, which were viewed as more dangerous than elsewhere in the Lancashire and Cheshire coalfield, the Federation had little hesitation in nominating 'Little Stee' to stand for the seat of Ince in the 1906 election.

The local contest was a microcosm of the struggle that was developing across the country. Walsh's Tory opponent was Colonel Henry Blundell. Educated at Eton and Christchurch, Colonel Blundell owned the very pits in which Walsh had made a living. Standing against him was an act of great courage for that time.

Walsh was a canny organiser. On polling day, the Miners' Federation organised a strike within the coalfield, which helped ensure that everyone who was entitled could get to vote. At the age of 46, Walsh won a majority of 4,636, which was a massive 70 per cent plus of the total votes cast. One can only imagine the sense of joy the miners of Ince and their families must have felt, first at having defeated their wretched employer, and second at having elected one of their own to Parliament. It was to be the first Labour victory in the only seat that has enjoyed uninterrupted parliamentary Labour representation since then.

From 1906 to 1987, the seat had always returned a working miner as the Labour candidate. When I was elected in 1987, I was the first non-miner to be elected, although I had strong connections with the National Union of Miners (NUM) and had been brought up in one of the Scottish coalfields with members of my family who had been working miners.

Walsh, like his fellow 1906 MP Thomas Glover who won in St Helens, owed little to the socialist traditions of the Independent Labour Party, drawing his power and inspiration instead from the solidarity of the Lancashire miners. Nor was Walsh beholden to the 1906 electoral pact with the Liberals as the Tory Blundell had been elected unopposed in 1900. Accordingly, how Walsh cast his vote in Parliament was dictated by life experiences rather than dogma. He supported causes he felt to be just.

In 1908 he successfully introduced a private member's bill that won an eight-hour day for miners. He also pushed through the 1911 Miners Act, which, amongst other measures, improved ventilation in pits, saving the lives of a great many miners.

He supported the First World War, campaigning enthusiastically for conscription. He joined the Coalition government as Minister for National Service even though many of the policies he found himself voting for were reviled by the unions. He stood for election in 1918 as a supporter of the Coalition and its policies even though his own son lost his life in active service earlier that year.

Walsh was a key player in the early days of the new party. In 1906 the national Miners' Federation had overwhelmingly voted against affiliating to the Labour Party, preferring to continue to hedge their bets on the Liberal Party. However, in 1908, inspired by the actions of the 29 Labour MPs, shocked by Taff Vale and moved by a rousing appeal by Stephen Walsh, the Federation balloted on the issue again and decided to affiliate. The eventual support of the miners ensured that only the Labour Party could lay claim to representing the organised working classes. It also ensured that the new party did not fail as had the previous efforts at ensuring independent representation for working people.

Walsh served on the National Executive Committee of the party and was Vice-Chairman of the Parliamentary Labour Party. He was a moderate influence on the fledgling party, often putting the national interest before party or union interests. However, unlike other MPs on the trade union right, he believed that the new party could challenge the political establishment and (supported strongly by his local party) he broke decisively from Lloyd George after a lasting peace was secured.

When the King asked Ramsay MacDonald to form the first Labour government, Walsh's wartime experience made him the automatic choice as Secretary of State for War. Although criticised by some Labour backbenchers for being too close to the Generals, he was recognised as an extremely competent Minister. He was unfortunate to find himself in the middle of a series of crises that brought down that government. A communist had written a prominent editorial calling on soldiers to disobey orders to fire on other workers; the government resisted taking action but Walsh pushed for prosecution. The affair added to the political melee that eventually returned the Conservatives to power.

Walsh remained active in opposition, in particular speaking up for the miners, but he never again enjoyed the same national profile. He died in 1929 just a few months before the next Labour victory. He was survived by his wife Anne, three sons and four daughters and is buried at Holy Trinity Church in Downall Green, North Aston, now in the St Helens North constituency.

Walsh is little remembered today but was much missed in the past. Studying the events of a century ago offers pertinent lessons for today's party. Then, as now, the fortunes of the trade unions and the party were inextricably linked. Then, as now, it was only the Labour Party that could deliver change for working people.

Delivering the eulogy at Walsh's funeral, Canon Raven summed up the significance of the achievements of Stephen Walsh and the other 1906 MPs: 'There are those who claimed that they could not turn poor stock into good, and that they could not get out of a slum, anything but a slum mind. Thank God Stephen Walsh stood as a witness to the fact that both these statements were untrue.'

Little Stee should be remembered as part of a generation that proved that working people are not 'ordinary people' but extraordinary people who can achieve extraordinary things. His was a generation of trade unionists and socialists who overcame massive political and personal obstacles to put their collective values into action. They formed a party that continues to give a voice to the voiceless and offer power to the powerless.

Walsh never lived to see the great achievements of his party – the NHS, the welfare state, the minimum wage – but these were steps on a journey that his generation began. It is not enough only to remember the heroes of 1906. We must honour their memories by showing the same aspiration, ambition and commitment to our timeless common values.

As I researched the life of Stephen Walsh, I was struck by the many coincidences in our lives. Both Stephen and I were elected to the local council before representing the Makerfield and Ince constituency in Parliament, we both married women named Anne, we both lost sons in tragic circumstances and we both stood at 5 feet 1 inch tall.

Ian McCartney
MP for Makerfield

Ian McCartney

GEORGE J. WARDLE. M. P.

*George Wardle:
MP for Stockport,
1906–20*

Chapter 27
George Wardle
1865–1947

T HE POLITICAL CAREERS of many of the Labour movement's historical figures are beset with controversy; the career of George Wardle, poet, preacher, journalist, railway clerk and MP for Stockport from 1906 to 1920, is no different. On his long journey from the factories of West Yorkshire to the beaches of the Sussex coast, Wardle would achieve individual success, secure his place in history at the birth of the Labour Party and be honoured by his country. But he would also face financial and physical hardship, political disgrace in the eyes of his trade union, for whose members he had fought so vigorously throughout his life, and the loss of his religious faith. From being Acting Chairman of the Labour Party from 1916 to 1917, Wardle's death in 1947 was not deemed worthy of mention in the union paper he had edited for two decades.

The second of eight children, Wardle was born in Newhall, Derbyshire, on 15 May 1865. His father, also George, was a collier and later a railway horse-keeper. When Wardle was 8 years old, the family moved to Keighley, in the heart of West Yorkshire's textile country. Wardle was sent to work in a woollen factory, where he spent the first seven years of his working life. He continued to be educated at the Wesleyan Day School in Keighley, but was forced to reject the offer of a scholarship on three separate occasions because the family could not survive without Wardle's factory income. The scholarship, as it transpired, could have cost Wardle the success he was later to achieve, potentially robbing him of the socialisation into nineteenth-century working life that would inspire his career.

The most important and formative years of Wardle's political life were between the ages of 15 and 30, after he followed his father into the railway industry to work as a clerk for Midland Railway. Indeed, it seems unlikely Wardle ever stopped thinking of himself as a railway clerk, even through his career as a journalist, MP, minister and charities campaigner. In his 15 years in the job, Wardle's political beliefs were forged and he became highly active in political life. Amidst the repression and intimidation of trade unionists, which were widespread among management in the railway industry, Wardle was one of the first clerks to join the Keighley branch of the Amalgamated Society of Railway Servants (ASRS), which became the National Union of Railwaymen (NUR) in 1913 after amalgamation with the United Pointsmen and Signalmen's Society (UPSS) and the General Railway Workers' Union (GRWU).

During his time as a clerk, which also saw his marriage to Atla Matilda Terry, he became involved in the co-operative movement and in the Keighley Labour Union, working alongside Philip Snowden, who was elected MP for Blackburn in 1906 and later became Chancellor of the Exchequer in the first two Labour governments. Wardle was the first editor of the *Keighley Labour Journal* in 1893, a post he held for four years. But it was the railways, inevitably, that gave Wardle his first big break in public life. In 1897 he was appointed as the editor of the *Railway Review*, the official paper of the ASRS, on a salary of £3. 10*s*. a week.[1] He edited the *Review* until his appointment as a minister in 1917, and it flourished under his leadership for many years, with circulation reaching 40,000 copies a week.

Alongside an emerging political career, both religion and poetry had, for a time at least, a strong hold over Wardle. A Methodist, he was a both a Sunday-school teacher and lay preacher in early manhood. However, doubts in later years caused Wardle to abandon all formal connections with Methodism. His first collection of poetry, *Problems of the Age and Other Poems*, was published in 1897. The greatest of his passions, his love–hate relationship with the railways, would influence this aspect of his life also: he edited a collection of poems in 1904 entitled, *A Railway Garland*.

Around the turn of the century, at a time when the Labour movement was still attempting to find its proper place in British politics, Wardle had long been an advocate of independent Labour representation in Parliament. He promoted the issue in the pages of the *Railway Review*, and in 1900 he seconded Keir Hardie's amendment in favour of 'a distinct Labour group in Parliament' at the London conference of trade unions and socialist organisations. Although later strongly committed to Lloyd George's Coalition government during and after the First World War, Wardle was adamant earlier in his career about the need for Labour to be strictly separate from the Liberal Party. 'We shall stand by ourselves. If the Liberals wish to help we shall make no objection, provided they don't ask for any alliance. We intend to be a distinct party, and whether hostile or friendly depends on how we are met,' he said after being chosen as the Labour candidate for Stockport in 1903.

In the historic General Election of 1906, Wardle was elected at the head of the poll in the two-member constituency of Stockport. He was joined in Parliament by two fellow ASRS members, Walter Hudson and Richard Bell. Over time, Wardle became associated with the moderate wing of the Parliamentary Labour Party (PLP), with opposition to the positions he took often coming from both his constituency party and his trade union. However, Wardle's opinions on the regulation of the rail industry, always the main focus of his attention, were hardly moderated throughout the entirety of his career.

Wardle was an early advocate of nationalisation, calling for it in his Stockport adoption speech of 1903 and a pamphlet he authored in 1908. Working hours in the industry were a particular concern. This was the subject of his first parliamentary utterance in 1906, in a question to the President of the Board of Trade. In 1907, Wardle tabled an amendment to the 1893 Railway Regulation (Hours of Labour) Act, proposing much stricter controls. Lamenting the industry's refusal to introduce even modest reforms, Wardle quipped: 'The Secretary of War said there was as much superstition in regard to certain things connected with the Army as there was in theology, and so there is as much superstition in regard to the

---

1   Perhaps about £300 a week now.

maximum day for railway employees.' In this debate, Wardle was in direct opposition to his ASRS colleague, Richard Bell, a prominent Lib-Lab Member. Although goals were shared between Labour and Lib-Lab Members, tactics could vary, and so it was in the Bell–Wardle conflict. Bell organised opposition to Wardle's working hours amendment for the Liberal government, aiming to win the favour of rail companies in order to secure union recognition.

Wardle was a tireless campaigner. In 1907, the Railway Clerks' Association (RCA), asked him to act as their representative in Parliament. His popularity in the union, a rival of his own, was high: between 1905 and 1908 Wardle was instrumental in the organisational changes that transformed the RCA into a more effective campaigning force. In Parliament, Wardle pushed for improvements in working conditions for railway workers. Following research showing that clerks were more prone to tuberculosis, caused by poor office environments, Wardle presented the Railway Offices Bill to Parliament in 1912. The Bill called for safe and hygienic working environments, as well as paid holidays, a standard working week of 42 hours, reductions in forced overtime and the abolition of night work for employees under 18 years of age. Although the Bill failed to reach the statute book, the publicity it generated did force some concessions from several railway companies, including Wardle's former employers.

Wardle was a strong supporter of women's rights with regard to union membership, going against the opinions of many trade unionists at the time. In 1915, female staff at the headquarters of the company Great Central Railway had their pay cut after joining a union. The company invoked its policy that employees in 'confidential positions' were not allowed to unionise. Wardle dismissed this as an insult to workers' integrity, and raised the matter in the Commons, as he had been doing for several years. A year after the outbreak of the First World War, the General Manager of Great Central Railway remarked that the whole energy of the House, instead of scrutinising his company, ought to be devoted to killing Germans. But Wardle's credibility, as a fervent supporter of the war effort, could not be undermined so easily. As well as the confrontation in Europe, Wardle declared, 'we ought to kill the Prussianism in our midst'. The company would buckle under the mounting pressure in Parliament and from the RCA directly, and finally allow all of its headquarters clerks to become union members.

It was the First World War, in fact, that became the defining period of George Wardle's career. At the outset, the Labour Party found itself divided once again, with MacDonald resigning from his position as Leader in protest at the party's support for the government. Fiercely patriotic, Wardle backed the war as one for 'freedom, honour, justice and truth'. Although he voted against conscription in Parliament, fearing a disproportionate burden for the working class, Wardle campaigned vigorously for military recruitment. He was made a Companion of Honour for his efforts in 1917. Also in this year, Wardle was given a post in the wartime Coalition government, as Parliamentary Secretary to the Board of Trade. His later refusal to relinquish the job would become, right or wrong, his most memorable act.

The Labour Party conference held at the end of the war resolved to end all co-operation with the Coalition. The eight Labour ministers were advised to leave the government: four complied, but the other four, including Wardle, refused. His union, the newly formed NUR, was furious and withdrew their financial support of him. Wardle was left to rely on allies within the RCA to secure a continued income, although he met reluctance here also. At the 1918 General Election, Wardle stood and won with the Coalition Labour group, for which ten MPs were elected. He remained in the government, moving to the Ministry of Labour in 1919. In 1920, Wardle's branch of the NUR sought to have him expelled from the union, without success. Later that year, the strains of the war years and ensuing struggles had taken their toll on Wardle's health to such an extent that he was forced to resign both his ministerial position and his Stockport seat. He retired to Hove, where he spent the remaining years of his life, becoming active locally in a number of charities. He died on 18 June 1947, survived by his son Reginald and daughter Ella.

Ann Coffey
MP for Stockport

Ann Coffey

ALEX. WILKIE. M. P.
COPYRIGHT Photo Brewis

Alex Wilkie: Labour MP for Dundee, 1906–22

LIFE AND EARLY CAREER

ALEXANDER WILKIE was born on 30 September 1850 at Leven on the coast of Fife. The son of William and Isabella Wilkie, both his parents died while he was still an infant. Alex received a sound elementary education at local schools where he did well winning a number of prizes. Through force of circumstance he left at the age of 13 to become an apprentice in the shipbuilding yard at Alloa. On completing his apprenticeship he followed the custom of the day by going to sea as ship's carpenter. Wilkie would say of those times: 'I had the unpleasant experience of finding myself at sea aboard a "coffin-ship" . . . the owners were surprised, if not pleased, when they heard of our safe arrival in port.'

Among places he visited were the West Indies and South America. He then found employment in Greenock, and later in Glasgow, where he joined the Glasgow Shipwrights' Society. He was very soon elected Secretary in 1872. At that time shipwrights were well organised in local unions in each separate shipbuilding centre.

From his early days as a trade unionist, Wilkie was a vigorous advocate of closer unity among the shipwrights' unions and in 1877 he became General Secretary of the Associated Shipwrights of Scotland. In 1882 he led the establishment of a national union, the Associated Shipwrights' Society, becoming its General Secretary. By the time Wilkie gave evidence to the Royal Commission on Labour in 1892, membership was nearly 12,000. He estimated that there were a further 4,000–5,000 shipwrights organised in local unions but still outside his national organisation.

Wilkie's industrial attitudes were typical of the majority of trade unionists during the closing decades of the nineteenth century. As he wrote much later, he worked all his life 'for conciliation and peace'. He supported the successful attempt in 1890 by Robert Knight, Secretary of the Boilermakers, to combine 13 unions into the Federation of Engineering and Shipbuilding Trades. The main aim was the resolution of inter-union conflicts, especially over matters of demarcation disputes and collective bargaining rights.

On the issue of strikes Wilkie favoured the formation of courts composed of equal numbers of employers and trade unionists with a neutral Chairman. He was strongly against any government compulsion. With the experience of the largely ineffective Conciliation Act of 1896 Wilkie began to argue for a larger degree of government control over arbitration procedures. It was the failure to persuade either employers or government to accept more positive arrangements that helped to push Wilkie like so many moderate colleagues into support for an increased independent Labour representation in Parliament.

Wilkie visited the United States twice. His first visit in 1899 as the TUC delegate to the annual conference of the American Federation of Labor (AFL), the second as a member of the Mosley Industrial Commission in 1902.

WILKIE'S ENTRY INTO POLITICS

Wilkie had first been appointed to the Parliamentary Committee of the TUC in 1890–91. He served again from 1895 to 1903 and then from 1904 to 1909. During 1897–98, he held the role of Chairman. He was one of the main architects of the General Federation of Trade Unions established in 1899 and he was a leading figure in the founding conference of the Labour Representation Committee (LRC) in February 1900.

Wilkie was prominent among the group of Lib-Lab trade unionists of the TUC Parliamentary Committee who were anxious to diminish the role of the Socialists in the new projected Labour Party. However the establishment of a Parliamentary Fund by the LRC in 1903 was a major contributory factor in ensuring the independence of their group. Each union would thereafter raise a voluntary levy of 1p per affiliated member to be paid into the LRC fund. By 1904, societies covering more than half the affiliated membership of the TUC had sent in contributions for the Parliamentary Fund. At this point the Executive of the LRC made the contributions compulsory and retrospective thus establishing a distinct separation of the LRC from the TUC Parliamentary Committee: in effect the birth of the modern Labour Party. All LRC candidates had to sign the party pledge to secure the election of candidates to Parliament and to organise and maintain a Parliamentary Labour Party.

Wilkie was on the Executive Committee of the LRC until 1904. This position together with his membership of the Parliamentary Committee meant that he was in a strong position to encourage a 'moderate' approach to problems of the day. Wilkie had stood as Labour candidate for Sunderland in the General Election of 1900, the invitation coming from Sunderland Trades Council. It was a two-member constituency and Wilkie fought the election from the same platform as Liberal candidate G.B. Hunter of the shipbuilding firm Swan and Hunter. Each failed to win by a narrow margin. Wilkie would however retain a close association with the North East.

Six years later Wilkie stood as LRC candidate for Dundee, another two-member constituency. This time he faced two Liberals and two Unionists – the latter modern-day Conservatives. In his personal manifesto he made no claims to be a radical Socialist, espousing free trade and the free exchange of commodities. He called for a system of free education and a universal old age pension. Curiously his only direct reference to 'Labour' was in relation to foreign policy where he commended Labour's commitment to international peace and to amity and friendship with all nations.

ELECTION TO PARLIAMENT

Wilkie's 1906 campaign was impressive. The calibre of his organisation, a committee of 400, hierarchically organised from ward level with a Central and an Executive Committee, was both admired and criticised by opponents and commentators alike. The *Dundee Advertiser* went as far as to state that Wilkie was not to be congratulated on 'the use of novel and sensational electoral methods that belong rather to England than to Scotland and does not improve our political atmosphere'. Yet Winston Churchill, who would be elected as Liberal MP for Dundee in 1908, later mimicked his methods and challenged him for his industry.

Dundee was a two-member seat with eligible voters casting two votes each. Evidence points to early tactical voting that would become commonplace in the constituency. Wilkie shared 3,183 votes with one of the Liberal candidates yet only 124 with the other. In analysing the results, only 37 per cent of the voters had supported the two Liberal candidates and 19 per cent the two Unionists. Nearly 20 per cent had backed Robertson, the sitting Liberal MP, and Wilkie together while 16 per cent had plumped for Wilkie alone. These 'plumpers' as they were colloquially known would later come to form the core for Wilkie's electoral support. Wilkie's ultimate victory came from the support of 6 per cent who also voted for a Unionist, causing the Liberals to comment '1,000 Unionists, anxious to cause a diversion in the Liberal ranks, deserted their party for that of Labour'. History has questioned the true sentiment of that claim, and events to come would prove it a hollow outcry.

Local commentators had thought Wilkie's election improbable and had argued that a vote for him would only damage the Liberals and help the Unionists. Some suggested that the practice of holding elections in stages throughout the country had advanced Wilkie's cause. Undeniably, when at last Dundee went to the polls, 21 Labour MPs had already been elected nationally. Yet Alexander Wilkie remains the first Labour MP elected in Scotland – an achievement of note and a significant marker for the party's political fortunes north of the border.

In subsequent elections Wilkie would become in the eyes of many an effective running mate of the Liberal Churchill. When Labour ran a candidate against Churchill in the Election in 1908, Wilkie did not support this. He claimed that he had been against a Labour candidate in the interests of the Labour Party and that Labour had no right to ask for more than a share of the representation of the city. In 1918, 80 per cent of those who voted for Wilkie also voted for Churchill – the two halves of the Dundee constituency. After 1908 as long as Wilkie stood there was only one Liberal against him: in effect, a pact.

In a curious twist of fate one of the Unionist candidates defeated by shipwright Wilkie in 1906 was Lieutenant Ernest Shackleton. The budding explorer had sailed with Captain Scott to the Antarctic on RRS *Discovery*, a vessel built on Dundee's River Tay, and recently restored to the City of Discovery as part of its 800th anniversary celebrations.

DUNDEE'S POLITICAL RADICALISM

To understand Wilkie you must understand Dundee. The politics of Dundee were driven by the burgeoning jute industry, the harsh impact of the city's geographical isolation and the predominance of the working class in its demography. Dundee had been Liberal since the creation of its parliamentary seat in 1832. Whereas by 1900 in other great Scottish cities Unionism was eating into Liberal support, in Dundee Liberalism held firm. Wilkie's 1906 victory was one of only two seats the party won that year in Scotland. Incredibly it was one of only three the party would hold north of the border before the First World War. Yet Wilkie's success came amidst a new political radicalism that would begin the process of building the base for Labour's eventual successes in the 1920s and beyond.

By 1910 Dundee was recognised as the 'least Liberal city in Scotland'. By 1922 – the year of Labour's electoral breakthrough across Scotland – Dundee was far more left wing than any other city: with half voting Labour, Prohibitionist or Communist compared to a third elsewhere in Scotland. Early advances had been slow. Both the Independent Labour Party (ILP) and the Scottish Party had polled badly for Westminster and failed to put forward candidates for municipal elections. Dundee's first LRC municipal representative elected in 1905 challenged this and set a train. Labour movements were not politically backward but lacked the organisation and numbers to advance change. Economic and social dependency on the jute mills and the often harsh attitudes of owners were obvious factors in resisting change. Indeed many of the 'Jute Barons' stood as Unionist and Liberal candidates in Dundee's municipal and parliamentary elections.

Change would come quickly to Dundee through a volatile combination of new political ideologies and a growing sense of 'class'. The relative strength of the Liberals over Unionism and the clear association both had with the jute industry proved a fertile breeding ground for Labour. By the time of Wilkie's 1906 election Labour support was substantial and eating into the Liberal powerbase. Wilkie's previous experience in working with the Liberals, his trade union background and willingness to seek new electoral 'arrangements' rather than direct confrontation may well have helped Labour ride the tide of political change.

TROUBLES A-PLENTY – PROHIBITIONISTS AND A WORLD WAR

The Dundee constituency had, as one study put it, 'an evil reputation for drunkenness. The innumerable public houses with their stale stench of beer, sawdust floors, spittoons, and salt fish kept on the counter by the publican to give his customers a thirst, promised a brief illusory comfort and accordingly did a roaring trade'. At weekends 'police were kept busy with their specially constructed wheelbarrows carting away the casualties after the battles had subsided'. Even Churchill who was progressive in his approach to social problems would comment 'he had never seen parallel to any part of the United Kingdom' of such 'bestial drunkenness'.

Just as Labour had used municipal elections to build support, so too did those seeking to address the problems of alcohol and the social damage it caused. Within the Temperance Movement nationally, Dundee was inseparably associated with the Scrymgeour family. James the father was a Unionist and dismissed by many as an eccentric, but it was his son Edwyn, a man who had flirted with Socialism and the Independent Labour Party prior to forming the Scottish Prohibition Party, who would eventually have a major impact on politics in Dundee for the next 20 years. The curious nature of municipal representation in Dundee at the time meant that business acumen, reputation, social character and participation were as important as political allegiance. Scrymgeour and his supporters made great use of this becoming a constant irritant in Wilkie's side.

During the First World War Wilkie had supported the British Workers' League and voted for conscription. A 'patriot' to some, he faced considerable opposition for his actions. By 1918 the combined pressures of divisions within Labour support, the increasing influence of the prohibitionist

Scrymgeour and the impact of war found Wilkie in a precarious position. In the 1918 election campaign, the fiercely patriotic *Dundee Advertiser* referred to the 'good Britishers' Churchill and Wilkie condemning 'all the Bolsheviks and pacifists of the city' arrayed against them. Wilkie was even heard at meetings to urge voters to give their second vote to candidates who had helped to win the war, a clear call to support Churchill. One commentator reported remarkably that 'Churchill accompanied by Wilkie, was given a rousing reception at each of the polling stations' visited on election day 1918.

WILKIE AND THE JUTE WORKERS

With his strong trade unionist background Wilkie was a natural supporter of the jute workers in Dundee. In 1908 he played a major role in the establishment of the Jute and Flax Workers Union. In doing so he developed a close working relationship with John Sime, its Secretary Organiser from 1908 to 1940, and a man regarded by many as the most powerful figure in Dundee's working-class history. Wilkie also played a high profile role in helping to resolve a number of industrial disputes for the jute workers and for the local shipbuilding unions.

The workforce of the jute mills consisted mostly of women and children, neither of whom had the vote. Sime would however ensure that strong union support for Wilkie in the 1906 and 1910 Elections would carry him to victory. In the 1918 Election women were given the vote, a fact that would be reflected in the substantial increase in Wilkie's support. Thereafter the rapidly changing face of Labour politics in Dundee began to undermine his position.

It will never be known if the support of women voters would have carried Wilkie to victory in the General Election of 1922. He announced his retirement in 1920 and was succeeded in the Commons for Labour by E.D. Morel. With his retirement, Labour – and Sime in particular – were free to enter battle with the Liberals on a more traditional Socialist platform.

THE LATER YEARS

For the remainder of the 1920s Wilkie continued trade union work despite worsening ill-health. Not long before his death he was succeeded as General Secretary of the Shipwrights' Association by W.F. Purdy. Many decades later, through a process of amalgamation, the union Wilkie had done so much to shape would become the General, Municipal and Boilermakers Union. In keeping with the contradictions of his earlier political career Wilkie deplored the General Strike of 1926 and counselled his members to remain at work.

Wilkie had always been involved in local affairs wherever he lived. In his Glasgow days he had served for many years as a delegate to the Trades Council. When he moved to Newcastle in 1900 he served for a number of years on the School Board. In 1904 he was elected to Newcastle City Council where he paid special attention to education. All through his time as MP for Dundee he retained close links with the city and the North East. In 1912 he was made a magistrate in the city of Newcastle and in 1917 he became a Companion of Honour. On leaving national politics he returned to Newcastle where he was made an alderman.

Wilkie married Mary Smillie, the daughter of a labourer, in 1872. She died in 1921 leaving Wilkie and their only son, William, who was a draughtsman. Wilkie himself died on 2 September 1928 at his home in Heaton, Newcastle, where he was subsequently laid to rest. He left effects valued at £11,302.

WILKIE'S ACHIEVEMENT

One hundred years on it is difficult to be overly critical of the 29 MPs elected for Labour in 1906. We currently enjoy a third consecutive Labour administration and a highly developed and diversified economy where rights, freedom and opportunities for all are basic expectations. The contrast for Wilkie and his peers is stark and daunting. It is difficult to imagine the problems that faced each of them at that time. Alexander Wilkie is by no means a stellar figure in the history of the Labour movement. Some might question whether he was in fact a true believer in the principles of our great movement at all. But therein lies a key to his and Labour's achievement.

Wilkie was a pragmatist who fought hard to win his seat, and harder still to keep it. He made enemies, lost friends, kept the occasional strange bedfellow and utilised every available political shenanigan to build and maintain his majority. He did all this to advance a broad social and political agenda to benefit his constituents. He fought the clamour of a belligerent press, vested business interests resisting demands for improved workers rights and a political establishment deaf to the needs of ordinary people. He also survived 16 years in the political maelstrom that was Dundee.

Alexander Wilkie was in many ways a thoroughly modern politician. As much Old Labour as New Labour, as much Lib-Lab as fierce trade union advocate, he took from the Right, the Left and the Centre. Wilkie could be parachuted into any era of Labour politics of the last century and sit comfortably with all around him. His achievement mirrors that of Labour: fixed principles, diversity of ideology and background, fluid and creative willingness to move and adapt with the times. Above all, a determination to make the life of the weakest and poorest better.

Ernie Ross
MP for Dundee, 1979–2005

Ernie Ross

W. T. WILSON. M. P.

COPYRIGHT PHOTO CROSBY

W.T. Wilson: Labour MP for West Houghton, 1906–21

Chapter 29
W.T. Wilson
1855–1921

WILLIAM TYSON WILSON was one of the 29 working men elected as Labour MPs in 1906. He became the 'Handy Man of the Labour Party', so named as he, 'did not mind what he was called on to do if it was for the betterment of the people'.[1]

Wilson, a carpenter by trade, was a senior figure within the union movement before standing as the Labour candidate for West Houghton[2] in 1906 when he ousted the incumbent Conservative (and Postmaster General), Lord Stanley, with a 3,128 majority. He retained the seat in both elections in 1910 and again in 1918, representing the constituency of West Houghton until his death in 1921.

As an important and popular figure within the newly formed party, Wilson's work gained cross-party recognition and respect. By 1915 his seniority and experience of the parliamentary system were rewarded when he became a Labour Party Whip and again in 1919 when he was appointed Chief Whip. His commitment to justice for all was similarly recognised in 1909 when he was appointed a JP for Lancashire.

Wilson was born on 8 December 1855 in Undermillbeck, a village in Westmorland in the Lake District, where his father was a Master Tailor. Apprenticed as a carpenter and joiner in Hawkshead, Wilson later practised his trade in various towns in Lancashire. As Wilson matured, he found that he had more than an in-depth knowledge of the practicalities of his trade; he also had a great understanding of the issues that affected people in the trade's workforce.

By the time Wilson had settled in Bolton in 1889, he was actively involved with the trade union movement. The establishment of the Bolton Building Trades Federation (BBTF) in the 1890s is testament to this as he was an influential founding member. He also took a leading part in establishing the Central and National Conciliation Board for Settlement of Disputes in the building trade. Wilson's involvement with the BBTF led him to represent the Federation's views to the Bolton Trades Council, of which he later became Vice-President.

---

1   *Bolton Journal and Guardian*, 10 January 1919.
2   The area now known as Westhoughton was known at this time as West Houghton.

In 1893, he was elected to the Executive Council of the Amalgamated Society of Carpenters and Joiners (ASCJ) having been a member since 1877, when his interest in union affairs was sparked by his time in Barrow-in-Furness. He became the Chairman of both the General and Executive Councils of the ASCJ from 1898–1906, and was appointed as the National Chairman in 1910. Wilson represented the ASCJ at the TUC as well as at several meetings of the Ship Building and Engineering Trades Federations, travelling all over the UK assisting in the settlement of disputes.[3]

With his background in championing the rights of working people within the union movement, Wilson was a natural candidate for public office. In 1902 he stood in the Bolton municipal elections, although this first election campaign ended unsuccessfully.

In 1905 the ASCJ sponsored three candidates including Wilson who was nominated by the Labour Representation Committee to stand for the very mixed constituency of West Houghton; it surrounded the town of Bolton but also included the borough's freeholders:

> The largest town, Horwich, contained the extensive locomotive works of the Lancashire and Yorkshire Railway Company; but West Houghton itself and two smaller towns, Aspull and Little Lever, were engaged in mining and Turton had cotton interests. There was an important but declining agricultural vote. Until after 1900 this was a safe Conservative seat; and although the Bolton freeholders and the agricultural vote might have contributed to this, much of the Conservative support must have come from the industrial working class.[4]

Wilson understood the uniqueness of the constituency's make up and recognised that a Labour candidate representing working people could remove the incumbent Lord Stanley. The Conservative, in his capacity as Postmaster General, had been attacking working people, describing postal workers as 'bloodsuckers' in the Commons on the 6 July 1905.[5] When Wilson attended the opening of a Labour Club in Wingates, West Houghton, he spoke to the party's activists as their newly selected candidate, saying that he could assure them they had no small thing on hand and he and a good many others would have fought shy of a contest in such a division as that. There had, however, been a great Labour awakening in the past few years and there would be a great struggle when the election came, so he hoped that, when the results were known, they should be able to congratulate the West Houghton Division on a most memorable and glorious victory.[6] Wilson recognised that the working-class electorate would be willing to support a Labour candidate if they truly believed that the candidate would work hard for their rights.

One of the central themes within the 1906 Labour Party manifesto[7] was that the House of Commons should represent the views of the population, and that the most democratic way to achieve this would be for ordinary working people to sit there: 'The House of Commons is supposed to be the people's House, and yet the people are not there.' It also questioned

---

3   M. Stenton and S. Lees (eds), *Who's Who of British Members of Parliament, Volume III, 1919–45*, Harvester Press, 1978, p. 386.
4   J. Bellamy and J. Saville (eds), *Dictionary of Labour Biography*, vol. 3, Macmillan, 1976.
5   *Bolton Journal and Guardian*, 7 July 1905.
6   *Bolton Journal and Guardian*, 19 May 1905.
7   See Appendix.

why Labour was not represented in Parliament as '[l]andlords, employers, lawyers, brewers, and financiers are there in force. Why not Labour?' Why not Wilson? In Wilson they had a candidate who advocated a 'system of Government which would give everyone who wished to work an opportunity of working and would also give the producers of the wealth of the country a fair share of the wealth they produced'.[8]

Wilson's views and those of the Labour Party did not go unchallenged. An article in the *Daily Chronicle* on 17 January 1906 urged readers not to vote for Wilson saying that a vote for him:

> Is a vote for Home Rule and separatism. It is a vote for Godless education in Elementary Schools. It is a vote for the spoliation of the church and the weakening of religious life of the country. It is a vote for a man who has played fast and loose with the licensing question and tried to play Jack-on-both-sides. It is a vote for an aggregation of men who have disgraced the Division by resorting to methods of rowdyism and hooliganism and a campaign against freedom of speech and thought.[9]

Wilson's emphatic victory surprised even his most ardent supporters as well as Wilson himself, as he did not believe every ward had been fully prepared for the election campaign. But when the crowds gathered to receive the election results outside the Town Hall it was evident that Wilson was their clear favourite with Lord Stanley's supporters in a distinct minority. As the votes were counted, there was a chorus of:

> Good-bye Stanley dear, good-bye
> Good-bye Stanley dear, don't cry
> You're a bloodsucker so true
> And we've had enough of you
> Good-bye Stanley dear, good-bye.[10]

As soon as the result was declared Wilson said: 'I attribute my victory primarily to the determination of the workingmen . . . Lord Stanley's attitude towards trade unions has made the workers have no trust in him, and the manner in which, as Postmaster General, he treated the postal employees, has had a certain weight'.[11]

As the news of Wilson's victory spread throughout the borough there were reports of men cheering until they were hoarse, shaking each other by the hand and throwing their hats and canes in the air. One reporter even noted that 'for some minutes everyone seemed to be mad with delight'. Wilson's supporters, who had congregated at the Starkie Arms, saluted the Conservative Club with red and white favours before they walked along Tonge Moor Road with 'boisterous enthusiasm', disturbing many households. The reporter witnessed windows being thrown open and the occupiers making enquiries as to the result of the poll: 'Who's won?' cried a female voice, 'Wilson' came the reply, which was greeted with 'hooray'. Another Wilson supporter said: 'By gum . . . Stanley won't forget this in a hurry.'[12]

  8 *Bolton Journal and Guardian*, 17 August 1906.
  9 Extract from the Wilson family biography.
 10 *Bolton Journal and Guardian*, 21 January 1906.
 11 Ibid.
 12 Ibid.

The new MP began his career as a parliamentarian in earnest with the issue of school meals. Wilson's direct involvement with the Education (Provision of Meals) Bill, of which he moved the Second Reading on 2 March 1906, is remembered as one of his greatest achievements. It was the first time that Wilson was recorded in Hansard, but as the reporting of debates was not verbatim it cannot be said with certainty that this was his maiden speech. The Education (Provision of Meals) Bill aimed to ensure that school children who went without food or who were undernourished received some form of nourishment whilst they were at school, so they would be able to focus on their studies. The Bill, which received Royal Assent on 21 December 1906, created the earliest form of school meal service. The Bill was described as the high point of Wilson's career and it was deemed that the Bill's final enactment was the result of his 'skill and patience'.[13]

On a more local level, Wilson's commitment to the provision of meals during a working day for all was demonstrated by him opening the first canteen in Bolton dedicated to the needs of working people. He felt that, from a business point of view, money spent on feeding children and workers would be wisely invested as they would be 'better equipped for fighting the battle of life',[14] and also in the years to come the expenditure on asylums, workhouses and prisons would be considerably reduced, therefore the money invested would be returned with interest.

Wilson's interest in education did not end with school meals; he was also concerned about how schooling was delivered. In 1909, he spoke at the Bolton Co-operative Society's fiftieth anniversary celebration saying that education should be provided by the local council and the burden should not rest solely on the shoulders of the Co-op.[15]

When in his constituency, Wilson was a regular feature in meeting halls, attending as many as his schedule would permit and speaking about a wide variety of issues from the state subsidising trade to the reform of the House of Lords. He spoke about the latter on numerous occasions throughout the constituency, saying at one such meeting:

> It was high time that the people of the country considered whether the present system of a second chamber was satisfactory. Under the existing conditions the Conservative Party (and he did not wish to say anything which was offensive to any party) were always in power, for the simple reason that the Conservatives were in the majority in the House of Lords and they could either amend or reject Bills sent up by the House of Commons.[16]

Wilson went on to say that he would vote in favour of abolishing the House of Lords.

Wilson regularly earned praise in a daily column in the *Bolton Journal and Guardian* called 'local chat', which recorded the daily 'goings on' in the Borough of Bolton. The comment section, which recorded the voice of local people, regularly said that Wilson had a wealth of support, had a genuine character and worked tirelessly for the people in his constituency. For example during the 1918 election campaign 'local chat' recorded that:

13 *Bolton Journal and Guardian*, 15 August 1908.
14 Hansard, Education (Provision of Meals) Bill Second Reading, 2 March 1906.
15 Information found in Co-op papers held by a current member.
16 *Bolton Journal and Guardian*, 15 November 1909.

'Mr Tyson Wilson is not afraid of work and has a deep sense of duty he owes to the electors and even when there is little possibility of a contest [in the 1918 campaign] he was going round the constituency and giving an account of his stewardship.' Noting that the supporters of Wilson's Conservative opponent were in 'a rather cock-a-whoop mood', it continued that it was doubtful they knew what they were up against, given the level of support that Wilson commanded.[17] In that year's election address, Wilson said to the people of West Houghton:

> If you are in favour of a higher Standard of Life for the people of this country, and securing for them the full fruits of their Labour, if you are against going back to the old condition of semi-starvation wages, then I ask you to give me your support. Thanking you for the confidence you have reposed in me in the past, and hoping to retain it in the future.[18]

It is evident that Wilson worked tirelessly in the Commons for his constituents as well as for the working people of Britain. His involvement with committees and debates is recorded in Hansard and the sheer volume of entries is impressive. He clearly pursued certain priorities including the provision of school meals, trade union matters, pensions and pension rights, the Post Office and anything affecting West Houghton. Nevertheless, he did not allow these core interests to command all his time, but diligently attended to the whole spectrum of issues raised in the House with equal vigour. A reporter noted:

> Altogether the Honourable member has driven home from first to last several hundred notes and queries. From Birmingham to Bermuda, from Bolton Post Office to Bristol Telegraph Office, from Glasgow shipbuilding to Glasgow telephoning, from Chatham to Devonport, he has carried the House of Commons; work in the dockyards and wages in the Post Office, income-tax assessment and magisterial delinquencies, have all alike received the attention of our political Argus of West Houghton.[19]

Wilson was well liked and respected throughout Parliament, his local paper recording that: 'The selection of Mr Tyson Wilson as Chief Whip of the Labour Party is welcomed by everybody and it is safe to say that never was an appointment more popular even amongst those politicians opposed to him.'[20] However, the Wilson family biography notes 'for all his good qualities [he] lacked the ruthlessness which was necessary to make a success of that job'.

His family remembers that one of his strongest characteristics was as a man of great integrity, with a true understanding of social responsibility, and that he was always willing to involve himself in unearthing the wrongdoings of public figures. One observer noted: 'It is only necessary to glance at his voyages in troubled waters to see how full the world is of wrong doing in the shape of tyranny and spoliation.'[21] Clearly Wilson was never

17 *Bolton Journal and Guardian*, 6 December 1918.
18 Wilson's 1918 election address was found amongst family documents.
19 *Bolton Journal and Guardian*, 24 December 1909.
20 *Bolton Journal and Guardian*, 10 January 1919.
21 *Bolton Journal and Guardian*, 24 December 1909.

afraid to stand up for his beliefs, his great grandson likening him in contemporary terms to the late Lord Wigg for his role in identifying malpractice. Leyland Booth refers to an incident where Wilson was responsible for revealing the unethical appointment of Miss Douglas Lee Pennant by her lover in the Royal Air Force, Sefton Branckner.[22]

Reflecting on Wilson's work as an MP for West Houghton for 15 years, his trade union experience had not only stood him in good stead for a successful parliamentary career, but had also influenced the parliamentary questions he asked and the points he raised in debates, becoming affectionately regarded, 'throughout Parliament as the mouthpiece of the carpenters' interests'.[23]

Wilson's commitment to his working background, his constituents, the Labour Party and, of course, his family placed a heavy burden upon him and ultimately on his health. When William Tyson Wilson died suddenly of a heart attack on 14 August 1921, the Coroner said that Wilson was:

> a gentle man who commanded the highest respect and esteem. One might almost say he had died in harness, though possibly his anxiety to do his duty caused him to work when otherwise he would have been resting. The country had indeed lost a man whose sole endeavour was to do his best not only for his own constituency but for his country generally.[24]

The Coroner's words were echoed by Wilson's family as his dedication and commitment to being a Labour Party MP often spilled over from the office and into the family home. Leyland Booth remembers that his 'Grandmother [Wilson's daughter, Gertrude] often recalled times when Keir Hardie and other Labour pioneers took over the family home, along with constituents . . . [but] although life was hectic, she always supported her father'. That support was necessary when the family was separated because of his parliamentary duties. Wilson himself admitted, to an audience at the Carnegie Hall in West Houghton, that he had been, 'reluctant to leave London as he believed it was his job as a parliamentarian always to be there when the House was sitting'.[25]

When Wilson died, his loss was felt deeply within West Houghton. People who knew him or knew of him saw him as a 'man of the people' but not one who 'craved a great share of publicity'.[26] Although Wilson did not wish to be in the public eye, after his 15 years as an MP he had found a place in the hearts and minds of the people he represented. Furthermore, he achieved cross-party recognition: both the local Conservative and Liberal Clubs had their flags at half-mast when they heard the news of his death.

The Labour Party's annual report eloquently summarises Wilson and the impact he made, as well as the legacy he left:

> Our own immediate Executive membership has suffered the loss of Tyson Wilson, one of the few of our ranks who have come straight from the workshop to Westminster and who pursued his daily work in

22 Leyland Booth, Wilson's great grandson who still lives in the area, assisted in the writing of this biography. His assistance is greatly appreciated.
23 *Bolton Journal and Guardian*, 24 December 1909.
24 *Bolton Journal and Guardian*, 19 August 1921.
25 *Bolton Journal and Guardian*, 1 November 1909.
26 *Bolton Journal and Guardian*, 19 August 1921.

Parliament during the last fifteen years much in the spirit of that same workshop . . . He remained a labouring man to the end as straight and fearless in Committee with his friends and colleagues as he was across the floor of the Commons with the Government powers that be.[27]

William Tyson Wilson, remembered today as a 'great man' and a 'labour pioneer', was survived by his wife Frances Tyrrell, whom he married in 1882, one of his four sons, Arthur, and his daughter, Gertrude.

The values that Wilson advocated in his first election in 1906 still ring true for me and the party today. Wilson and the other 'founding fathers' are an inspiration to all of us who continue with the Labour Party's journey, working hard to represent the British people in the 'people's House'.

Ruth Kelly
MP for Bolton West

Ruth Kelly

27 Labour Party Annual Report, September 1922.

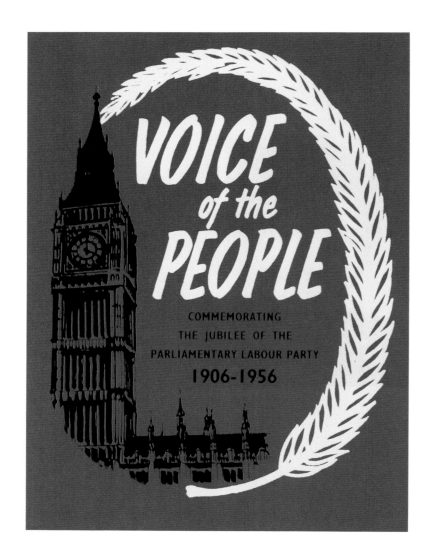

The original front cover of Voice of the People

Voice of the People[1]
50 Years of the Parliamentary Labour Party

ONE DAY IN 1892, so the story goes, when Keir Hardie, newly elected independent Member for West Ham, arrived at the House of Commons wearing the famous cloth cap, a policeman halted him at the entrance. Roof repairs were in progress and the constable pointed round the corner to the workmen's entrance. 'You working on the roof, mate?' he asked. 'No, on the floor, mate' replied Hardie laconically. And the small, squarely-built figure passed into the precincts to continue his lonely job as 'member for the unemployed'.

To the elegant members of the Government and Opposition benches Hardie was regarded as a rare and, they hoped, temporary curiosity who could at best be relied upon to provide those very necessary and most welcome diversions from the gentlemanly boredom of the debates. What they saw was a bearded, shaggy figure in a blue serge suit who could certainly have taken his place with the workmen on the roof. They could not see beyond him.

What they heard on his entrance to Parliament was the quavering note of a solitary cornet playing the 'Marseillaise'. What they did not hear was the drum-roll of history.

'A SPLOTCH OF RED'

Indeed, Sir William Vernon Harcourt, a Cabinet Minister who occasionally expressed that rare and dangerous quality among politicians, a sense of humour, once genially referred to Hardie's presence in the House as 'the little splotch of red from West Ham'. The phrase was taken up aptly by the rhymester of Hardie's paper, the *Labour Leader*, in the following prophetic lines:

> A splotch of red. Sir William V.
> Only a little splotch of red
> Your friends sit back and broadly smile

1 This is a very slightly edited version of the original, which was produced by the Labour Party for the Golden Jubilee of the PLP in 1956.

As you the weary hours beguile
With little jokes – but time will be
When you'll not treat so jestingly
That tiny little splotch of red.
A hearty, healthy little splotch
And growing fast, full firmly bent
On turning out the fools that sport
With simple men and women's woes
Your office is your only thought
Your friends but on their seats intent.
Think you it can be ever so?
Sir William V., we tell you, no;
And all your mocking Parliament.

For James Keir Hardie was the precursor of the mightiest single event of the British Parliament. Fourteen years later, in 1906, before an astonished and incredulous House, he led 29 Labour men on to the floor of St Stephens. Overnight Labour had become a living political power. The little group of four Members in 1905 had been replaced by a strong and determined Parliamentary Party. The 'little splotch of red' had become a vivid banner. The old Labour Representation Committee, which had blazed the trail to this great climax, ceased to be. The 'committee' had become a great political movement. The Labour Party was born.

The victory was hailed with joy and expectation in the homes and workplaces of all Labour's well-wishers, but no one dreamed then that the famous 29 – a sevenfold increase over their previous parliamentary strength – were merely the advance guard of an even greater army. Behind the victory, so bravely won, there was a long, proud and often tragic history that reached back through the centuries; a story of tremendous trials, effort and faith; of victory and bitter defeat; of courage and betrayal; a story of the human suffering of men and women for the right to live decently and freely; for the right to share fairly in the wealth they produced and to secure the future and happiness of their children. A story in which the weapons of want, poverty, imprisonment and transportation had been wielded mercilessly to crush the spirit of freedom. It was ever a story of struggle, and more often than not a story of defeat, but now the first great victory had been won. Britain's Parliament, so long the prerogative of the rich and privileged, was at last to hear the voice of the people.

A PROPHECY

Immediately the great news was known, there was an irresistible movement from every part of the country to celebrate the tremendous event. Socialists, trade unionists and co-operators flocked to London to a great demonstration on 16 February 1906, at which Arthur Henderson declared amid terrific enthusiasm: 'What has been too long a capitalist citadel is now going to be made not only a Commons' House, but a house of the common people'. And Hardie added: 'The sleeping giant is awakening, and in days to come, in the very near future, Labour will be the dominant factor in politics, not only potentially but actually and in fact'.

It was no idle prophecy. Thirty nine years later Labour swept into power with a massive majority, pledged to lay the foundations of socialism in Britain. Today [1956], despite temporary setbacks, Labour stands as the greatest political movement in the country and the most powerful social democratic movement in the world. At the 1950 General Election it polled more votes than any party had ever polled before. In 1906, it was the size of the Labour vote, as well as its representation, which shook the capitalist parties. The Labour poll was 323,195 – 37% of the total poll in the seats contested.

And now the great names, which have long been written into our history, began to claim public attention. With Hardie (elected for Merthyr Tydfil) came Henderson at Barnard Castle, MacDonald at Leicester, Jowett at Bradford, Snowden at Blackburn, Shackleton at Clitheroe, Clynes at Manchester NE, Crooks at Woolwich, Thorne at West Ham South, Bowerman at Deptford, Barnes at Glasgow, Hodge at Gorton, Walsh at Ince and 16 others who were to make their mark. They may not have known it then, for they were nearly all raw and untried in Parliament, but they made as powerful and tough an opposition team as any government has had to cope with for many a long year. Hardie was elected Leader, with Shackleton as his deputy, MacDonald was secretary of the party, but in his absence on a colonial tour, Henderson combined the duties of secretary with his own function as Whip.

The modest resources of the new Labour Party at that time allowed for only a very small permanent staff. Two young men were the principal assistants who were destined to serve the party faithfully and well throughout the whole course of their working lives until within a year of its greatest triumph in 1945. They were H. Scott Lindsay who in 1906 was appointed Assistant Secretary of the Parliamentary Party until 1918, when he became Secretary; and James Smith Middleton who was Assistant Secretary at Head Office from 1903 to 1934, when he succeeded Henderson as Secretary. Both retired in 1944.

THE TEST

The new and enthusiastic parliamentary group faced an endurance test of the most severe kind. Would they be able to operate as a single independent group, or would they become 'a tail of the Liberals' as many newspapers unkindly suggested? There were many precedents for Labour-Liberal co-operation including a resolution moved by Hardie at the 1900 Conference, which declared for a policy which would 'embrace a readiness to co-operate with any party which for the time being may be engaged in promoting legislation in the direct interest of Labour, and be equally ready to associate themselves with any party in opposing measures having an opposite tendency'.

An amusing altercation followed the moving of this resolution. Hardie, supported by Wardle and Wilkie, argued that it laid down the principle of a completely independent Parliamentary Labour group; others took the view that it did the exact opposite. Burns shouted bewilderedly: 'I want to know where we are now'. 'The Memorial Hall', a chorus of voices replied. 'I know that perfectly well', snapped Mr Burns, his sense of humour deserting him, 'But I want to know where we are in this debate'. So did a good many others. The matter was straightened out by a revised statement at the 1903 Conference which declared for a 'distinct group in Parliament, with its own whips and its own policy on Labour questions to abstain strictly from identifying themselves with or promoting the interests of any section of the Liberal or Conservative Parties'.

After a year of work, Hardie was able to report: 'We have supported the Government and opposed the Government just as we deemed the interests of the workers required'. Labour was determined to be a completely independent party 'without adjective or qualification'.

THE MINERS COME OVER

The party's unity of purpose made a deep impression on the Miners' Federation whose MPs had been elected with the support of the Liberals. And in 1909 the Federation affiliated to the party. Now Labour truly spoke with the voice of the people. It was a power to be reckoned with in everything that the Liberal Government did and, by the next election in 1910, Keir Hardie could point to many progressive measures in which Labour had taken the initiative or backed with their powerful support. Meals for school children, old age pensions, the Miners' 8-Hours Act and the Labour Exchanges Act were all measures which laid the foundations for the dramatic social advances of later years.

In the autumn of 1909 there were ominous signs that the House of Lords intended to reject Asquith's budget, and the Labour Party immediately began to lay plans to fight the coming election on a wider front. The miners were in the party now, and their strength brought the total of Labour candidates up to 78. Labour emerged from the 1910 election with 40 MPs, 16 of them miners, a net loss of five seats which, in the circumstances of the new and growing organisation, was regarded as a satisfactory result. Later in the same year a second election came as a surprise to the party. This time Labour had a net gain of two seats although only 56 were contested.

THE HATED JUDGMENT

'We were severely handicapped both by the old register and the financial impediment which the Osborne Judgment placed in our way', the Executive Report declared. Despite an extremely difficult and exhausting year, the Labour Party entered the new Parliament with an even greater zest than on previous occasions. They were determined to reverse the hated Osborne Judgment which ruled that a trade union could not spend money in support of the Labour, or any other, party. So long as the law remained unaltered, all the long effort to secure an alliance of unions and socialists for lawful parliamentary action appeared doomed.

Hardie set the keynote for the campaign in a characteristic statement which went right to the heart of the matter. 'If the Labour members were being paid by brewers or landowners, or railway directors, or financiers, to represent their interests in the House of Commons', he said, 'no objection would have been taken. It is only because they are being paid to represent an interest which is dangerous to all the other interests that the issue is being forced upon us'.

The agitation reached such a pitch that the Liberal Government agreed to a Bill to reverse the judgment, but was unwilling to go as far as Labour demanded. There was a two years' delay and it was not until 1913 that the Trade Union Act became law and permitted trade unions to engage in certain political activities.

LABOUR ON THE MARCH

The door to progress was opened once more – not wide – but at least open, and Labour, with its rightful resources now available, prepared to fight the next contest with renewed strength. At the same time, the women's suffrage movement had reached the peak of its dramatic campaign for votes for women. Labour was closely allied with the movement, through the Women's Labour League, which was founded in the same year as the Parliamentary Party. The *Daily Herald* was struggling to life, while the Socialist International added to its prestige by organising a 'War Against War' Conference at Basle.

Labour was on the march. But others were marching too – the German Army. The tragic outbreak of war in August 1914 had a shattering effect on the Labour Movement, both nationally and internationally. By tradition pacifist in outlook, most of the ILP members could not support the war in any circumstances. Keir Hardie took this view, and others, while not being outright pacifists, did not feel that Labour had any part in an imperialists' war, and wanted only an end of hostilities and a negotiated peace. MacDonald resigned the chairmanship of the Parliamentary Committee and turned to journalism and the ILP. At the stormy meetings he addressed, he used Wordsworth's famous lines:

> Were half the power that fills the world with terror
> Were half the wealth bestowed on camps and courts
> Given to redeem the human mind from error
> There were no need for arsenals or forts.

But the majority of Labour MPs, though opposing the foreign policy that led up to the war, took the view that with the country in peril their duty was to help to ensure a successful and speedy end to that dire and bloody event.

Henderson took this line and became Chairman of the Parliamentary Committee in MacDonald's place. From this moment, the tide of events flowed swiftly. With the collapse of the Socialist International and the mounting crisis of the war, Labour was faced with a momentous decision. A Coalition Government was formed in 1915 and Labour was invited to participate. Henderson accepted the post of President of the Board of Education with a seat in the Cabinet, and two other Labour MPs, W. Brace and G.H. Roberts, were given appointments. Thus, less than ten years after its formation in Parliament, Labour took its part in the government of the country.

Hardie, who had believed implicitly in the power of the workers of all countries to counter and stifle the outbreak of war by declaring a General Strike, was so shocked by the turn of events that he took no further part in parliamentary debates. His life was spent, his work done, and in his 60th year, in the second month of the second year of the Great War which he had tried so desperately to avert, he died.

Criticism of Labour's action came from many quarters but it proved the undoubted ability of Labour men, and stood the party in good stead when, after the war, the great 'Coupon Election' of 1918 was rushed upon the nation. Labour won 57 seats and nearly 2¼ million votes. A fair result considering the many divisions that the war had caused within the movement.

LABOUR REORGANISES

In this election MacDonald and Snowden, who had opposed the war, went out. Henderson accompanied them. In the later stages of the war, he had clashed with Lloyd George over a proposed international socialist peace conference and resigned. Urgent work awaited him in the confused situation in the party. While Empires were tottering in Europe, and Russia rocked with revolution, Henderson applied himself quietly to the immediate need of reorganising the party on a national basis with individual membership and constituency organisation as we know it today.

In the same year the party adopted and issued its first detailed socialist programme, 'Labour and the New Social Order'. It was the work of Sidney Webb, representative of the Fabian Society on the National Executive.

THE OFFICIAL OPPOSITION

Three years later the 1922 election brought its reward. Labour emerged with 142 members and achieved the distinction, even before it had come of age, of becoming His Majesty's Official Opposition. The party reverted to its old Leader, Ramsay MacDonald, who had been returned in the election, and a turbulent Parliament faced the Tory administration of Bonar Law.

GOVERNMENT

General elections fell thick and fast in those post-war years. There was yet another in 1923 — a fateful one for Labour. This time the representation reached another record with 191 members. The Liberals had restored their position to 158, but the Tories dropped to 258. A combined Labour-Liberal vote on the Address defeated them and MacDonald was called upon to form the first Labour Government in Britain's history.

It was a government without power and dependent for its majority on the Liberals. It is hardly surprising that it was not permitted to survive for very long. But here it was. A government of socialists grown up from nothing in half a lifetime. Jack Lawson, who with Attlee worked under Stephen Walsh, the first socialist War Minister, has this to say of it:

> When we think of the gallant unknowns of the 19th century who assailed the conditions then prevailing, only to go down in defeat, we know in truth how fortunate we are who have lived to see a Labour Government. There were strange doings in Britain in those days, and particularly in that official part of it which had ruled us all, but was no longer official. There they were, the owners of land, banks, factories, pits, ships — one might almost say the possessors of the great places of learning — there they were, dazed with the thing that had happened, as though something had gone wrong with the laws of nature. From century to century they had ruled, wealth and possessions the token of their right; Westminster the abiding place of their power. And now — tinkers and tailors, to say nothing of sailors, sat in their places. Then the enemy recovered — the Campbell case and the Zinovieff letter revived them. What they were about would mean nothing to the reader — in fact they meant nothing to anybody. But you should have heard the row, and didn't they scare the wits of folk — including the workers.

You have to see a political panic to believe it. So beware of the ghost.
It will surely walk again – at midnight.

Labour lost seats in the stunt 'Red Letter' election of 1924, being
returned with a total of 151 members, but its poll increased by more than
a million votes.

In came the Tories under Stanley Baldwin, determined to stifle the
growing power of Labour. The single event which distinguished that indifferent administration was the great General Strike of 1926. Baldwin thought
he could call the bluff of the unions who had threatened a general stoppage
if the government carried into effect its intention to remedy the crisis in
the coal industry by wage reductions and an increase in the weekly working
hours. But on 30 July 1925, the leaders of the railway and transport
workers issued notices to refuse to handle coal after midnight on 31 July.
The issue of the notices had an electric effect on the Prime Minister who
beat a hasty retreat and granted a further nine months of subsidies to the
mining industry.

The nine months of grace which the Tories had obtained for themselves
were deliberately used as a period of preparation for the inevitable conflict
with Labour when the subsidies were exhausted. When the time came, the
government was fully prepared for the emergency and the battle was joined
at midnight on 4 May 1926. A State of Emergency was declared and the
government moved in with full powers to crush the strike and then introduced the vicious Trade Disputes Act of 1927 which crippled the industrial
power of the unions and aimed a murderous blow at the Labour Party
finances. It was not until 19 years later that the Act was repealed by the
first majority Labour Government.

THE SECOND LABOUR GOVERNMENT

But the sands were running out for the reactionary and vacillating Baldwin
Government. In 1929 came the reckoning. Labour won 287 seats in the
general election, and although still in a minority position was, for the first
time, the biggest single party. Again Ramsay MacDonald formed a government, relying on the Liberals – only 59 of them this time – to keep Labour
in office.

In America and Europe the last act of a great drama was being played
out. The post-war industrial boom had come to an end. Unprecedented
speculation in industrial and financial securities resulted in a fall in prices
and profits in the autumn of 1929 and the American economic structure
collapsed.

TRAGEDY

Distrust, unrest and financial depression spread throughout Europe. Hitler
scored a spectacular victory at the German Election of 1930, increasing his
Nazi strength from 14 to over 100 members. In Britain, growing concern
within the government led to a serious division of opinion between Ministers
and three of Labour's leaders – MacDonald, Snowden and Thomas – who
went over to the Tories and formed a 'National' Government. This was a
black year for Labour. At the bitterly contested election in 1931, the party
suffered the greatest blow of its history, dropping in strength from nearly
300 seats to a mere 46. The most serious loss was in the defeat of its leader,

Arthur Henderson. But the vote held well; even in this time of extreme adversity the party still commanded the loyalty of nearly 6½ million voters.

After the terrific strain of his work throughout the foundation and development of the British Labour Movement, Henderson fell ill and in 1935 he died, leaving a record of service to the growth and organisation of the Labour Party which has no equal. In the year before his death, he was awarded the Nobel Peace Prize for his widely-recognised services to the cause of disarmament and peace in which he so passionately believed.

THE RISE OF ATTLEE

By this time, Hitler and his Nazis were in the saddle in Germany. His acts of naked aggression were an open invitation to the Fascists in Italy and Japan to follow suit. The Labour Party campaigned strongly for action to halt the brutal audacities which, if unchallenged, could only end in another world war. But Lansbury, who had succeeded Henderson as Leader, was a sincere and convinced pacifist. He found himself more and more at variance with the official policy of the party and was unable to continue as Leader. Clement Attlee was elected in his place and was almost immediately faced with leading the party into a general election at the end of 1935.

With four changes of leadership in so short a period, Attlee had the double task of establishing himself as a Leader, in the eyes of the party and the public. Not long after the 1935 election in which the party recovered some of its lost ground with the return of 154 Members, he published his *Labour Party In Perspective*, which left no doubt as to his socialist convictions.

LABOUR AND SOCIALISM

'It is necessary to bear in mind the historical position of the Labour Party', he wrote. 'It is not the creation of a theorist. It does not propagate some theory produced in another country. It is seeking to show the people of Great Britain that the socialism which it preaches is what the country requires in order in modern conditions to realise to the full the genius of the nation'. Within five years he was Deputy Prime Minister.

The march of events which led to Labour's historic decision to join Churchill's war administration need not be itemised. What happened in those critical years has left its mark upon the lives of all of us. Under Attlee's leadership after 1935, Labour stuck determinedly to its faith in collective security as the only guarantee of peace, but, ironically, it was in the fire of war that the implements of the future socialist administration were forged. With Attlee as deputy to Churchill, Bevin as a powerful Minister of Labour, Morrison equally successful as Minister of Supply and later Home Secretary, Alexander at the Admiralty, Greenwood as Minister without Portfolio, Dalton as Minister of Economic Warfare (among whose assistants was a vigorous and determined young Labour candidate named Hugh Gaitskell) and Jowitt as Solicitor General, the Labour representation in the Coalition established a sound reputation for wise and efficient administration.

BRITAIN'S GREATEST GOVERNMENT

Labour's solid work in the difficult days of the war Government, combined with the great revulsion against the disastrous record of pre-war Toryism, resulted in a magnificent Labour victory at the 1945 election. Forty years of struggle, hard work, great joys and great sorrows lay behind that memorable day in July 1945, when Clem Attlee arrived at Transport House to be told by Morgan Phillips (who had succeeded Middleton as General Secretary of the party) that Labour was in power with 393 seats, an overall majority of 147. Attlee's reaction was characteristic. He looked at the results and murmured one word: 'Good'.

The feelings of those who had fought, thought, worked and prayed all their lives for this day could not adequately be put into words. Appropriately enough, the programme on which Labour had been elected bore the historic tide of 'Let Us Face The Future'. That phrase, more than any other, summed up the spirit of the new and powerful Parliamentary Party which took its place on the government benches in August 1945.

With its new young Secretary, Mr Carol Johnson, who had been appointed after Scott Lindsay's retirement in 1944, and Willie Whiteley and his team of Whips, the new Parliamentary Party embarked upon a gigantic programme of legislation which was without precedent in parliamentary history. To say that the first majority Labour Government worked hard is an understatement. The pace was terrific, and at times got so hot that the Tories yelled for mercy. Legislation was framed and passed in record time, bringing the basic industries of the nation into public ownership: coal, electricity, gas, civil aviation, the railways, road transport, steel as well as the Bank of England. A great Agriculture Act was introduced.

On the massive foundations of the National Insurance Acts, National Health Service Act and the National Assistance Act, the great edifice of the Welfare State began to rise. Within a few years it was a going concern and an established part of our social life, which, while Labour remains strong, no reactionary government dare destroy. Housing, education, family allowances, new towns, new and re-deployed industries all took their part in the programme. Justice cannot be done to this record in such limited space, nor can a mere list of Acts of Parliament tell the story of Labour's tremendous work for the development of the Colonies, and the conferring of freedom and independence upon India, Ceylon and Burma. Suffice it to say, in this brief tribute to the party in Parliament which carried a truly tremendous task to a successful conclusion, that Britain's first majority Labour Government has written a new and proud chapter in the history of our land which has gained the respect and admiration of every free nation throughout the world.

ADVERSITY

It is perhaps characteristic of the turbulent and chequered history of Labour in Parliament that, after achieving an unprecedented record of beneficial legislation in the most difficult and exhausting circumstances of post-war Britain, the 1950 Election brought Labour's majority down from 147 to a mere six. The Tories, who had learnt a bitter lesson in 1945, spent their five years of Opposition in assailing the Labour Government for all the temporary privations which were the inevitable result of the material exhaustion and financial bankruptcy which followed the war. However, that is the way of democracy.

Attlee carried on until October 1951. In this election, economic factors told heavily against Labour and the Tories came in with a majority of 21 and reaped the benefits of the gruelling spade-work which the two Labour Governments had put in. They carried on while fortune favoured them, but as soon as their own Tory-made difficulties began to beset them they rushed to the country in May 1955, with the notorious 'sunshine' budget which distributed largesse in return for a favourable verdict at the polls. Now Nemesis is overtaking them. But that is another story.

Now, after 20 years of splendid service as Labour's Leader, Earl Attlee has been succeeded by Hugh Gaitskell, and the party is preparing for a victory at the next election that will open the way to a further advance towards the final goal of socialism.

JUBILEE

And so we have come down the arches of the years to the party's Jubilee in Parliament, with 270 Members in place of the original 29, and 12½ million votes in place of the original 323,000.

Let us look back over the way we have come. Many names have been missed, many events, great at the time, obscured by the demands of space. It is fitting to return to the source of all our strength, all our past and all our future, for every MP has been a candidate, perhaps against hopeless odds, every candidate has been an ordinary party worker on the doorstep, the street corner and in the cold committee room, sharing in the toil of the ordinary members who have always provided the spirit, the purpose and the very life of our party.

Ben Hanford, an old socialist, once coined the name 'Jimmie Higgins' to personify the Trojan spirits who carried the socialist banner everywhere and never sought reward, and of whom he wrote:

> Jimmie Higgins never had a front seat on the platform; he never knew the tonic of applause nor the inspiration of opposition; he never was seen in the foreground of the picture. But he erected the platform and painted the picture; through his hard, disagreeable and thankless toil, it had come to pass that liberty was brewing and things were doing. Jimmie Higgins. How shall we pay, how reward this man? What gold, what laurels shall be his? There's just one way, reader, that you and I can 'make good' with Jimmie Higgins and the likes of him. That way is to be like him.

And so to Labour men and women everywhere who have given so much of their lives to build up Labour's strength in Parliament, to that great and valiant band of pioneers and defeated candidates whose names have passed unsung into oblivion, and to the comrades who now carry the banner, this tribute is sincerely and humbly addressed.

Labour's Early Days

By Lord Shepherd

A Sallon Caricature produced by courtesy of the "Daily Herald"

N.C.L.C. PUBLISHING SOCIETY LIMITED
TILLICOULTRY, SCOTLAND
(Publishers for the National Council of Labour Colleges)

PRICE ONE SHILLING

The original front cover of Labour's Early Days

Labour's Early Days[1]

By Lord Shepherd[2]

BIRTH OF THE PARTY

IN 1945, NEARLY 12 MILLION PEOPLE knew the Labour Party sufficiently well to elect it with a majority to form an independent Labour government. Hundreds of thousands of people know the party intimately, even though a large proportion of them secured their knowledge by practice rather than by study. Very few people, however, have much knowledge of the party's early days and the factors that brought it into existence. Here we set out the most interesting features of the period during which the party took shape.

The middle classes, in the Reform Act 1832, secured the first fruits of 19th century political agitation, but their working class supporters had to wait until 1868 and 1884 for their enfranchisement in the towns and the counties respectively. Afterwards, the trade unions, still influenced by their old associations with the radical reformers, made their earliest attempts to secure working class representation by arrangement with the Liberal Party. It was not until 1909 that the Miners' Federation of Great Britain, the last of the big unions to do so, broke away from the old traditions and affiliated to the Labour Party for complete independence in politics.

Notwithstanding the tendency of the unions to secure representation in Parliament as the poor relations of the Liberal Party, there came into existence during the 1880s two socialist organisations which had great influence on working class opinion. They were the Social Democratic Federation (SDF), with the full doctrine of Karl Marx, and the Fabian Society, which sought, by permeation, to influence the Liberal Party into a more generous mood, and to provide programmes for the unions which the Liberal Party might be persuaded to accept. In 1893, the Independent Labour Party (ILP), pledged to socialist principles and bitterly critical of the Liberal Party, took its rise at Bradford. Its chief aim was to lead the organised workers to complete independence by the creation of a working class party, both in

---

1   This is a slightly edited version of the original, which was published by the NCLC in 1950.
2   Lord Shepherd, as George Shepherd, was for many years the National Agent of the Labour Party.

and out of Parliament. The ILP soon captured the imagination of most active spirits in the unions and, as a result, resolutions in favour of independent political action appeared on the agenda of the Trades Union Congress (TUC). Eventually, at the Trades Union Congress of 1899, the following resolution was adopted by 546,000 to 434,000:

> That this Congress, having regard to its decisions in former years and with a view to securing a better representation of the interests of labour in the House of Commons, hereby instructs the Parliamentary Committee to invite the co-operation of all the co-operative, social-istic, trade union and other working organisations to jointly co-operate . . . in convening a special congress of representatives from such . . . organisations as may be willing to take part to devise ways and means for securing the return of an increased number of Labour Members to the next Parliament.

The sentiment in the Congress was strikingly in favour of the motion, only two speakers taking the floor against.

The administrative authority of the TUC was vested in a Parliamentary Committee. The title is indicative of the political aspirations of the unions associated with Congress. It would be a mistake to assume that the trade unions had no political outlook or sphere of political activity prior to the establishment of the Labour Party. They clearly had, but the idea behind the Parliamentary Committee was that the work should be undertaken, not on the green benches at Westminster, but in the lobbies of the House of Commons. The work of the Committee covered such matters as the Shops (seats) Bill, Old Age Pensions, Half-Timers' Bill, Amendment to Compensation Act, Miners' Eight-hour Bill, Workmen's Cheap Trains Bill, Boilers Inspection and Registration Bill, Bakehouses (Hours) Bill, Early Closing (Shops) Bill, Steam Engines and Boilers (Persons in Charge) Bill, Watermen's Bill, Anchors, Chains and Cables Bill, and other questions, including Electoral Reform, Taxation of Ground Values, Banking of Trade Union Funds, Sweating in the Public Service, Amendment to Factory Act, and Victimising of Railway Servants.

The Parliamentary Committee, as directed by Congress, convened a special Conference on Labour Representation in the Memorial Hall, London, on 27 and 28 February 1900. 129 delegates, appointed by 69 organisations, with a total membership of 568,177, considered an agenda drawn up by: Sam Woods MP, W.C. Steadman MP, Will Thorne, C.W. Bowerman and Richard Bell representing the Parliamentary Committee; Keir Hardie and Ramsay MacDonald, from the ILP; R.H. Taylor and H. Quelch, the Social Democratic Federation; and E.R. Pease and George Bernard Shaw, representing the Fabian Society.

There is no published report of the discussions of this committee, but it can be inferred from its composition that the agenda which emerged was an attempt to secure the greatest common agreement possible, and that may account for the tentative and timid nature of the items which were included. There were amongst the committee Liberal-Labour men, Marxist doctrin-aires, permeaters and political independence men. That such a committee actually got down to writing out an agenda is one of the most surprising things in the Labour Party's history. The first resolution submitted to the Conference read:

> That this Conference is in favour of the working classes being repre-sented in the House of Commons by members of the working classes

as being the most likely to be sympathetic with the aims and demands of the Labour Movement.

The resolution is merely an expression of opinion in favour of the working class being represented in Parliament by members of the working class themselves. It is hard to conceive of anything less ambitious. Clearly, it was an attempt to keep men of incompatible views in something like marching order. However, subject to an amendment moved by the Engineers to add 'whose candidatures are promoted by one or another of the organised movements represented by the constitution, which this Conference is due to frame', it was carried by 102 votes to 3.

The principal discussion of the Conference centred round a resolution:

> [I]n favour of establishing a distinct Labour Group in Parliament, who should have their own Whips and agree upon their policy which must embrace a readiness to co-operate with any party which, for the time being, may be engaged in promoting legislation in the direct interest of Labour and be equally ready to associate themselves with any party in opposing measures having an opposite tendency.

The resolution was challenged from the extreme right and the extreme left. The Social Democratic Federation moved a resolution in favour of a Parliamentary Group separate from the capitalist parties and having for its ultimate object the socialisation of the means of production, distribution and exchange, and empowered the Parliamentary Group to formulate its own policy for practical legislative measures in the interests of Labour. The resolution, whilst proposing co-operation with other parties in Parliament, nevertheless bound the Group to recognise the full implications of the class war.

The Shipwrights, on the other hand, proposed that the Labour Group should have a platform of four or five planks, embracing questions upon which the vast majority of workers could unite, but that, outside of those questions, the members of the Parliamentary Group should be left entirely free on political questions.

It soon became clear that the original resolution could not secure unanimity – but it was also obvious that the motions of the SDF and the Shipwrights could not secure a majority. So it was left to the ILP, through Keir Hardie, to put forward an amendment to the original resolution by the addition of the words 'and further, members of the Labour Group shall not oppose any candidates whose candidature is being promoted in terms of resolution 1'. After some debate, Hardie's amended resolution was carried unanimously and thus provided for the establishment of the first Parliamentary Labour Party (PLP).

The Committee of the conference proposed that the business of the conference, and of any subsequent conference, should be reported annually to the TUC, and to the annual meetings of the national societies connected with the Committee. The effect was to make the Labour Representation Committee (LRC) not an independent political party, but an organisation subsidiary or ancillary to the TUC. Although objection to this procedure was entered by G.N. Barnes of the Engineers, the proposal was accepted by the Conference, but it did not continue in operation very long. The development of propaganda and the extension of electoral activities rapidly gave to the LRC a status of its own.

There was one other resolution of the first Conference. The Railwaymen proposed that Trades Councils should be invited to send delegates to the next Conference on the basis of one delegate for every 25,000 members affiliated to each Council, and on payment of an affiliation fee of £5 for each 25,000 members. The resolution was amended to include Co-operative Societies, and was agreed by 218,000 to 191,000. To-day it is difficult to appreciate the attitude of the minority. One may wonder how Labour's representation was to be secured in Parliament if there existed no electoral machinery to carry the candidates to victory in the constituencies. The time had not yet arrived for the establishment of Constituency Labour Parties, and the first conference had no alternative but to seek the assistance of the Trades Councils for organising the electorate.

Much of the conference business was transacted in a happy-go-lucky way and the lack of ordered procedure showed little promise of future stability. This was especially the case in the appointment of the Secretary of the LRC. John Ward of the Navvies enquired whether Mr Woods, then acting as Secretary of the Parliamentary Committee of the TUC, would undertake the work. This was found to be impossible, because Woods' trade union had not sent representatives to the Conference, and the Conference remembered that Woods was a Liberal MP. Mr Brocklehurst, of the ILP, suggested that two secretaries should be appointed, but met with no support. John Hodge of the Steel Smelters moved that Brocklehurst himself should act as Secretary, *pro tem*, but Brocklehurst declined and nominated Ramsay MacDonald who was elected unanimously.

The selection of MacDonald, casual as it seemed, was perhaps the most important decision taken by the Conference. Perhaps no other man could have brought such influence and power to the Secretaryship of the LRC in the early years. His very presence, his splendid voice and his grasp of affairs, coupled with ability of the highest order, lent to the Labour Party a leadership and direction which attracted, quite apart from the active spirits within the movement, millions of citizens to support of the party's programme. Not many people appreciate the importance of the decision which appointed MacDonald to such a post at such a time.

The first Conference of 129 delegates was rich in strong personalities. Amongst the delegates were the enlightened leaders of the union movement, whose battles on the industrial field had given them character only noticeable in men who have been through bitter struggles. No less than 26 of the delegates were afterwards to reach Westminster and, of these, MacDonald became Labour's first Prime Minister; Snowden Labour's first Chancellor of the Exchequer; Barnes a Member of the War Cabinet, 1914–18; Hodge the first Minister of Labour; Jowett, the Minister of Works; and Clynes became Home Secretary.

James Keir Hardie and Richard Bell of the ASRS entered Parliament almost immediately. Hardie became the pioneer leader of working class independence in the country, and after 1906 Leader of the Labour Party in Parliament.

W.C. Steadman, who presided over the Conference, and at the time sat in Parliament as a Liberal-Labour MP, was Secretary of the TUC, but he was not to join the Parliamentary Party. John Burns, then an MP, was to become the first working man to enter a British Cabinet as a Liberal. Richard Bell, the cause of much early trouble in Labour's political ranks, ceased quite early to be recognised as a Labour Member of Parliament.

Amongst others who later achieved prominence were C.W. Bowerman, the future Secretary of the TUC; James Sexton of the Liverpool Dockers; Ben Tillett of the Dockers; Will Thorne and Pete Curran of the Gasworkers, and Alex Wilkie, who united a multitude of local Shipwright Societies into a powerful trade union.

THE FIRST CONFERENCE

The Labour Representation Committee, elected in February 1900, had hardly got into its stride before it was confronted with the khaki general election of the same year. The Committee was ill-prepared for the contest and, as the unions were backward in selecting their nominees, a national challenge to the old political parties could not be made.

The Committee decided that it could support only those candidates run by affiliated Labour organisations and that, whilst it would be no bar to a candidate that he was receiving the support of either of the non-Labour political parties, his candidature was not to be promoted by either of them, and that he would accept the conditions laid down by the London Conference.

The constituencies contested, and the candidates approved by the LRC, were:

Derby	Richard Bell
Merthyr	J. Keir Hardie
Gower	John Hodge
Sunderland	Alex Wilkie
West Ham	Will Thorne
Blackburn	Philip Snowden
Bradford	Fred Jowett
Halifax	James Parker
Leicester	Ramsay MacDonald
Manchester, S W	F. Brocklehurst
Preston	J. Keir Hardie
Bow & Bromley	George Lansbury
Ashton	J. Johnson
Leeds (East)	W.P. Byles
Rochdale	A. Clarke

Hardie was nominated for two constituencies – a privilege which no longer exists. Two candidates were elected, the protagonists respectively of political dependence and political independence: Richard Bell (Derby) and J. Keir Hardie (Merthyr). Most of the candidates polled remarkably well, with a total Labour poll of 62,698, out of an aggregate poll in the 15 constituencies of 177,000. Given the war time circumstances, and the fact that no local organisation existed, the results were very satisfactory.

The LRC issued the first of a long series of election manifestos, but its total national expenditure amounted to no more than £33.[3] This very trifling sum was looked upon as exceptional, and in the Committee's report to the first Annual Conference, lest the delegates should think there had been extravagance, the expenditure was referred to in an apologetic note. The modern conception of an electoral campaign had not been thought of at the turn of the 19th century.

Bell and Hardie were not the only working class representatives sent to the 1900 Parliament. There had been elected, chiefly by individual union enterprise, nine other working class MPs. They did not, however, owe allegiance to the LRC and, although the relations of the nine with Bell and Hardie were cordial, the nine did not accept the whips of the organised movement.

It will be useful to recall earlier parliamentary representation. In the 1874 Parliament, following the first election with the parliamentary franchise

---

3   Perhaps the equivalent of £3,000 in 2006 values.

being given to working men in the Boroughs, two miners – Thomas Burt and Alex MacDonald – were returned. In 1880, they were joined by Henry Broadhurst. Following the 1884 enfranchisement of working men in the counties, the number of working class representatives in the Commons gained headway slowly: 1885: 11; 1886: 9; 1892:15; 1895:12; 1900:9.

The figures indicate the fallacy of the view that the chief hope of working class representation depended on accommodation with other political parties, and they furnished the principal propaganda for the advocates of political independence which led to the TUC decision to convene the London Conference in 1900.

The first annual conference of the Labour Representation Committee took place in Manchester in 1901 when the Committee reported the following affiliations:

	membership
Trade unions	339,577
Trades Councils	94,000
Fabian Society	861
Independent Labour Party	13,000
Social Democratic Federation	9,000

There were 82 delegates. The Co-operative Movement had decided not to join in the attempt to build up an independent political party and was therefore unrepresented.

MPs received no payment from the State, and the maintenance of Labour Members gave rise to much discussion. The Fabian Society moved:

> That the Conference expresses general approval of a scheme for a Labour Members' Maintenance Guarantee Fund . . . and instructs the Executive Committee . . . to assist in its formation . . . .

The ILP moved an amendment to delete the words after 'Fund' and to add 'but considers the time is not ripe for the Executive Committee to assist in its formation'. The amendment was carried by 227 votes to 106. The Social Democratic Federation then attempted to establish of a special sub-committee to arrange the details of a scheme of maintenance, but this resolution fell.

However, the subject was of too much importance to be shelved. In the following year at Birmingham, the Executive Committee were instructed to prepare a plan for submission to the 1903 Newcastle Conference, where approval was given for the establishment of a Maintenance Fund. The Fund was provided by a levy of 1d (one penny) per member on national organisations and, after the Fund had accumulated a sum of £2,500, payments were made not exceeding £200[4] per annum, to each MP whose organisation had contributed its share. The Fund was something more than payment of relief to existing MPs. Its principal effect was to extend the choice of candidates by bringing to selection conferences men of merit, irrespective of their own wealth or that of their promoting organisations. It had an equalising result consonant with the principles of a party forming the spearhead of democracy.

The ILP was especially active in the first annual conference, and it commenced the work of converting the movement to a socialist programme,

---

4   Worth between £16,000 and £17,000 in 2006.

employing its big propaganda guns. Philip Snowden introduced a resolution on municipal trading, John Penny a resolution on electoral reform, Joseph Burgess a resolution on imperialism. All were carried unanimously. The big discussion took place, however, on another ILP resolution, on 'Collectivism', moved by Bruce Glasier, which read:

> This Congress . . . recognising that the inevitable tendency of privately owned capital is towards combination in monopolies known as Trusts, is of the opinion that the ownership and control of such vast aggregations of capital by private individuals are disastrous to the welfare of the consuming public, inimical to the social and political freedom of the people, and especially injurious to the industrial liberty and economic condition of the workers, must be to transfer all such private monopolies to public control as steps towards the creation of an Industrial Commonwealth founded upon the common ownership and control of land and capital and the substitution of co-operative production for use in place of the present method of competitive production for profit.

To this, the SDF moved an amendment to add:

> And this Congress further declares that no candidate for Parliament should receive the support of the Labour Representation Committee who is not pledged to the above principles and to the recognition of the class war as the basis of working class political action.

Although the only outright opponents were John Ward of the Navvies and James Sexton of the Dockers, the tender digestive system of the conference would accept neither resolution nor amendment. The decision was accepted by the ILP with patience and a waiting policy, whilst the SDF characteristically withdrew its affiliation from the LRC soon afterwards. The ILP thus proved itself the more practical party of the two, and went on to make further history.

THE FIRST BIG VICTORY

During the first years of the LRC, the federal conception of its functions persisted, despite an urge from left wing sources to the contrary. Annual conferences were prepared to pass single resolutions on one subject or another, but they steadily refused to be drawn into a declaration of ultimate objects, or into the drafting of a programme. The moderate elements took the line that, as the TUC had passed many resolutions during its long life, there appeared to be no necessity for the LRC to do other than string them together as occasion demanded. The ILP continued its almost Fabian method of conversion from within, whilst the SDF, though it had withdrawn from the LRC, persisted in seeking a declaration on ultimate objects through its members who represented other affiliated organisations at the conference.

Ultimately in 1905, due to the persistence of the SDF from without, the following was carried without discussion:

> The annual conference of the LRC hereby declares that its ultimate object shall be the obtaining for the workers the full results of their labour by the overthrow of the present competitive system of capitalism

and the institution of a system of public ownership of all the means of production, distribution and exchange.

No one can now explain why the LRC, after strenuously opposing similar resolutions during the years, allowed the motion, pledging it to a socialist basis, to go through as if unnoticed. Despite the resolution, the Labour Party has not been socialist from 1905. Indeed, until 1918, Left criticism continued to be levelled on platforms and in the press against both the LRC and, subsequently, the Labour Party as a Liberal-Labour organisation.

Even the 1905 conference continued to decline to adopt a public programme, and, following the important 1906 election, repeated its decision. Notwithstanding this reluctance, electors were left in no doubt as to the ultimate course to be followed politically by the organised workers. The ILP grew strong both in numbers and in influence; its propaganda intensified, and working class electors were drawn into the pursuit of political power.

The Executive Committee of the LRC took steps in January 1905 to hold conferences on unemployment, and the feeding of school children. These preceded the annual conference and were held in the same town. It can be claimed, therefore, that these conferences formulated the first public policy as distinct from a programme to be put forward by the movement as a whole. With the approach of the 1906 Election, the discussions attracted public attention, and the resolutions passed on unemployment certainly influenced the results. The first resolution declared:

(a)   That unemployment is not caused by scarcity of land, of capital, of national wealth, or by incapacity to consume.

(b)   That unemployment prevails in protectionist and free trade countries alike.

(c)   That the presence of aliens in Britain is not a cause of unemployment amongst British workers.

(d)   That unemployment . . . is due to the existence of monopoly, and the burdens which the non-producing sections impose on the industrious classes, together with the lack of such an organisation of industry as will prevent alternate periods of overwork and unemployment.

MPs, in a second resolution, were urged to secure powers for local authorities to acquire and use land; to reorganise local administrative machinery for dealing with poverty and unemployment; and *to create a Labour Ministry*. Shackleton moved a third resolution which declared that local authorities should execute public work when the labour market was depressed, and should schedule improvements and housing schemes, and where possible employ direct labour, on standard union rates and conditions.

To Keir Hardie we owe Labour's first agitation against the prevailing unemployment. In Parliament, and in the country, he awakened the public conscience, and, poor and weak as the Unemployed Workmen's Act of 1905 now appears, its place upon the Statute Book is a tribute to the memory of a man who felt deeply and spared himself no effort in the cause of the unemployed.

The present writer has a vivid recollection of being taken by Hardie into the House of Lords for the second reading of the Bill. There was a poor attendance of Peers, and at the Bar the only MPs showing any interest were John Burns, Arthur Henderson, Will Crooks and Hardie. The only strangers were Frank Smith (Keir Hardie's secretary) and myself. Crooks indulged in a running commentary on the debate which was a joy to listen to, and especially so during the speech of the Marquis of Aylsbury, whose voice provided Crooks with a splendid target for his robust wit.

One other subject influenced the LRC and its supporters between the elections of 1900 and 1906. The Taff Vale Railway Company, aggrieved at a strike supported by the Amalgamated Society of Railway Servants, sued the Society in the courts and was awarded heavy damages. This decision was of serious consequence to the unions and severely curbed their actions. The award was attacked in Parliament and throughout the country, and many unions not hitherto moved to political action for social reform were so outraged that they joined the LRC, bringing its membership to more than one million. The Railway Company enjoyed a brief period of exaltation, little understanding that it had forced the organised working class movement to seek redress through parliamentary action, and had helped it to make up its mind to secure political power to take over whole industries in the name of the nation.

The General Election of 1906 brought results that startled the whole world. Fifty candidates had been nominated and approved by the LRC. Unlike their 1900 forerunners, these candidates were no scratch nominees. They had been officially promoted by affiliated organisations and selected by constituency organisations in time to make preparations for the fight. 29 were elected, and the new members not only looked like a real Parliamentary Party, but acted as one. The House of Commons, remembering the four lone figures representing Independent Labour in the old Parliament, were greatly impressed by Labour's new strength.

A glance at a photograph of the first Parliamentary Labour Party, while recollecting the socialist rejoicing at the victory, also shows that time has taken its dread toll. Not a single Labour Member of the 1906 Parliament figured in the 1945 parliamentary majority of 393.

When the new PLP met in 1906, Keir Hardie was chosen as Leader. With Roberts and Jowett as his Parliamentary Secretaries, the parliamentary party took its work very seriously, and established a system of four Standing Committees: the Municipal Committee; the Government Workers' Committee; the Estimates' Committee and the Government Contracts' Committee. During the Session, special Sub-Committees were appointed to deal with the Notification of Accidents Bill, the Workmen's Compensation Bill, the Trade Disputes Bill, the Education Bill, Provision of Meals for School Children Bill and Railway Rates.

At the 1906 annual party conference, the Parliamentary Party submitted the first of the Parliamentary Reports which have been such a feature of annual conferences ever since. The historical importance of this lies in the constitutional status acquired by the Parliamentary Party to the party conference. The Parliamentary Party, having direct access to conference, is not now, and has never been, subject to the direction of the National Executive Committee.

It was at this 1906 Conference that a decision was taken to drop the name 'Labour Representation Committee' and to adopt the name 'Labour Party'. No better title could have been chosen to convey to the working classes a sense of their ownership of a political party. A working man may be a Conservative, a Liberal or a Socialist, but he will always look upon those words as something additional, as something that can be discarded at will. But to be a Labour man is another matter altogether. A working man is a Labour man inevitably, and he naturally belongs to the Labour Party. He may disagree with its policy at times, but he is not tempted to leave the party because he is a vital part of its organisation.

ORGANISING THE PARTY

Since 1929 the selection of parliamentary candidates has been governed by an elaborate form of procedure, involving the National Executive Committee (NEC), affiliated organisations, Constituency Parties and individual members. The procedure has been supervised by the National Agent's Department and its staff of District Organisers who are in close touch with every section of the party.

A Labour candidate must be an individual member of the party; if eligible, he must be a member of a trade union affiliated to the TUC or recognised as a *bona fide* trade union; accept and conform to the constitution, programme, principles and policy of the party; undertake to accept and act in harmony with the Standing Orders of the Parliamentary Party; not be a member of a political party or organisation declared by the conference, or by the NEC, to be ineligible for affiliation to the Labour Party; in an election he must designate himself as a Labour Candidate only, and give prominence in his election address and campaign to the issues defined in the party manifesto; his promoting organisation must accept financial responsibility for his candidature.

Resolutions submitted to the preliminary 1900 Conference gave life to the LRC. So tentative were the initial steps that no provision was made for a written constitution. It was not until 1903, after a number of difficulties had arisen in the promotion and selection of parliamentary candidates, that attempts at constitution-making were started.

In 1901, the Executive Committee warned the party conference that it could only support candidates run by affiliated Labour organisations, and that while it would be no bar to a candidate that was supported by either of the non-Labour parties, it must be understood that his candidature was not promoted by either of them, and that he accepted the conditions of the second resolution of the 1900 London Conference. In 1902 there were considerable difficulties in a by-election at Dewsbury, caused by attempts to select a representative candidate on behalf of the whole Labour movement in the absence of any rule governing the procedure.

By 1903, the Executive had accepted the need for a written constitution, but so careful was the Committee not to disturb affiliated organisations that the first draft did no more than paraphrase the original resolutions. The Committee did, however, indicate its fear that the draft was weak and invited the annual conference to strengthen the draft by amendment.

As there had been one or two incidents which excited a good deal of interest, affiliated organisations needed no second invitation to send in amendments. Those incidents were a challenge to the independence of the party, and could not be ignored, especially in the case of the Fawcett Association, and its leading member, W.E. Clery. The Association (later part of the Union of Post Office Workers) had, in accordance with the resolutions and the ruling of the NEC, decided to promote the candidature of Clery, and to undertake responsibility for his election expenses. Clery, however, allowed himself to be selected as a Liberal candidate by the Deptford Liberal Association believing that, as the LRC was a federal body interested in sending working men to Parliament, the Committee could not object even though a working class representative had been selected by one of the capitalist parties. The Fawcett Association reported Clery's selection to the NEC and asked for the endorsement of his candidature by the LRC. The NEC argued with the Fawcett Association but, notwithstanding its own warning to the 1901 conference, finally decided that it had no authority to refuse endorsement. However, it agreed to advise the next conference not to allow Clery's case to become a precedent.

The Gas Workers promptly submitted a motion on the party's independent position which was adopted and became part of the constitution:

> To secure, by united action, the election to Parliament of candidates promoted . . . by an affiliated Society or Societies in the constituency, who undertake to form or join a distinct group in Parliament, with its own Whips and its own policy on Labour questions, to abstain strictly from identifying themselves with or promoting the interests of . . . the Liberal or Conservative Parties, and not to oppose any other candidate recognised by this Committee. All such candidates shall pledge themselves to accept this constitution, to abide by the decisions of the Group in carrying out the aims of this constitution, and to appear before their constituencies under the title of Labour Candidates only.

The debate on the resolution was notable, the principal protagonists being John Ward, for the Liberal-Labour supporters, and Hardie for the Labour Independents. Ward urged that the Labour Party should follow the lead of the Irish Nationalist Party under Parnell. 'Everybody knows', said Ward, 'that Parnell always kept himself absolutely clear of any such resolution as that under discussion. Parnell always supported Liberals and Tories as the occasion demanded. [This] resolution would not allow them to take such action as Parnell did so successfully in his time. They would strangle themselves if they passed such resolutions, as they would absolutely choke the movement in its inception'.

Keir Hardie had a longer vision, and dealt with Ward in a trenchant fashion. He said they were being 'advised to use any weapon, honourable or dishonourable, in order to win seats in the House of Commons'. It was not true to say that they were justified in doing anything to win a seat. There was but one weapon which would stand the test of time and prove effective – adhesion to honest principle. Any departure from that would ruin their Labour movement. They all – Liberal, Tory and Socialists – rejoiced at the magnificent conference gathered together. What was the principle that enabled them all to come together and discuss this matter? – INDEPENDENCE. If the Socialists had insisted that all should be Socialists, there would be no such gathering. Had the Liberals insisted that all should be Liberals, they would have had a like result. They had fixed upon a common denominator, that 'when acting in the House of Commons, they should be neither Socialists, Liberals nor Tories, but a Labour Party'.

The constitutional clause agreed continued to cover parliamentary candidates. A candidate, on completing his Nomination Paper for a Selection Conference, signs his name to the following words: 'I accept nomination . . . and, if selected, will accept the stipulations relating to candidatures as set out in the Labour Party Constitution and Rules'. No one now questions the essential need for independence *vis-à-vis* the Liberal and Conservative Parties. In those early days, however, the pledge caused immediate repercussions and it strongly influenced the Judges acting in the Osborne Case.

In 1904, Bell of the Railwaymen, having declined to give the required pledge, took provocative action which led to his elimination from Labour Party politics, and to a fuller endorsement by the party of the constitutional clause. In the 1904 Norwich by-election, George Roberts of the Typographical Association had been nominated by the Labour forces in the city. A request was sent to Bell, through the Amalgamated Society of Railway

Servants, inviting him to speak in support of Roberts' candidature. Although Bell had been associated with the creation of the LRC – he was its first Treasurer – and despite being the General Secretary of one of its strongest affiliates, he replied to his Norwich Branch regretting the intervention of the Labour Candidate and expressing an opinion favourable to the Liberal nominee. This letter found its way into the press from the London end, and Bell was charged with being responsible for the leak. Whether the charge was true may never be known, but on the successful election of the Liberal candidate, Bell sent him a letter of congratulation.

The LRC asked Bell's union to take action. Unfortunately, although the union refrained from appointing Bell to future LRC conferences, it continued to allow Bell, its General Secretary, to go his own way politically, whilst keeping itself in touch with the LRC. In the 1906 Parliament, the union found itself in an embarrassing situation, when its two Labour MPs, Hudson and Wardle, moved an amendment to a trifling resolution on railway conditions moved by Bell.

The introduction of the candidates' pledge proved an acid test for the Liberal-Labour element in the party. A majority, faced with the personal decision, swallowed the pledge and committed themselves to Labour independence. A minority (including W.C. Steadman and John Ward) refused to take the pledge, and so had their endorsements withdrawn by the LRC. All the duly-nominated candidates at the succeeding election were pledge-bound under the party constitution, and those who were elected lived up to their pledge.

Members of the Labour Party cannot resist the temptation of constitution-mongering and at every conference until 1928 the agenda was never free from some motion for a change. The party, however, by 1928 had had enough annual constitutional reviews and in the redrafted constitution of that year included a clause restricting proposed constitutional amendments to every third conference.

Two further changes were made in the early days. In 1906 the clause set out above was amended to bind candidates to abstain from identifying themselves with or promoting the interests of any party not eligible for affiliation. The initiative was taken by the Belfast Trades Council to deal with their own brand of political parties but the effect was to bar association with any party unrecognised by the Labour Party as an affiliated organisation.

In 1908, at Hull, the NEC proposed an addition to the constitution to govern selection conferences. Although Trades Councils and Local Labour Representation Committees were eligible for affiliation, these bodies had not been provided with local rules. Consequently difficulties arose out of the local conferences convened for the selection of parliamentary candidates. The NEC recommendation was:

> That all branches of affiliated organisations within a Constituency . . . covered by a proposal to run a Labour candidate must be invited to send delegates to the conference and that the local organisation responsible for calling the conference may . . . invite representatives from branches of organisations not affiliated but eligible for affiliation.

This clause continued for many years and was only superseded by the adoption of model rules for constituency parties approved by the party conference in 1918.

The 1908 Hull Conference discussed the appointment of a National Agent to conduct the party's electoral activities. The debate centred round a demand for local autonomy. It was feared that having a National Agent under the direction of the NEC would lead to over-centralisation. The question had been submitted by the previous conference to the NEC, but the Committee refrained from making a recommendation. By a narrow majority, the Hull Conference agreed to appoint a National Agent. There is no evidence that any delegate, except Henderson, had any conception of the importance of the office thus created. Henderson's early political activities had been in the Liberal Party, where he had acted as a Constituency Agent. In its first 41 years of existence, only four persons . . . occupied the post of National Agent: Arthur Peters, formerly of the Liberal Party but later Labour Agent for Barrow-in-Furness; Egerton P. Wake, whose early life had been spent in Labour circles at Chatham but who followed Peters as Labour Agent at Barrow; myself, and R.T. Windle, the present holder of this important office.

ATTACKS BY THE LAW

The 1946 repeal of the 1927 Trade Disputes and Trade Unions Act was a great moment for the Labour movement. It restored to the unions much of their former industrial independence, and gave certain unions the right the 1927 Act denied them, of linking up with the TUC. The repeal also deleted those restrictions which Churchill, in a moment of triumph and in the interests of the Tory Party, fastened round the Labour Party and its affiliated organisations. These followed earlier attempts reactionaries made through the courts to defeat the Labour Party by sapping its strength at source. From the enfranchisement of working men in the towns in 1868, unions had engaged in political activities, and had nominated members at parliamentary and local elections with varying degrees of success. Until 1906, feeling perhaps that they were sufficiently strong to prevent the election of working class candidates in great numbers, political opponents took no advantage of the law. But with the growth of the LRC, and the approach of the 1906 Election, the courts were brought in to assist in the defeat of the rising political force.

Action was first taken against those unions which had become active in politics without going through the formality of securing authority through the adoption of appropriate rules. So awkward did the situation become that in 1905 the LRC circulated to unions a Model Rule, sanctioned by the Chief Registrar of Friendly Societies, and urged its adoption. The Model Rule read:

> The object of this Society is to regulate relations between workmen and employers and between workmen and workmen in the trade; to relieve its members when unemployed; to create benefits for sickness, accident, or superannuation; to bury its dead; and to these ends it adopts the following methods: (a) The establishment of a fund or funds; (b) The giving of legal assistance in connection with . . . the above objects . . . (c) The securing . . . of legislation for the protection of its trade interests and for the . . . welfare of its members; (d) The adoption of any other legal method . . . in the . . . interests of the members as declared by a majority voting by ballot.
>
> For the purpose of promoting these objects and of making these methods effective, the Society may aid and join with other trades or other Societies, or Federation of Societies, having for their object . . . the promotion of the interests of workmen within the scope of the Trade Union Acts.

It made no reference to the Labour Party, nor to the promotion of parliamentary candidates, but the wording is so wide that it gave elbow room and sufficient authority to join the Labour Party and to engage actively in politics.

The adoption of the Model Rule only brought a brief period of quiet. Big business is not in the habit of pulling its punches when intent on a kill, and the resumption of its attack later is not a matter for surprise because the work of the Labour Party in Parliament offered a daily challenge to employers and a rallying point for their employees. In 1909 the half-feared and the fully-expected bomb-shell fell. A member of the Amalgamated Society of Railway Servants, named Osborne, sought an injunction to restrain the union from levying its members to support the Labour Party, on the grounds that the statutory objects in the Trade Union Act 1876 did not give unions authority to engage in political action. Those objects were:

> The regulation of the relations between workmen and master, or between workmen and workmen, or between masters and masters, of the imposing of restrictive conditions on the conduct of any trade or business, and also the provision of benefits to members.

Mr Justice Neville, who presided over the Court, thought that the statutory objects did not prevent the adoption of other objects, and he refused the injunction. Osborne took the case to the Court of Appeal which reversed the decision of the lower Court. It mattered not to the Appeal Judges that unions had been active politically for 40 years, or that many of their members had been elected to Parliament. To the Court of Appeal the statutory objects limited unions to industrial action, and therefore any form of political action became *ultra vires*.

The Labour movement was aroused to high fury because the decision of the Court of Appeal would prevent unions sending members to lobby MPs at Westminster, and their branches would no longer be able to participate in Trades Councils. It was decided with unanimity that the case be taken to the House of Lords in the hope of a more reasoned judgment. The case was finally decided in December 1909, and – to the disgust of the unions – the decision of the Court of Appeal was upheld. In the three Courts, no less than nine Judges had to decide for and against the union claim 'That political action comes within the meaning of the Trade Union Acts and is, therefore, not *ultra vires*'. Only two Judges answered in the affirmative, six answered in the negative, and one Judge was neutral.

Following the House of Lords judgment (which involved the movement in costs exceeding £4,000[5]) the Labour Party had to decide what action to be taken to free the trade unions. Quick action became imperative because more than a score of unions were taken through the Courts and had injunctions forced upon them following the House of Lords judgment. The NEC proposed, firstly, a modification of the constitution of the Labour Party, and secondly, to secure the passage through Parliament of a new Act granting unions their proper and necessary political rights. The alteration to the constitution was submitted to the 1911 Party Conference at Leicester. There had been great play in the Courts about pledge-bound MPs; the Leaders felt that if Parliament had to be won over to new legislation, MPs had to be freed from any noticeable obligation to an outside body. There were heated discussions and the NEC's proposals were only adopted after

5   Perhaps around £⅓ million in 2006 money.

a great struggle. Hitherto parliamentary candidates had been obliged to sign the following undertaking:

> Candidates and Members must accept this constitution; agree to abide by the decisions of the parliamentary party in carrying out the aims of this Constitution; appear before their constituencies under the title of Labour Candidates only; abstain strictly from identifying themselves with or promoting the interests of any parliamentary party not affiliated, or its candidates; and they must not oppose any candidate recognised by the National Executive of the party.

Following the Leicester Conference, no signature by a parliamentary candidate became necessary and the amended rule read:

> Candidates and Members must maintain this Constitution; appear before their constituencies under the title of Labour Candidates only; abstain strictly from identifying themselves with or promoting the interests of any other party, and accept the responsibilities established by parliamentary practice.

The attack on the proposed change was led by Bruce Glasier in a closely reasoned and penetrating speech. MacDonald replied with great debating power. Hardie then followed, supporting Glasier's attack, and Henderson replied on behalf of the platform. Opposition to the proposed change was because it was thought unwise to bow the knee to the Bench, and that Parliament would be more likely to listen to a fighting party than one that trimmed its sails.

Despite the partial dependence of the government on Labour votes, it was not until 1913 that the Osborne judgment was reversed by Act of Parliament. Although the new Act did not give the Labour movement all its demands, it largely clarified the union position in the political field. To the statutory industrial objects of unions were added specific political objects. Unions could spend money: (a) on the payment of expenses incurred by a candidate or prospective candidate for election to any public office, before, during, or after the election in connection with his candidature; or (b) on the holding of meetings or the distribution of literature to support any such candidate; or (c) on the maintenance of an MP; or (d) in connection with the registration of electors or the selection of a candidate; or (e) on the holding of political meetings, or on the distribution of political literature, unless the main purpose of the meetings or of the distribution of the literature is the furtherance of statutory objects within the meaning of this Act. The Act made it clear that the statutory political objects named were without prejudice to the furtherance of any other political objects.

It also enabled a union to establish a political fund raised either by a political levy on its members or by the transfer of money from other union funds. Members who objected to political action could either claim exemption from the payment of the political levy or could have their contribution cards credited with the equivalent of their share of monies transferred to the political fund. It was the business of the unions to make this privilege known.

The repeal[6] of the Trade Disputes and Trade Unions Act 1927 has thrown the union movement back on to the Trade Union Act 1913. There is now

---

6   By the Labour Government elected in 1945.

much more money for unions' political funds to expend on political propaganda; and on the promotion of candidates for parliamentary and local
government elections, to say nothing of the political education of union
members. In the year following the passing of the Trade Disputes and Trade
Unions Act 1927, because of the substitution of 'contracting-in' for
'contracting-out', the affiliated membership of the Labour Party fell by more
than one million. The affiliated membership will be greatly strengthened as
the unions will be able to affiliate on a membership almost as big as that on
which they affiliate to the TUC. The total affiliated membership of the two
bodies will not be the same exactly because, apart from those members
who 'contract-out', a number of TUC-affiliated unions are not affiliated to
the party.

THE VOTERS

In winning a parliamentary majority for the first time in 1945, the Labour
Party had spent 46 years in the preparatory work. In the life of the nation
that period of time is of little consequence but for those who joined the
party at the beginning, it may seem a pretty long process consuming practically the whole of their working lives.

Sidney Webb's view is that in Britain a new idea normally takes a period
of 25 years to reach fulfilment. But if so, how is it that the Labour Party
idea took twice the normal period to reach a parliamentary majority? The
answer is in the restricted franchises of the first two decades of the 20th
century. During those years, the electoral basis for achieving a Labour
government did not exist because the small electorate was over weighted
by the rich, by the middle class and by the more elderly members of the
working class. A glance at the elections following the 1819 extension of the
franchise, and subsequent extensions, shows that Labour's increased votes
and representation in Parliament have coincided with them. In 1915 the
total electorate, including the whole of Ireland, amounted to just 8½ million
men as against the 33 million men and women on the 1945 Register. The
1915 electorate comprised:

(a) The Ownership Franchise (freeholders, copyholders and lease-
holders) – 644,110 men
(b) The Occupation Franchise (occupiers of land or premises of the
annual value of £10; householders; service occupiers) – 7,162,491 men
(c) Lodgers occupying unfurnished rooms of the annual value of
£10 – 144,656 men.
(d) Freemen – 54,919 men
(e) University Electors – 51,471 men

All women and most of the young men being excluded, the comparatively
slow progress of the party until the 1920s is understandable; despite the
setback of 1931, the later progress due to a more effective response to
Labour's propaganda from the younger people is recognisable.

Curiously enough, the Labour Party appeared to take little interest in
electoral reform until the outbreak of the First World War. Motions
inspired by Arthur Henderson were on to the 1909–10 conference agendas,
but the interest was lukewarm. The party did not appreciate that the existing
franchise laws were heavily weighted against Labour's advance. Henderson's
major proposals were:

(a)   The enfranchisement of all adults, male and female
(b)   The shortest possible qualifying period for registration
(c)   The payment of MPs
(d)   The holding of all parliamentary elections the same day, and only one vote for each elector
(e)   The strengthening of the Corrupt Practices Acts
(f)   The prevention of the election of members by a minority of votes

Regarding the 6th proposal, 'The prevention of the election of members by a minority of votes', subsequent conferences debated Proportional Representation, the Alternative Vote and the Second Ballot but all were turned down at Glasgow in 1914. Recurring attempts to interest the party in Proportional Representation met with a similar fate, although in 1930 the Labour Minority Government reached agreement with the Liberal Opposition, as a price for its support in the lobbies, in favour of the Alternative Vote. Fortunately the Bill never reached the Statute Book, and Labour's advance to political ascendancy has not been hamstrung by the inter-party electoral arrangements to which that system would have given rise.

Discussions on the franchise did arise out of the militant campaigns of the Suffragettes. From 1904 until 1908, there were annual debates on proposals to extend votes to women on the same terms as men. The opposition came from the supporters of Adult Suffrage, chiefly because they thought the demands of the women would merely enfranchise the well-to-do. Apart from the 1906 party conference, when women advocates nearly carried the day by 432 votes to 435, annual conferences voted by large majorities in favour of Adult Suffrage, and with this they appear to have been content. Not even the eloquence of Keir Hardie, who in 1907 pleaded for the enfranchisement of women and who believed that 1¾ million working women would receive the vote as against ¼ million well-to-do women, could alter the decision of conference.

The two Parliaments elected in 1910 gave rise to many difficulties in the PLP and in the movement. The Liberal Party, which in 1906 had the largest majority of modern times, suffered losses in both general elections. It had to rely either on the Irish Nationalist Party or on the Labour Party, or both, to maintain its legislation against the Tory attack in both Houses and to fulfil its pledges to Ireland. The Labour Party, desiring to clear the Irish demands out of the way, had its own reason for continuing the Liberal Government in office. It wanted an amendment to the trade union laws, which was eventually carried in 1913. Moreover, the Parliament Act, which was an attempt to destroy the absolute veto of the House of Lords, seriously modified the relationship of parties in co-operation, however loosely, one to another. As MacDonald pointed out in 1914, an agreement of parties to support a Home Rule Bill likely to meet with obstruction in the Lords really meant an agreement to cover three parliamentary sessions. Consequently a party bound in that way had less parliamentary freedom. That situation should be remembered in assessing the merits of the pressure of the Women's Social and Political Union[7] on the Labour Party and the interruptions at meetings addressed by Labour MPs, and especially the meetings of the men who had been most prominent in their advocacy of women's enfranchisement. This pressure on the party, coinciding with deeds of violence, sought to compel the Labour Party to vote against the Liberal Government on every issue unless the government gave women the vote. This the party declined to do.

7   The militant organisation of the Women's Suffrage Movement.

In 1912, George Lansbury, MP for Bow and Bromley, gave himself completely to the women's cause. To force the hands of the party, he resigned his seat in Parliament to obtain a verdict in favour of the women's case. This dramatic action, taken without any consultation with his parliamentary colleagues, caused enormous embarrassment, especially as he issued circulars to affiliated organisations calling on them for support. During the by-election, the NEC decided that he should not receive the support of the Labour Party. Lansbury, who had formerly had a majority of 863, lost the seat by 751. The party continued to support Adult Suffrage, but the 1911 conference, on a motion from Henderson, asked the PLP to make it clear that no Bill would be acceptable which did not include women. The resolution met with bitter opposition from the miners led by Robert Smillie. They believed it would be politically silly to vote against Manhood Suffrage merely because the government refused to grant the franchise to women. The resolution was adopted by 919,000 to 686,000. The battle was resumed at a later conference when a similar case against the Henderson position was made by Stephen Walsh.

Such troubles ceased on the outbreak of the Great War. The dimensions of that struggle absorbed the whole nation, except those who supported the outlook of the ILP. Political passions died down and, under the electoral truce and the cessation of the campaign of the militant women suffragettes, electoral reform appeared of minor importance. Not until the appointment of a Speaker's Conference in 1916 to consider redistribution and the franchise was interest again aroused. Labour's representatives at the Speaker's Conference were Wardle (MP for Stockport); Goldstone (MP for Sunderland) and Walsh (MP for Ince).

The 1917 Annual Party Conference took cognizance of the Speaker's Conference, and demanded:

(a) adult suffrage, including women
(b) short periods of qualification and continuous registration
(c) the provision of facilities for candidates to put their views before soldiers and munition workers and facilities for these electors, and others having to be absent, to be able to vote
(d) redistribution of electorates
(e) no election on the existing register, or before the above changes had been made.

The Speaker's Conference reported to the Prime Minister in a series of resolutions. The NEC held a joint conference with the TUC's Parliamentary Committee when, though reiterating their former demands, the two bodies agreed that the PLP should support the resolutions, provided that the enfranchisement of women, including women wage earners and widows, was agreed. The January 1918 Conference accepted the new Bill, as a compromise only, and demanded further reforms.

The 1918 Representation of the People Act altered the franchise considerably. Men at 21 years of age became qualified as electors if they had been resident in a constituency for six months; or if they had been in occupation of business premises of the annual value of £10 for six months; or if they were graduates of a university. Women were granted the franchise if they were 30 years of age, and entitled to be registered as local government electors in respect of the occupation of land or premises (not being a dwelling house) of a yearly value of not less than £5, or of a dwelling house, or as the wife of a husband entitled to be registered. A woman at

30 could also be entitled under certain conditions to registration in a University Constituency.

The extension of the franchise, though well short of adult suffrage, increased the electorate enormously. 21,370,316 men and women were included in the register for the 1918 Election. The importance of that increased electoral register did not show itself completely in the new House of Commons, but the total vote given to a much larger number of Labour candidates rose from 370,802 in December 1910 to 2,244,945 in 1918. The results would have been much greater if it had not been for the division in Labour's ranks over the war. Indeed, because of that, the PLP lost some of front rank members including MacDonald and Snowden, and a substantial number of seats.

Whilst a Labour Government under the old franchise might have been a forlorn hope, the developments of 1918 paved the way to a constituency in which the youth, uncommitted to past prejudices, looked forward to political developments which would make for freedom and the abolition of poverty.

THE STRUGGLE FOR UNITY

The Labour movement, growing from small beginnings, finds itself cluttered up with conflicting organisations which, from time to time, give birth to clashes. The various types of operating machinery created vested interests which are difficult to remove. Men have become so attached to the associations they formed during the years, that they are prepared to fight for their retention to the last ditch. We look here at attempts to secure some unifying agency to enable the movement to speak with one voice.

In February 1906 at Caxton Hall, Westminster, a meeting between the TUC's Parliamentary Committee, the Management Committee of the General Federation of Trade Unions (GFTU) and the NEC of the Labour Representation Committee, decided to form a National Labour Advisory Board. An Agreement was reached whereby:

I.   All candidates adopted by the LRC shall receive the loyal and hearty support of all sections of the Labour Party

II.   All Labour and trade union candidates approved by the TUC Parliamentary Committee shall receive the support of the LRC . . . in the same manner as T. Richards, in West Monmouth

III.   Members of the LRC shall not be considered disloyal in refusing to support any Labour candidate adopted on any party platform except that of Labour; . . . the candidates approved by the three committees shall offer no opposition to each other

IV.   That the LRC make it clear that their constitution does not require abstention by electors in constituencies where no Labour candidate is running.

The reference to T. Richards covered a decision of the South Wales Miners' Federation which, although not affiliated to the LRC, had decided to run its candidates as Labour candidates, on the understanding that its MPs should work in conjunction with the PLP. Paragraph IV arose out of the LRC's declaration of independence; in the absence of a Labour candidate in any election, the party gives no direction to its membership or followers as to how they should vote.

Later in the year, a further Agreement decided:

I.   That every effort should be made by the three Committees to prevent overlapping

II.   That . . . on all matters relating to political resolutions, political policy and action in Parliament, the three Secretaries should more frequently confer together. It would be advisable . . . that the offices of the three organisations should be in the same building

The National Labour Advisory Board served a useful purpose, although the partnership established had uneasy moments because of differing customs and the different relationships existing between the committees and their respective affiliated organisations.

A proposal was made during 1907 for the establishment of headquarters to provide offices for the three national committees but this was not achieved, because the Parliamentary Committee of the TUC saw no useful purpose in bringing the three committees under one roof. Attempts were also made to prevent overlapping in the functions and activities of the three committees, with industrial matters being the prerogative of the Parliamentary Committee, banking operations the concern of the Management Committee of the GFTU, and political affairs the responsibility of the Labour Party. The Joint Board, as the Advisory Committee became known, however, failed to agree upon any plan to prevent overlapping.

In 1908, the Joint Board was vested with other responsibilities. Much controversy had arisen out of the acceptance into affiliation by one or other of the national committees of unions not recognised by the others. Frequently these unions were breakaways, and their existence gave rise to bitterness. Additionally, there had been political difficulties arising out of independent pronouncements from the several national committees. A new constitution was, therefore, approved, including:

The Joint Board shall be the body to determine the *bona fides* of any trade union affiliated, or applying for affiliation, to any of the constituent organisations.

The Joint Board shall report as to whether new societies connected with trades already covered by existing organisations shall be encouraged or otherwise.

The Joint Board shall decide references made to it . . . [on] questions affecting them jointly, or about which some . . . difference may have arisen as to which body they properly belong to.

The Joint Board shall . . . agree upon joint political or other action when such is deemed to be advantageous . . . and is agreed to by the constituent bodies.

The Joint Board may, in cases of trade disputes, with the concurrence of the Executive of the union or unions affected, use its influence to bring about a settlement.

Much water has flowed under bridges since 1908. To-day the GFTU has no political interests, and takes no part with the Labour Party or the TUC in national decisions. It has been easy, therefore, under the constitutions of the TUC and the Labour Party to deal with the status of trade unions. In fact, the responsibility for deciding whether a union is a *bona fide* organisation is now vested in the TUC, and every application from a union for affiliation to the Labour Party is dependent on whether the union is affiliated to the TUC or is recognised by its General Council as a *bona fide* union. The co-ordinating body of the movement is now the National Council of Labour.

At the 1910 party conference, a resolution from the St Helens Trades Council favoured the fusion of the Labour Party and the TUC. An amendment was submitted by the Gas Workers' Union to include the GFTU. The motion and amendment were referred to the NEC which, in 1911, adopted three resolutions for submission to the Joint Board:

> That the present practice of three Annual Conferences held at separate times of the year is expensive, leads to much waste of effort and to divergence of policy, and the amalgamation of the national bodies, without delay, should be aimed at.
>
> That a scheme for a central building in Westminster, to be used by the Labour Movement, should be prepared.
>
> That a Committee be appointed to consider . . . the above proposals, and to report to a joint meeting of the three Executives within the next three months, with a view to its submission to the three national conferences.

The Joint Board decided that until these resolutions had been placed before the three national conferences, they could not be carried further. The resolutions were accepted by the Congress, the Labour Party Conference and the Annual Council of the General Federation. Unfortunately, in 1912, before the decisions could be implemented, the TUC decided in favour of the elimination of the GFTU from joint activities and thus placed the Joint Board, which included the GFTU, in an embarrassing situation. At the subsequent Annual Council of the Federation, it withdrew its support from the proposed amalgamation. Further, at the Newport TUC, in a mistaken attempt to expedite matters, a proposal was put forward by the Boiler-makers' Society in support of unification and was heavily defeated. These decisions ended the first real attempt to unify the trade union and political movements into one national organisation.

One other attempt at co-ordination took place. The Co-operative Union, which with its constituent bodies had refused to affiliate to the LRC or to the party, made overtures in 1912 for the establishment of a Joint Committee in the mutual interests of both movements. In 1913 the following was agreed:

> That this Joint Conference of representatives of the Co-operative Union, the Trades Union Congress Parliamentary Committee and the National Labour Party, is of opinion in order to assist in the promotion of the social and economic conditions of the people, it is advisable that there should be closer mutual effort – educational and practical – between the three sections represented at the Conference.

The objects of the United Co-operative and Labour Board which emerged, included (a) the promotion of a better understanding, (b) a joint programme for education, (c) the preparation and distribution of literature to influence officials of the movement to take a more active interest in Co-operation, (d) to influence friendly relationships between all branches of the Co-operative Movement and their employees, (e) to secure the practical exploitation of surplus capital for the promotion and development of co-operative enterprise, (f) to examine the facilities for banking offered by the co-operative movement, (g) to consider how to ensure the distribution

of food or the payment of benefit during trade disputes, (h) special conferences to influence public opinion in support of questions affecting the social
life of the people, (i) an exchange of fraternal greetings at annual conferences.

Unfortunately, when the Constitution of the Board was submitted to the
Co-operative Congress at Aberdeen, the proposed Board was turned down
by the following resolution:

> That this Congress, while approving concerted action with trade unions
> and other organised bodies for raising the status of Labour, cannot sanc-
> tion union with the political Labour Party, and that the Central Board
> be instructed strictly to maintain the neutrality of the movement in
> respect of party politics, so that political dissension may be avoided.

Years were to elapse before further attempts were made to secure
co-ordination between Co-operatives, trade unions and Labour Party
organisations, but in 1917, at the Swansea Co-operative Congress, a decision
was reached to enter the political arena. This led to further discussions
between the three movements to avoid unnecessary friction in the constituencies, and years later to the establishment of the National Council of
Labour embracing the trading, industrial and political wings of the Labour
movement.

First PLP Minutes[1]
12, 13 and 19 February 1906

THE LABOUR PARTY

Minutes of Parliamentary Meetings

On a Summons issued by the Executive Committee of the L.R.C. the Labour Party met in Committee Room No 12 of the House of Commons on Monday the 12th of February at 3.0pm.

There was a full attendance of Members and also the members of the Executive Committee of the L.R.C., and Mr. Henderson as Chairman of the Executive Committee occupied the Chair.

Resolved: That we sit on the Opposition side of the House on the two front benches below the gangway, if possible.

Attitude to other Labour Members:

Resolved: That we do not form a separate section in the House with the other Labour Members, but that we express our readiness to co-operate with them on all purely Trade Union objects.

The Labour Members of Parliament sitting alone proceeded to transact the following business:-

Chairman: W. Crooks moved 'That D.J. Shackleton be the Chairman'. This was seconded. G.N. Barnes moved 'That J. Keir Hardie be the Chairman'. This was seconded, and a vote being taken, there voted, 13 for D.J. Shackleton, and 13 for J. Keir Hardie. A ballot was then taken when there voted 14 for D.J. Shackleton and 15 for J. Keir Hardie.

J. Keir Hardie thereupon took the Chair, D.J. Shackleton being declared Vice-Chairman and called for nominations for Whips.

Resolved: 'That there be two Whips and a Secretary'.

---

1   The original minutes, hand-written by H. Scott Lindsay (presumably under the direction of Ramsay MacDonald) are in the Labour Archive Centre in Manchester.

Moved: 'That J. Ramsay MacDonald be the Secretary and one of the Whips'.

Moved: 'That A. Henderson be a Whip'.

There being no further nominations the meeting resolved accordingly.

After a discussion upon Bills, Resolutions etc. the meeting adjourned until 11.0am on Tuesday the following day.

The Members of the Party met in Committee Room No 12 at 11.0am on Tuesday the 13th of February, 1906. J. Keir Hardie in the Chair.

Correspondence: A letter was read from the New Reform Club offering the use of the Club to Members.

Resolved: 'That the letter lie on the table.'

A letter from the Park Studio requesting the Members to agree to be photographed.

Resolved: 'That the Secretary arrange for the Party to be photographed on The Terrace at 1.30pm.'[2]

Bills and Motions. The following subjects were agreed to as being those upon which the Party propose to draft Bills or Motions:-

     Trades Disputes
     Women's Suffrage
     Canals Nationalisation
     Unemployed Amendment Act
     Compensation Act
     Steam Enginemen's Boiler Bill
     Mines – Employment of Boys
     Women's Local Government
     Mines Regulations
     Miners' Eight Hours
     Taxation of Land Values
     Child Feeding
     Old Age Pensions
     Housing
     Shops Bill

Resolved: 'That the Party meet after the King's Speech and then decide what action to take on these matters'.

Resolved: 'That the Secretary ask that the Party be furnished with an early copy of the King's Speech.'

Resolved: 'That there shall not be more than one Official Amendment.'

Resolved: 'That the Party meet on Monday, the 19th of February at 12.30pm to finally decide these matters.'

Liberal Whip.

2   The outcome of this decision is the iconic photograph, reproduced on the cover of this book and p. ii.

Resolved: 'That in reply to a communication from the Liberal Whip, the Secretary courteously inform him that our Members prefer not to receive his Whip.'

Expenses.

Resolved: 'That we ask the Executive Committee of the L.R.C. to furnish the cost of printing, clerical assistance, postage etc. involved in the Party's work in the House'

Whip's Room

Resolved: 'That the Whips be instructed to approach the Commissioner of Works with a view to obtaining from him the use of a room in the House for the Party.'

The Party met in Room 13 in the House of Commons on Monday, the 19th of February, 1906. J. Keir Hardie in the Chair.

Resolved: 'That the following nominations be made for the Committees:–

> Committee of Selection :– A. Henderson.
> Standing Orders:– D.J. Shackleton.

These were agreed to unanimously.

Public Accounts. The following were the nominations and voting:–

	1st vote	2nd vote
G.N. Barnes	5	5
P. Snowden	4	5
F.W. Jowett	1	
W. Crooks	4	5

G.N. Barnes then withdrew and there voted 8 for P. Snowden and 6 for W. Crooks.

P. Snowden was declared elected.

> Kitchen   W Thorne

Debate in the House.

Resolved: 'That the Chairman be authorised to make a statement on the General Debate.'

Resolved: 'That if any Official Amendment is moved it will be upon one of the following questions:–

> Unemployment
> Trades Disputes
> Compensation
> Chinese.'

The meeting adjourned until 1.0pm. next day.

Appendix

LIST OF CHAIRMEN AND SECRETARIES OF THE PLP, 1906–2006

Chairmen

1906–07	J. Keir Hardie MP
1908–09	Arthur Henderson MP
1909	George Barnes MP
1911–14	J. Ramsay MacDonald MP
1914	Arthur Henderson MP
1916	George Wardle MP
1917	Arthur Henderson MP
1918–20	W. Adamson MP
1920–22	J.R. Clynes MP
1922–23	J. Ramsay MacDonald MP
1923	R. Smillie MP
1924–28	J. Ramsay MacDonald MP
1929–30	Harry Snell MP
1930	Rev J. Barr MP
1931–34	George Lansbury MP
1934–40	Clement Attlee MP
1940–42	H.B. Lees-Smith MP
1942	F.W. Pethick-Lawrence MP
1942–45	Arthur Greenwood MP
1945–46	Neil Maclean MP
1946–50	Maurice Webb MP
1950–51	I.W. Glenvil Hall MP
1951–55	Clement Attlee MP
1955–63	Hugh Gaitskell MP
1963–64	Harold Wilson MP
1964–67	Emanuel Shinwell MP
1967–74	Douglas Houghton MP
1974	Ian Mikardo MP
1974–79	Cledwyn Hughes MP
1979–81	Fred Willey MP
1981–87	Jack Dormand MP

1987–92	Stan Orme MP
1992–97	Doug Hoyle MP
1997–2001	Clive Soley MP
2001–05	Jean Corston MP
2005–	Ann Clwyd MP

Secretaries

1918–44	H. Scott Lindsay CBE
	He started work for the PLP (as Assistant Secretary) in 1906. Total service: 38 years.
1944–59	Carol Johnson CBE
1959–79	Sir Frank Barlow CBE
	He started work for the PLP in January 1937. Total service: 42 years 6 months.
1979–92	Bryan Davies
	Now Lord Davies of Oldham.
1992–2004	Alan Haworth
	Now Lord Haworth. He started work for the PLP in February 1975. Total service: 29 years 9 months.
2004–	Fiona Gordon

LABOUR PARTY 1906 MANIFESTO

Drafted centrally and circulated to candidates on 6 December 1905, each LRC candidate was then to put it out to the local electorate as his manifesto.

TO THE ELECTORS –

This election is to decide whether or not Labour is to be fairly represented in Parliament.

The House of Commons is supposed to be the people's House, and yet the people are not there.

Landlords, employers, lawyers, brewers, and financiers are there in force. Why not Labour?

The Trade Unions ask the same liberty as capital enjoys. They are refused.

The aged poor are neglected.

The slums remain; overcrowding continues, whilst the land goes to waste.

Shopkeepers and traders are overburdened with rates and taxation, whilst the increasing land values, which should relieve the ratepayers, go to people who have not earned them.

Wars are fought to make the rich richer, and underfed schoolchildren are still neglected.

Chinese Labour is defended because it enriches the mine owners.

The unemployed ask for work, the Government gave them a worthless Act, and now, when you are beginning to understand the causes of your poverty, the red herring of Protection is drawn across your path.

Protection, as experience shows, is no remedy for poverty and unemployment. It serves to keep you from dealing with the land, housing, old age, and other social problems!

You have it in your power to see that Parliament carries out your wishes. The Labour Representation Executive appeals to you in the name of a million Trade Unionists to forget all the political differences which have kept you apart in the past, and vote for [candidate name inserted].

Bibliography

Asquith, Margot, *The Autobiography of Margot Asquith*, vol. 2, Thornton Butterworth, 1922

Bagwell, Philip, *The Railwaymen – the History of the National Union of Railwaymen*, George Allen and Unwin, 1963

Barnes, Eric, Article on the 1903 by-election, unpublished (used in the Arthur Henderson chapter)

Barnes, George, *From Workshop to War Cabinet*, Herbert Jenkins, 1923

Barnes, George, *Industrial Conflict: The Way Out*, Pitman, 1924

Bealey, Frank and Pelling, Henry, *Labour and Politics 1900–1906: A History of the Labour Representation Committee*, Macmillan, 1958

Bell, Lady Florence, *At the Works: A Study of an Industrial Town*, Edward Arnold, 1907

Bellamy, Joyce M. and Saville, John (eds), *Dictionary of Labour Biography*, vol. 3, Macmillan, 1976

Benn, Caroline, *Keir Hardie*, Hutchinson, 1992

Bottigelli, Emile (ed.), translated by Yvonne Kapp, *Frederick Engels, Paul and Laura Lafargue*, vol. 2, Foreign Languages Publishing House, 1959

Brivati, Brian and Heffernan, Richard, *The Labour Party: A Centenary History*, Macmillan Press, 2000

Brockway, Fenner, *Socialism over Sixty Years (1864–1944): The Life of Jowett of Bradford*, G. Allen and Unwin for the National Labour Press, 1946

Brockway, Fenner, *Towards Tomorrow*, Hart-Davies MacGibbons, 1977

Brown, K.D. (ed.), *The First Labour Party: 1906–1914*, Croom Helm, 1985

Chase, Malcolm, 'Profile of Charles Duncan', in Batho, G.R. (ed.), *Durham Biographies*, vol. 1, Durham County Local History Society, 2000

Chesterton, G.K., 'Introduction' to George Haw, *From Workhouse to Westminster: The Life Story of Will Crooks MP*, Cassell, 1907

Christian Commonwealth, 9 February 1910

Clark, David, *Victor Grayson: Labour's Lost Leader*, Quartet, 1985

Clegg, H.A., Fox, A. and Thompson, A., *A History of British Trade Unions since 1889*, vol. 1, Oxford University Press, 1964

Clynes, J.R., *Memoirs 1869–1949*, vols 1 and 2, Hutchinson & Co., 1937

Clynes, J.R., *When I Remember*, Macmillan, 1940

Coleman, Charles, 'The Coming of Labour', *Amalgamated Engineers Monthly Journal*, vol. 2, 1906

Craig, F.W.S., *British Parliamentary Election Results 1918–1949*, Macmillan, 1977

Craig, F.W.S., *British Parliamentary Election Results 1885–1918*, Dartmouth Publishing, 1989

Cross, Colin, *Philip Snowden*, Barrie & Rockcliff, 1966

Davies, A., *To Build a New Jerusalem*, Abacus, 1996

Donaldson, F.L., 'The Church and the "Labour Church"', in Hunt, William Henry (ed.), *Churchmanship and Labour: Sermons on Social Subjects*, Skeffington, 1906

Dugdale, Blanche E.C., *Arthur James Balfour, First Earl of Balfour*, vol. 1, Hutchinson, 1936

Espinasse, Margaret, 'John T. Macpherson', in Bellamy, Joyce M. and Saville, John (eds), *Dictionary of Labour Biography*, vol. 5, Macmillan, 1979

Fowler, Edith Henrietta, *The Life of Henry Hartley Fowler, First Viscount Wolverhampton*, Hutchinson, 1912

Fox, Allan, *A History of the National Union of Boot and Shoe Operatives 1874–1957*, Basil Blackwell, 1958

Frow, E. and R., *To Make that Future – Now!: A History of the Manchester and Salford Trades Council*, E.J. Morton, 1976

Gardiner, A.G., *Prophets, Priests and Kings*, Dent and Sons, 1914

George, E., *From Mill-Boy to Minister: The Life of the Rt Hon J.R. Clynes MP*, T. Fisher Unwin, 1918

Hamilton, Mary, *Arthur Henderson*, Heinemann, 1938

Harrison, Brian and Matthew, H.C.G. (eds), *Oxford Dictionary of National Biography*, Oxford University Press, 2004

Haw, George, *From Workhouse to Westminster: The Life Story of Will Crooks MP*, Cassell, 1907

Hayter, Dianne, *Fightback! Labour's Traditional Right in the 1970s and 1980s*, Manchester University Press, 2005

Hodge, John, *Workman's Cottage to Windsor Castle*, Sampson Low & Co., 1931

Howell, David, *British Workers and the Independent Labour Party 1888–1906*, Manchester University Press, 1983

Jeffreys, J.B., *The Story of the Engineers*, Lawrence & Wishart, 1945

Kemp, John, 'Red Tayside? Political Change in Early Twentieth Century Dundee', in Miskell, Louise, Whatley, Christopher and Harris, Bob, *Victorian Dundee, Image and Realities*, Tuckwell Press, 2000

MacDonald, J. Ramsay, *Socialism and Society*, Independent Labour Party, 1905

Manchester Faces and Places, Vaughan Chambers, Manchester, vol. 2: 6, March 1891

Marquand, David, *Ramsay MacDonald*, Richard Cohen Books, 1997

Martin, David E., 'Charles Duncan', in Joyce M. Bellamy and John Saville (eds), *Dictionary of Labour Biography*, vol. 2, Macmillan, 1974

Martin, David E., 'George Davy Kelley', in Bellamy, Joyce M. and Saville, John (eds), *Dictionary of Labour Biography*, vol. 2, Macmillan, 1974

Martin, David E., '"The Instruments of the People"?: The Parliamentary Labour Party in 1906', in Martin, David and Rubinstein, David (eds), *Ideology and the Labour Movement*, Croom Helm, 1979

Martin, Ross, *The Lancashire Giant: David Shackleton, Labour Leader and Civil Servant*, Liverpool University Press, 2000

Masterman, C.F.G., *The Condition of England*, Methuen, 1909

Meeres, Frank, *Norfolk in the First World War*, Phillimore, 2004

Middleton, J.S., 'Clynes, John Robert (1869–1949)', in *Oxford Dictionary of National Biography*, Oxford University Press, 2004

Morgan, Kenneth O., *Keir Hardie – Radical and Socialist*, Weidenfeld & Nicolson, 1975

Morgan, Kenneth O., 'Inaugural Keir Hardie Memorial Lecture', Workmen's Institute, Trecynon, South Wales, 2 November 1985

Morgan, Kenneth O., *Labour People – Hardie to Kinnock*, Oxford University Press, 1987

Mowatt, J. and Power, A., *Our Struggle for Socialism – A Short History of the Barrow-in-Furness Labour Party*, Guardian Printing Works, 1949

Muller, William D., *The 'Kept Men'? The First Century of Trade Union Representation in the British House of Commons, 1874–1975*, Harvester, 1977

Nicolson, Harold, *King George the Fifth: His Life and Times*, Constable, 1952

Paterson, Tony, *A Seat for Life*, David Winter & Son, 1980

Pelling, Henry, *Social Geography of British Elections 1885–1910*, Macmillan, 1967

Quelch, Henry, *Social-Democracy and the Armed Nation*, Twentieth Century Press, 1907

Radice, E.A. and G.H., *Will Thorne: Constructive Militant*, George Allen and Unwin, 1974

Reid, J.H.S., *The Origins of the British Labour Party*, University of Minnesota Press, 1955

Report of the Second Annual Conference of the Labour Representation Committee, LRC, 1902

Review of Reviews, 'The Labour Party and the Books that Helped to Make It', *The Review of Reviews*, vol. 33, 1906

Richards, Thomas, 'How I Got On', *Pearson's Weekly*, 26 April 1906

Rose, Jonathan, *The Intellectual History of the British Working Classes*, Yale University Press, 2001

Rosen, Greg (ed.) *Dictionary of Labour Biography*, Politico's, 2001

Rubinstein, David, *The Labour Party and British Society 1880–2005*, Sussex Academic Press, 2006

Saville, John, 'Charles William Bowerman', in Bellamy, Joyce M. and Saville, John (eds), *Dictionary of Labour Biography*, vol. 5, Macmillan, 1979

Schneer, Jonathan, *Ben Tillett: Portrait of a Labour Leader*, Croom Helm, 1982

Schofield, Gerald, *Philip Snowden 1864–1937*, www.cottontown.org

Shinwell, Emanuel, *Conflict without Malice*, Odhams Press, 1955

Shipwrights Records, Bulletin 3, General, Municipal and Boilermakers' Union

Smith, Frank, *From Pit to Parliament – J. Keir Hardie MP*, People's Penny Pamphlets, No. 4, The Specialist Press, 1909

Snowden, Philip, 'The Man Who Made the Labour Party – An Intimate Sketch of J. Keir Hardie', *John O'London's Weekly*, 15 April 1922

Snowden, Viscount Philip, *An Autobiography*, vol. 1, Ivor Nicholson & Watson, 1934

Spring, Howard, *Fame is the Spur*, Fontana Books, 1969 (first published Collins, 1940)

Sproat, T., *The History and the Progress of the Amalgamated Society of Lithographic Printers & Auxiliaries of Great Britain and Ireland*, Offset, 1930

Spy: Serio-Comic and Free Lance for Manchester and Surrounding Towns, 7 May 1892

Stenton, Michael and Lees, Stephen, *Who's Who of British Members of Parliament, Volume II: 1885–1918*, Harvester Press, 1978

Stenton, Michael and Lees, Stephen, *Who's Who of British Members of Parliament, Volume III: 1919–1945*, Harvester Press, 1979

Stewart, William, 'Review of "J. Keir Hardie: A Biography"', *The Nation & the Athenaeum*, 5 November 1921

Stewart, William, *J. Keir Hardie: A Biography*, Cassell, 1921

Thompson, Laurence, *Robert Blatchford: Portrait of an Englishman*, Gollancz, 1951

Thorne, Will, *My Life's Battles*, Georges Newnes, 1926

Tillett, B., *Is the Parliamentary Labour Party a Failure?*, Twentieth Century Press, 1908

Tsuzuki, Chushichi, *H.M. Hyndman and British Socialism*, Oxford University Press, 1961

Tyler, Paul, 'Will Crooks MP, Local Activist and Labour Pioneer', Greenwich Industrial History Society, Issue 30, 2003

Walker, William M., *Juteopolis: Dundee and its Textile Workers, 1885–1923*, Scottish Academic Press, 1979

Webb, Sidney and Beatrice, *The History of Trade Unionism*, Longmans, 1894

Wilkie, Alexander, 'How I Got On', *Pearson's Weekly*, 24 May 1906

Woolf, Virginia, *Mrs Dalloway*, The Hogarth Press, 1925

Wrigley, Chris, *Arthur Henderson*, GPC Books, 1990

Index

Page references in **bold** indicate illustrations.